Charles Dowding

No Dig

Nurture your soil to grow better veg with less effort

Photography by Jonathan Buckley

CONTENTS

INTRODUCTION

Simple is best and taking easier approaches that work well is clever rather than lazy. For four decades my gardening has not followed many of the "rules" that have been taught at horticultural colleges and recommended generally. I always search for a reason before doing something, and there are remarkably few good reasons to invest time and effort in digging and many other labour-intensive gardening jobs. I wrote this book to show you that no dig is a highly practical, effective, achievable, and economical alternative to gardening methods involving soil cultivation.

In the 1980s, when I started gardening, almost everybody was digging and experiencing sticky soil, masses of weeds, and time wasted on more soil preparation, with no extra reward for these difficulties. I started to discover both organic and no dig methods in 1981, after becoming vegetarian at university, which got me interested in nutrition. Having grown up on a farm I was aware of the tillage and synthetic fertilizers used to grow vegetables at that time. Wondering what synthetic chemicals were in the food we ate, and in the wider environment, led me to embrace organic methods. I became a market gardener in late 1982, with 6,000m² (7,176yd²) of beds that I maintained by hand after rotavating the pasture. I erected a large road sign by my garden which said simply: "Health from the Land".

I became aware of no dig through writings in the Soil Association magazine and the work of Ruth Stout in the USA, who wrote about her "no work" approach. Stout advocated mulching with hay and I bought some old hay to cover my beds, because I was afraid of weeds growing. The next spring I lost many plantings to slugs hiding under the hay, and quickly came to appreciate the value instead of covering soil with compost that does not harbour slugs, especially in the damp climates found around the UK. Next I found that no dig and annual mulching with compost quickly resulted in very little weed growth, to the point where many visiting gardeners were simply amazed. This reduced need for weeding is an enormous benefit of no dig and the most significant time-saving aspect of my approach.

My current garden at Homeacres, in Somerset, has been created using no dig methods since November 2012 and the cropping area now stands at 1,300m² (1,555yd²). Initially I spent 40 or more hours each week running the garden, with 40 hours part-time help for harvesting salads in particular. These salad leaves are supplied to local shops and restaurants, I sell boxes of vegetables locally, and a lot of the produce from the garden is also used to provide lunches for people who attend courses at Homeacres. I continue to spend many hours each week working in the garden, but because my drive to promote no dig also pulls me towards teaching, video making, and writing, I now employ a full-time helper.

Word is spreading about the benefits of no dig growing and it is attracting increasing interest, especially with new evidence that it helps to retain carbon in soil, and growing awareness of the role that microorganisms nurtured by no dig methods play in soil fertility and plant nutrition. Social media has allowed me to reach a significant and continually expanding audience, and the positive feedback I receive from all over the world motivates me further. Like-minded people are successfully adopting my methods in a huge range of climates, soils, and situations; from single beds in urban gardens, to community gardens, schools, and market gardens.

No dig saves time and allows gardeners to enjoy themselves more, while a simple annual mulch of compost improves soil fertility, its ability to hold carbon, and feeds the soil ecology, for a healthy balance between pests and predators. Best of all, this practical approach promotes robust growth of both vegetables and flowers, enabling you to grow a large harvest of super-healthy food in a beautiful, sustainable garden, with few weeds or pests.

At Homeacres, vegetables and flowers thrive year after year in no dig beds, with just an annual mulch of compost. By August, the garden is filled with second plantings made following earlier harvests – no dig makes this succession planting quick and easy.

CHAPTER 1

It all begins
with the soil

NO DIG: ACHIEVE SO MUCH MORE BY DOING LESS

No dig methods make it easy to create and maintain a healthy and productive garden, on sites of any size or soil type. One application of compost each year, on top of undisturbed soil, results in high yields from a minimal input of time and effort. Leaving soil undisturbed is fundamental to no dig growing and although planting and harvesting will sometimes cause surface disruption, this can easily be kept to a minimum. There isn't even any need to remove weeds when you begin, and the lack of digging combined with regular mulching significantly reduces the need for subsequent weeding.

What's the problem with digging?

There is a common misconception that plant roots need soil to be loose and fluffy to grow, but their growth is actually better when the soil structure is firm. What's more, digging and other types of cultivation break the existing structure of tiny channels within the soil and damage the networks of fungal growth, such as mycorrhizae, which help plant roots to access water and nutrients (see pp.16–17).

Dug soil's damaged structure means it soon slumps to a dense state, with little space for air between soil particles, especially after it's walked on. Digging also only reaches a certain depth, beneath which the soil is not disturbed, creating two layers of different density. This forms a "capillary boundary" through which water cannot flow freely from the crumbly surface soil to the denser soil below, resulting in poor drainage.

Soil disturbance stimulates weed growth by bringing buried weed seeds to the surface, where they quickly germinate to cover bare soil and "heal" the damage caused by digging. Weeds then need to be removed before sowing or planting. A further disadvantage is that disturbed soil sticks to boots; in my garden I rarely wear wellingtons.

No digging and less weeding leaves more time to plant vegetables and enjoy a varied harvest.

The principles of no dig gardening

The no dig method is simple and easy to practice, producing successful harvests with a significantly smaller investment of time and effort, when compared to digging. Avoiding soil disturbance is key as it allows the natural processes within the soil to work without interference. Ground can also be cleared of most weeds quickly and easily without digging, by covering with a light-excluding mulch (see pp.40–41). Only woody plants, such as brambles, need to be dug out before establishing a new bed.

A second aspect of treating soil well is to add a mulch of well decomposed organic matter just once every year to feed the diverse range of organisms that live out of sight (see pp.16–17). In forests and pastures, this happens through leaf fall and decay, but a mulch replaces this in vegetable gardens, where we harvest much of the surface growth. Organisms in the soil come up to eat the surface compost and excrete organic matter in forms more available to plant roots. In moving through soil these organisms build a structure of larger soil particles and air pockets, which improve both drainage and water retention (see pp.30–31).

I apply compost mulch to beds in late autumn or early winter, after removing the last autumn crops and any weeds, so that the bed surface is covered for winter and will be ready for planting in spring. Likewise I mulch the paths between beds with well-rotted wood chip to ensure that all ground is covered and the organisms within it are fed. Plants can extend their roots beyond beds and tap into this additional resource of path soil.

Mulch around the base of overwintering crops, like this purple sprouting broccoli.

IT ALL BEGINS WITH THE SOIL

Comparison of dig and no dig trial beds

Since 2013 I have used two adjacent 1.5 x 5m (5 x 16ft) beds to compare and demonstrate the differences between dig and no dig methods. Each year they are planted with the same vegetables at the same time and all harvests are weighed, providing a lot of data. Results vary with the weather, but the no dig bed consistently produces an equivalent total harvest to the dig bed, and usually 5–10 per cent more. All for less time and effort, because there are few weeds in the no dig beds, while the dig bed's disturbed soil is colonized by weeds, such as creeping buttercup. Watering is also noticeably easier because the compost mulch on no dig acts like a sponge, absorbing water freely into the soft surface. When the dig bed is watered in dry weather, water tends to run off the top (see pp.30–31).

In spring, I notice that growth of most vegetables, with the exception of potatoes, gets underway more quickly on the no dig bed. I imagine this is thanks to the established mycelial structures of soil fungi interacting quickly and easily with developing plant roots to help their early growth (see pp.16–17). The no dig bed also has a slightly higher soil

The no dig bed on the right equals or surpasses the yield of the dig bed opposite with less work (top). Snow melts faster on no dig soil (above).

temperature, thanks to both the dark layer of compost on the surface that absorbs the sun's warmth faster than the paler dug soil, and undisturbed capillary contact with warmer soil at greater depths. This is demonstrated after snowfall and during the melt, when it's noticeable that the dig bed remains white while the snow melts more rapidly on the neighbouring no dig bed.

As above, so below: there is a cosmos out of sight beneath our feet. If only it were visible, we would be amazed at the life and activity within the soil, and scientific research is allowing us to increase our knowledge of soil organisms, their interactions with plants, and their impact on soil health. No dig allows this soil ecosystem to develop undisturbed and every year I'm delighted by the growth in my garden, which occurs simply as a result of enabling natural processes.

SOIL FOOD WEB

American soil biologist, Dr Elaine Ingham, describes this life as a "soil food web", made up of plant roots interacting with insects, earthworms, and microscopic, sometimes single-celled organisms such as fungi, bacteria, and protozoa. These creatures play a role in processing both organic matter and minerals in the soil into forms that can be taken up by growing roots. Plants then return the favour by releasing from their roots exudates containing some of the products of photosynthesis, which form a "chemical currency" that provides the main food source, at least for the fungal networks.

Scientists classify soil-dwelling animals, or fauna, into three groups according to their size. Creatures from each group feed on soil organic matter or other soil animals: their excretions and movement contribute to soil structure and fertility. Macrofauna are 1cm (1/2in) or longer, like centipedes, millipedes, slugs, snails, fly larvae, beetles, and beetle larvae. Animals classed as mesofauna are 0.1–2mm (1/250–1/16in) long and usually inhabit the surface layer, where most organic matter decomposes. They include insect larvae, small spiders, land planarians, and springtails or collembolans. Microscopic microfauna enable decomposition, provide a food source for other soil fauna, and include the fungal network.

Organic mulches add organisms to the soil food web, and provide food for those already present. Enabling this biological network to work with plant roots ensures sufficient food for new growth, without any need for synthetic fertilizers which would harm soil organisms. Dr Ingham's research even leads her to assert that, "There is no soil on earth that is incapable of providing all the nutrients that plants require". The missing link in ostensibly "poor" soils may be the web of organisms that can transform organic matter into nutrients that are available to plants.

MYCORRHIZAL FUNGI

Fungi constitute a separate kingdom of life to plants, fauna, and bacteria. Fungal networks usually grow underground, cannot photosynthesize, and are visible above ground mainly when they produce mushrooms, their fruiting bodies. The fungi associated with plant nutrition are known as "mycorrhizal", a word that combines Latin "myco-", fungi, with Greek "rhiza", root. This reflects mutually-beneficial relationships they form with plant roots, which enable plants to access the water and nutrients they need from soil. When I started gardening in the 1980s, mycorrhizae were not considered important for vegetable crops, but today their role in the growth of almost all plants is widely recognized.

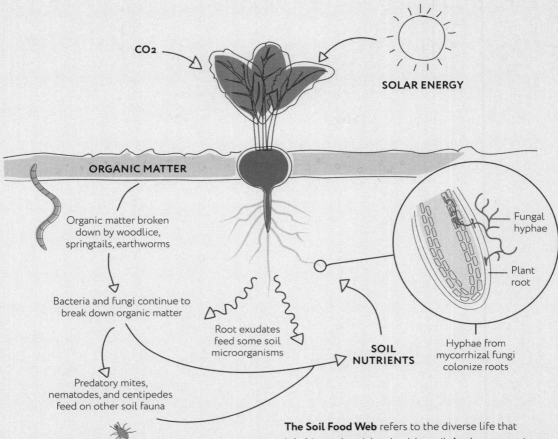

CO2

SOLAR ENERGY

ORGANIC MATTER

Organic matter broken down by woodlice, springtails, earthworms

Bacteria and fungi continue to break down organic matter

Root exudates feed some soil microorganisms

Predatory mites, nematodes, and centipedes feed on other soil fauna

SOIL NUTRIENTS

Fungal hyphae

Plant root

Hyphae from mycorrhizal fungi colonize roots

Mycorrhizal fungi form a mutual symbiosis with plants by physically joining their tiny filaments (hyphae) with plant roots (see above). The fungi supply water and nutrients from the soil to plant roots in exchange for sugars that the plant has manufactured during photosynthesis. This effectively expands the root systems of plants, providing them with access to existing networks of fungal hyphae within the soil. The easiest way to encourage this elegant natural system is to avoid digging, because disturbing soils will damage the fragile fungal growth that they contain. Some research suggests that chemical fertilizers are also detrimental to mycorrhizal associations, because the delivery of these instantly available, water-soluble nutrients directly to plant roots makes redundant the symbiotic relationship between plant roots and fungi.

The Soil Food Web refers to the diverse life that inhabits and enriches healthy soil. As these organisms feed on organic matter and other soil fauna, they make nutrients available in forms that can be taken up by plants. The hair-like hyphae of mycorrhizal fungi penetrate fine plant roots to deliver nutrients less easily accessible from the soil in exchange for sugars, in a relationship that is symbiotic.

Mycorrhizal fungi are naturally present in soils, although sometimes dormant as long-lived spores. The species present vary according to soil type, existing plants, and climate. Products containing mycorrhizal fungi in a dry pelleted form may not introduce species that are native to your area or useful to your plants. I prefer to add indigenous microbes to beds with an annual mulch of homemade compost, which will contain spores of both mycorrhizal fungi and saprophytic types that all play their own parts at different stages of decomposition and plant growth.

THE IMPORTANCE OF COMPOST

Compost is at the heart of a no dig garden, used both to create new beds and maintain the fertility of existing beds. You can make it yourself (see pp.52–57), but will almost certainly need to buy some to supplement your homemade supply, especially when you establish new beds. There are many types of compost to choose from and although some are described as "organic", this simply means they are organic matter, not that they are free from chemical residues.

What is compost?

Compost refers to any carbon-based material that is well decomposed. It may have started as garden waste, chipped wood, cereal straw, tree leaves, digester waste, or animal manure – all decompose eventually. Compost is described according to the principal material it was created from – the starting point. For example, when gardeners talk about using manure on their plot, what they mean is compost made from animal waste or manure, including any bedding materials. Compost varies in colour from pale brown to almost black and often has a lumpy texture rather than being uniformly fine. Colour, smell, and any visible materials are all clues about a product's original ingredients and the composting method used. More than anything they indicate the stage of decomposition. Traditional descriptions of "black gold" suggest that dark compost is better, but a black colour results from either strong heat of 70–80°C (158–176°F) or anaerobic decomposition, both of which favour certain bacteria and damage fungi, and does not guarantee that a compost is well decomposed. Any compost that is browner in colour is usually balanced with fungi as well as bacteria, and increases soil fertility more rapidly.

The process of decomposition generates heat, therefore warm compost is a clear indicator that microorganisms are still breaking it down. They require nutrients to do this, which means that applying partially decomposed organic matter in the rooting zone can deprive plants of some food they need, and result in a lack of growth or leaves turning yellow. Newly bought green waste and mushroom compost are often fresh and still warm, so they improve when left to decompose for at least a month before using. If compost is still above 35–40°C (95–104°F), allow it to decompose further before using

Compost with a coarse texture is ideal to mulch beds.

Spread a thin layer of well-decomposed compost on no dig beds every year to improve soil fertility.

Use your hand or a compost thermometer to check the temperature of compost before use.

it to make new beds with a thick 15cm (6in) layer of compost, where plants initially do not have access to the soil below. Warm compost can work as a 2.5cm (1in) surface mulch, decomposing more while plants root below it.

Why use compost?

Compost increases fertility by feeding the inhabitants of the soil, and they in turn improve structure – aeration, moisture retention, and drainage – and make nutrients available to plants (see p.24–25). Thanks to decomposition having already happened elsewhere, laying compost on the surface delivers organic matter in forms that are readily accessible for soil organisms to eat and excrete, converting them quickly into compounds that can be taken up by plant roots. I see the addition of compost as giving soil a deep contentment, leaving it well fed, and contributing to the absence of new weeds in established beds.

In damp climates compost mulches provide no habitat for pests, such as slugs, which are often a problem under straw and undecomposed materials. Compost's dark colour also absorbs heat from the sun in early spring, warming the soil quickly for earlier plant growth.

How much is needed?

Apply a larger amount of compost when you start out and smaller applications once a year after that. The existing fertility of your soil determines how much compost is worth using initially, to set beds up for good harvests over several years. On poor ground or where weeds are particularly strong, a 15cm (6in) layer of compost is an investment to increase yields in future years, reduce weed growth, and improve the moisture retention of soil. Such a thick mulch never needs to be applied again and in other circumstances you could start with less. When converting a lawn to beds, lay cardboard topped with 7cm (2¾in) of compost.

An existing vegetable plot may not need cardboard, and 5cm (2in) of compost will be enough. To create deep raised beds, use top soil as a base layer, because it holds its volume, and top beds with 20cm (8in) of compost.

Once beds are created, annual applications of roughly 2.5cm (1in) of mature compost are sufficient, without spreading more during the growing season, even when you plant follow-on crops in summer. The texture influences how thickly to apply it; a rough compost with pieces of straw or woody material can be spread a little more thickly. Small lumps and pieces of wood are fine and do not need to be sieved out.

WEEDKILLER CONTAMINATION

I now use less manure and purchased compost than before, because of the increased risk that they contain pyralid weedkillers, sprayed on grass eaten by livestock or on lawns. The herbicide stays intact during animal digestion and all composting processes, so that after mulching it causes pale, stunted growth of plant shoot tips, especially in legumes and solanums. Ask your supplier about pyralid weedkiller use, and test any compost you want to check by sowing broad beans into pots before it is spread. If pyralid weedkiller is present, beans grow slowly and show curling leaf tips within a month, depending on temperature. Soil microbes can eventually clear compost of this contamination.

Homemade compost is a great free resource and need not be sieved when used to mulch beds.

Compost types for soil fertility

These are the best and most easily available composts for mulching no dig beds. I make use of bought-in composts even though I produce a large quantity of my own. Leaf mould is also an excellent fine-textured compost with a high fungal content, but is not readily available and takes two years to produce. Another product marketed as "compost" is anaerobic digestate. I don't recommend its use, as it isn't compost, but finely chopped anaerobically processed material, which lacks microbial life.

1. HOMEMADE GARDEN COMPOST

I rate this as one of the best composts for garden use, especially when you make it in aerobic conditions. Its high microbial content is fantastically beneficial for soil (see pp.16–17), although it's not necessarily the richest in nutrients. The texture and content will vary depending on what you added and how you looked after it (see pp.52–57). I use it at 5–10 months old, counting from midway between the first and last application to the heap.

2. BAGGED COMPOST

Look for peat-free compost labelled multi-purpose, all-purpose, or potting and container compost. Avoid blends for seeds or cuttings, and ericaceous compost. Buy a product that suits your needs: potting compost is intended for sowing and potting on young plants and has a fine texture and higher nutrient content; composts for garden use suit mulching and have a lumpier texture, with fewer nutrients.

3. GREEN WASTE COMPOST

This black compost is made from garden waste that's been processed at specialist facilities, where large heaps reach around 80°C (176°F). This heat speeds up decomposition, but kills most life, except bacteria, giving the compost a lower microbial content. It is best used as a thin surface layer, where microorganisms in both the air and the soil can feed on it and improve soil fertility. This variable product can be surprisingly effective and rarely hosts weed seeds or pathogens, but may be contaminated with plastic or residual weedkiller.

4. MUSHROOM COMPOST

Also called "spent" mushroom compost, because it's no longer useful for mushroom cultivation, this dark brown mixture of decomposed horse manure and straw produces great results in the garden. Its fluffy texture quickly settles, so spread it 4–5cm (1½–2in) thick on beds. It is rich in fungal life, and although it can have a high pH if chalk has been used to cap the mushroom beds, this practice is now less common. Residual weedkiller contamination may be a problem.

5. COMPOSTED ANIMAL MANURE

Animal manure enhances plant growth by introducing different microbes and extra nutrients, to both compost heaps and soil. Either add it in small amounts to your compost heap, or create a dedicated manure heap and use it when it is a year old. Animal manure varies according to both the type of animal and the bedding used. Manure with straw should compost within 12 months, while wood chip bedding extends that to 24–36 months.

6. COMPOSTED WOODY MATERIAL

Any kind of woody material in small pieces can become compost within two or three years, so it's a great resource if you have a local supply and space for a heap. The smaller the pieces, the faster they will decompose. This is the only compost that might be worth sieving, to prevent larger pieces of wood accumulating and getting in the way on the surface of beds.

DELVE DEEPER NATURAL NUTRITION

No dig soil grows healthy plants by allowing their roots balanced access to nutrients as and when they are needed. The process begins when you leave soil undisturbed and spread just a single application of compost, which you repeat each year, whatever you plan to grow. This is much easier than trying to understand all the different needs of various plants through the growing season and tailoring a fertilizer regime appropriate to each one.

UNLOCKING NUTRIENTS

Compost is not fertilizer and is not used to feed plants directly. When laid on top of beds it feeds the diverse life within soil (see pp.16–17), which in turn produces complex organic compounds containing nutrients that plant roots can access whenever they need them, with help from the mycelial network of mycorrhizal fungi (see pp.16–17). This natural process, which is enabled through no dig, allows us to trust the soil to feed plants whenever they need it without any extra input. The complex carbon-based molecules containing nutrients are not water soluble and therefore do not leach away with rainfall or watering, unlike the nutrients in synthetic fertilizers, which need constant management.

DISPELLING THE MYTHS OF FEED

Any kind of digging or disturbance damages soil's ability to provide nutrients for plants. This means that frequent soil cultivation can make it necessary to apply fertilizers, which are not needed on soil where no dig methods are used.

In the past, soil was sometimes described as a "bank balance", where nutrients came in with fertilizers and manures, then went out to plants or were washed away in a process called leaching. Advice was based around anticipating each plant's needs at different stages of growth, then feeding to match that, giving more nutrients to plants considered "heavy feeders" and fewer to "light feeders". However, the water-soluble nutrients in synthetic fertilizers can wash away in heavy rain or be taken up in unbalanced amounts by plant roots, making them unavailable or producing undesirable effects, such as soft growth that is prone to damage by pests, following an excess of nitrogen.

Scientific research has also shown that the use of synthetic nitrogen fertilizers damages soil microbial processes, which results in poor plant growth in the long term. Even organic gardeners, who add organic matter to their soil and eschew the use of synthetic fertilizers, have often based their approach on this same understanding that plants need to be fed.

Confusion can also arise because digging exposes bacteria to oxygen so that they feed on carbon in the soil, making a short burst of nutrients available to plants. However, this quickly passes and, by halfway through the growing season, the damage caused to soil organisms and structure results in weaker plant growth, which can lead gardeners to think their soil is short of nutrients and that fertilizer needs to be applied.

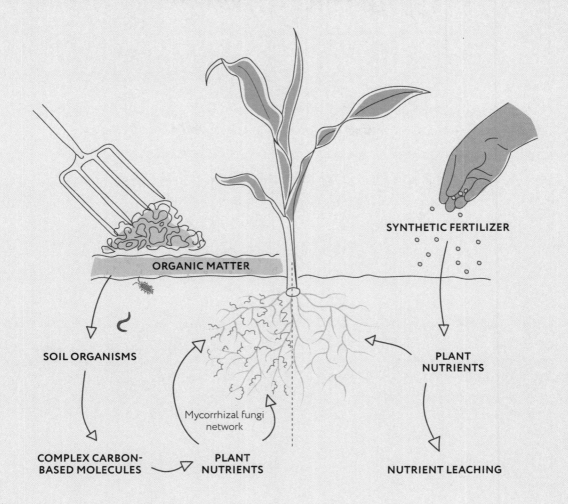

ORGANIC MATTER

SYNTHETIC FERTILIZER

SOIL ORGANISMS

PLANT
NUTRIENTS

Mycorrhizal fungi
network

COMPLEX CARBON-
BASED MOLECULES

PLANT
NUTRIENTS

NUTRIENT LEACHING

THE ROLE OF TEMPERATURE

Every plant tolerates a different range of temperatures. At the lower end of this range they are in survival mode and do not grow, but as the temperature rises growth switches into gear. Soil microbe activity decreases when the soil temperature is lower, especially below 6°C (43°F), preventing plants accessing nutrients and resulting in leaves looking paler. This is from a deficiency of warmth, not nutrients, so if leaves of plants that need warmth turn yellow after transplanting in cool spring conditions, this is not a signal to apply fertilizer – growth will get underway once the temperature rises. Sowing each vegetable at the right time will enable its roots to access the nutrients they need from the soil.

A mulch of organic matter versus synthetic fertilizer. When applied annually, organic matter feeds the diverse organisms of the soil food web, which gradually break it down to leave soil rich in a broad range of nutrients. These can be accessed by plants when needed with the help of a network of mycorrhizal fungi associated with their roots. In contrast, applying synthetic fertilizer to soil provides plants with a brief burst of specific nutrients, before they are used up or washed away, and damages populations of soil microbes, including mycorrhizae.

UNDERSTANDING WEEDS

Weeds are not bad plants, just plants growing where we do not want them, vigorously and without any encouragement! They're quick to colonize bare soil by spreading roots underground or dispersing large quantities of seed, competing with vegetable crops for water, light, and nutrients. Sometimes they harbour pests, but may also host helpful insects, such as ladybirds. No dig methods provide simple and effective ways to reduce weed growth, and it's enjoyable to keep them under control when they are few in number and pull out easily from compost mulches.

The characteristics of weeds

Weed species divide mainly into perennials and annuals. Perennial weeds persist year after year through either a network of creeping roots and runners that they use to colonize new areas, or large, persistent tap roots. They have the ability to regrow from just a small portion of root left in the soil. Perennial weeds also spread by seeding. Annual weeds multiply by producing seeds, often just a short time after they start to grow. It's vital to catch them before they drop seeds in their hundreds and thousands, otherwise they colonize soil very quickly and smother slower and lower-growing seedlings, such as carrots. A few garden flowers can become weeds if their seeds are allowed to mature after flowering.

Digging promotes weed growth

All soil contains weed seeds, which will be brought to the surface by any cultivation, where they quickly germinate. This weed flush will repopulate bare soil rapidly, leading to extra, time consuming work weeding soil that has become sticky because its structure has been disturbed. Trying to dig out established perennial weeds is even harder work, because their roots are deeply buried and often break readily, leaving portions in the soil to regrow.

Weeds as healers

No dig makes controlling weeds simpler, even on very weedy sites, and achieves this because it does not disturb soil. Following digging or other disturbance, soil quickly recovers or "heals" with a flush of small, fast-growing colonizer weeds. An example of this is chickweed (*Stellaria media*), whose roots bind to soil and are surprisingly strong for such a small plant. Farmers have a saying that "chickweed follows the rotavator", a tool that smashes the soil surface into fragments, which then need to be bound together by the roots of weeds to help soil regain its structure and life.

*A thick mulch weakens perennial couch grass (*Elymus repens*).*

No dig avoids weed problems

Preventing problems is always easier and healthier than curing them. When creating beds, the only weeds that actually need to be removed are woody plants (see p.40). Cover all other weeds with a mulch of light-excluding material, such as cardboard, and you can plant into the surface compost or the soil under the mulch immediately, while weeds are dying in the darkness underneath.

Weeds with no access to light cannot photosynthesize and supply energy to their roots. This kills shallow-rooted annual weeds within four weeks, but it takes longer to exhaust the deep and thicker parent roots of perennials, whose stored energy sends up new stems for months. For example, they may push up through decomposing cardboard, even two to three months after you laid it. Be wary of such root vigour and quickly remove any new weed shoots you see, before they produce leaves to feed the roots below.

Black plastic (top) and cardboard (above) deprive perennial weeds, like this field bindweed (Convolvulus arvensis), of light.

THE BENEFITS OF NO DIG BEDS

A well organised bed and path layout gives you demarcated areas, making it simpler to plan what to grow, and easier to manage plant growth and harvests. Thanks to the firm structure and stability of no dig soil, solid boundaries between beds and paths are unnecessary, and beds can be formed without sides. An absence of raised sides means better access; try it and you will notice that it's easier to reach into the middle of open-sided beds.

Bed dimensions

No dig methods give you flexibility when planning a bed and path layout, because it's possible to create beds of any width. Wider beds are no problem, because you can put a foot on the soil to reach the middle when planting or picking, without having to worry about compacting the soil or damaging its structure (see pp.30–31). The width of paths is also totally flexible and I notice that mine are generally narrower than I see elsewhere. This means less path to manage for weeds, and increases the proportion of bed to path in a growing space. Open-sided beds also permit plant roots to grow into pathway soil, which is never useless or compacted, but instead becomes part of the growing area.

The width and length of beds and paths are also determined by what fits into the space that is available for growing: you could create three beds of 1.5m (5ft) width, or four of 1.1m (3½ft) width in the same area, for example. Varying path width can adjust the overall fit.

Stable soil with a soft surface

Repeated applications of compost give no dig beds a soft surface with a settled, stable structure beneath, unlike soil loosened by digging. On sloping sites, dug soil is more likely to be washed away and eroded in heavy rain. The standard advice is therefore to run beds across a slope, to prevent loose soil washing downhill, but unless expensive holding boards are installed on the lower sides of such beds, their surface will still slope downhill. This allows loosened soil to wash over the sides quite easily. In contrast, I have found no dig soil's stability permits beds to be run up and down a slope. Some water and new compost will run down such beds, but will be retained along their length.

Open-sided beds and living paths

Creating beds without sides has many positives. Wooden bed sides decompose on the inside within three or four years. There are then cavities of rotten wood that make ideal hiding places during the day for slugs and woodlice,

Placing a foot on no dig soil to access the centre of wide beds does not damage its stable structure.

which then nip up to eat your plants at night. If using wooden sides at all, it's best that they are temporary and lifted off after a few months (see p.47).

In dry weather I notice that plants growing close to the edge of a bed are bigger than those in the centre, because edge plants have access to moisture and nutrients in the path soil. This shows how worthwhile it is to maintain the fertility of your paths, by mulching the surface with a thin layer of rough compost in the first year and old wood chip thereafter. This improves fertility and structure, holding soil open when you walk along paths and making it easy to push heavy wheelbarrows.

Cabbages thrive along a path edge (right).
Vary bed size to make best use of space (below).

DELVE DEEPER SOIL CARBON AND STRUCTURE

No dig methods not only boost the productivity of your soil and reduce weed growth, but also allow you to increase its ability to hold carbon and reduce the amount of carbon dioxide released into the atmosphere. Not disturbing the soil and using surface mulches of compost benefits soil structure by maintaining air-filled pores between soil particles that improve both drainage and moisture retention, as well as reducing run-off from the surface during watering or rainfall.

TYPES OF SOIL CARBON

Carbon is vital in life forms for its ability to form complex molecules. Our bodies are 18.5 per cent carbon, and healthy soil can have levels close to that when measuring both organic and inorganic carbon, the latter being stable carbonates such as limestone. Organic carbon is formed when plants fix atmospheric carbon dioxide during photosynthesis. It is then used for life processes within the soil as plants grow, die, decay, and are consumed by soil organisms, which is when we measure it as "soil organic matter" or SOM. This is the part of soil where organisms are active, and where plant matter decomposes.

Another form of soil carbon is biochar, a high carbon form of charcoal, which forms a very stable constituent of SOM and is therefore useful to retain carbon in the soil. I recently installed a small charcoal kiln in the garden and am learning how best to use the charcoal it produces. Currently, I add charcoal to my compost heaps, where its porous nature makes it a valuable site for life processes and store for dormant microbes, such as fungal spores.

A soil scientist, Jane Thatcher, is measuring soil organic carbon (SOC) in my dig and no dig trial beds as part of her postgraduate research. These beds have received the same amount of compost over the past nine years. She uses the loss-on-ignition method to determine the combustible carbon present in samples taken at a range of depths from each bed.

Her preliminary findings from samples taken at a depth of 0–10cm (0–4in) show more carbon in the no dig soil, at a statistically "highly significant" level. An increase in SOC in the top 5cm (2in) of no dig soil is not unexpected following the surface application of compost each year, but a "highly significant" increase in SOC was also found when samples from four depths, down to 40cm (16in), were analysed together. This analysis measures only one part of soil's complex living process. Even more can be learned about soil interactions by comparing plant growth and harvests.

THE ROLE OF GLOMALIN

One important component of SOM is a sticky, carbon-rich protein named glomalin. Not even known until 1996, glomalin was discovered by Sara F. Wright, a soil scientist working for the US Department of Agriculture in Maryland. It is produced by the underground filaments (hyphae) of certain mycorrhizal fungi (see pp.16–17). A coating of glomalin enables hyphae to transport water and nutrients, and holds them firm enough to span the pores between soil particles. Glomalin persists in soil for several years after fungal hyphae have degraded, and research suggests that it may account for up to a third of soil carbon.

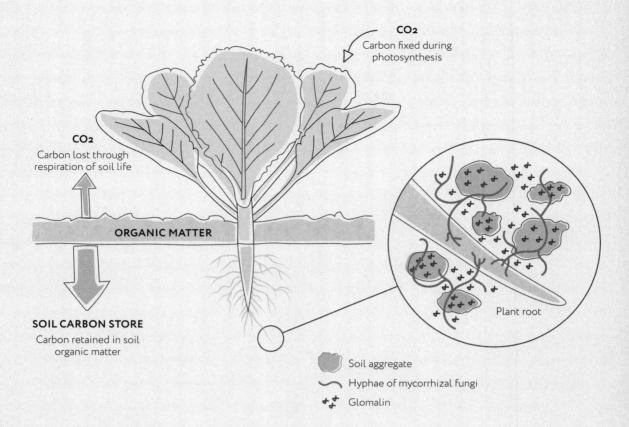

CO₂
Carbon fixed during photosynthesis

CO₂
Carbon lost through respiration of soil life

ORGANIC MATTER

SOIL CARBON STORE
Carbon retained in soil organic matter

Plant root

Soil aggregate

Hyphae of mycorrhizal fungi

Glomalin

IMPROVED SOIL STRUCTURE AND POROSITY

No dig methods add organic matter to the soil surface, where it promotes a healthy soil food web (see pp.16–17) in the underlying soil. The activities of undisturbed soil life result in improved soil structure, particularly the growth of glomalin-producing mycorrhizal fungi. Glomalin helps to bind soil particles and organic matter into water-stable aggregates of different sizes. The varied spaces between these aggregates improve the soil's structure and porosity. Larger pores hold air and enable drainage of excess water through soil, while smaller pores retain moisture in soil for plant roots to access.

When watering my comparison beds, it is also clear to see that no dig soil with a layer of organic matter on the surface absorbs water

No dig soil is an effective carbon store. The carbon that plants fix from the atmosphere during photosynthesis is better captured as soil organic matter in no dig soil, where soil life, including networks of mycorrhizal fungi, are allowed to thrive undisturbed. The sticky protein called glomalin, produced by the hyphae of mycorrhizae, is a major constituent of soil organic matter, an important carbon store, and helps to bind soil particles and organic matter together, creating a free-draining yet water-retentive soil structure that's ideal for growing.

more readily than soil that has been dug and has its organic matter incorporated. Water is more prone to run off the surface of the dig bed, making it unable to reach plant roots, and often washing away some loosened soil with it.

CHAPTER 2

Getting started

DECIDING WHAT TO GROW

The fun first step in this process is to write down what you and your family want to eat. There is no point growing beautiful Brussels sprouts if nobody likes them, but bear in mind that homegrown vegetables have better flavour. Also consider any limitations posed by likely weather conditions, the size of your growing space, and whether you can grow some plants under cover. Stick to what is feasible when you outline a plan and you will be successful.

Consider your climate

Temperature and rainfall influence plant growth throughout the seasons, and an understanding of your climate enables you to choose vegetables that can thrive. Discover when to expect the last frost in spring and first frost in autumn, dates which bookend the season for growing tender vegetables outdoors. In northern regions, where summers are short and cool, heat-loving crops like tomatoes and winter squashes might not give good returns outdoors. Hot, dry summers mean you need plenty of water for growing leafy vegetables, while a very windy location might rule out climbing beans and other tall plants. Before starting out, talk to neighbours or other allotment holders about their experiences to get an idea of what's possible. Check the profile for each crop you would like to grow in the second half of the book to assess its suitability for your climate.

My observations and recommendations are based on the climate at Homeacres, which is temperate and oceanic, often cloudy and damp, with few extremes of temperature. The last frost date is mid-May and the first frosts can be in mid-October. This is equivalent to US hardiness zone 8, but can be misleading, because Texas is the same zone yet has much hotter summers and potentially colder winters. Here in the UK, our winter temperatures are mitigated by ocean currents called the Atlantic Meridional Overturning Circulation (also known as the Gulf Stream), which brings warm surface water up from the Gulf of Mexico. At Homeacres, the average maximum summer

	Temperature min.°C/°F	Temperature max. °C/°F	Average °C/°F	Rainfall mm/in	Sunshine hours
Spring (Mar–May)	4.5/40	15.5/60	10/50	179/7	478
Summer (Jun–Aug)	11/52	21/70	16/61	190/7.5	591
Autumn (Sep–Nov)	7/45	14/57	10.5/51	249/10	319
Winter (Dec–Feb)	1.5/35	8.5/47	5/41	232/9	176
Average cumulative total	6/43	15/59	10.5/51	850/34	1564

Weather conditions at Homeacres 2013–2021.

Selecting crops to suit your climate makes success easier to achieve. See the same beds in early spring on p.29.

temperature is 21ºC (70ºF) and the average winter minimum is 1.5ºC (35ºF). Rainfall is remarkably constant throughout the year, which makes this a fantastic climate for all vegetables except those that thrive in hot summers. Light levels are low in winter, both due to the predominance of cloud and latitude of 51º north – equivalent to Newfoundland.

Get the most from your space

Even if your space is small, you can still grow a wonderful range of vegetables. Choose plants that are compact and continually productive, which includes all salad plants, along with leafy greens like kale, spinach, and chard. At the other end of this scale, just one courgette plant can take up 1m (3ft) of a bed, which works if that's what you want, but reduces your options. Large plants like Brussels sprouts, cauliflower, and many perennial vegetables, also demand plenty of space. Consult the vegetable and herb profiles for my recommended spacings, because you can often plant closer and crop more intensively than seed packets suggest. Try multisowing (see pp.78–79) beetroot, leeks, radish, and onions to grow more plants in a given space, and interplant when possible among maturing vegetables (see p.70). Most vegetables can mature in half a season, depending on climate, and that knowledge can be used to plan and grow a second follow-on crop, for two harvests per year in much of your space (see pp.68–69).

Salad leaves, including sorrel, chervil, and mustard, are compact and high-yielding.

Choose suitable varieties

Vegetable varieties are bred for different growing conditions and tastes, to mature at particular times, or to resist pests and diseases. An enormous choice is available, so seek out the varieties that best suit your needs. Look for those that mature early if your climate is cool, and dwarf varieties if your location is windy. Choose those with the best flavour if that is your main criterion, although vegetables grown in no dig soil often have better flavour than any you can buy.

Large courgette plants need warm summer weather to thrive; grey leaf markings are natural.

THE DIFFERENCE BETWEEN OPEN-POLLINATED VARIETIES AND F1 HYBRIDS

Open-pollinated varieties produce seeds as a result of natural pollination between selected plants with the desired characteristics, and will grow into plants with almost identical characteristics to their parents. After this happens over many generations they are sometimes referred to as "heritage" or "heirloom" varieties, and you can save your own seed from them.

An F1 hybrid is produced by cross-pollinating two inbred parent lines of the same vegetable, both with desirable traits, to give seed which grows reliably vigorous, uniform crops. The production of F1 hybrid seeds is not a natural process, but it is a method of plant breeding rather than any type of genetic manipulation. Seed saved from an F1 hybrid will not have the same characteristics as the parent plant. F1 hybrid varieties are more expensive, but reliable, so you will avoid disappointment. I often grow them where no good open-pollinated varieties are available (see pp.50–51).

Don't plan too much

I believe it's a mistake to begin the year with a spreadsheet showing precisely what you're going to grow where and harvest when, because changeable weather will almost always throw those timings out of the window, or something will be eaten by pests and leave a big gap in your plan. It's better just to have an overall outline by the end of winter – a plan or list showing roughly what you're going to grow where in spring. This helps you to get organized, while giving the flexibility to be creative, react to what's happening in the garden, and make any changes you feel are necessary; perhaps because vegetables have matured rapidly in a warm spring, or you've raised more transplants than expected and want to plant them all out.

PLANNING YOUR BEDS

Stable no dig soil is ideal for creating gently mounded, open-sided beds with edges that slope at an angle of approximately 30°. I use this method to minimize costs and pest problems. Beds can also be made at a convenient height using wood, plastic, or metal sides. Before creating beds, consider the slope of your site and how you will access pathways, to make moving water, compost, and other materials as easy as possible.

Laying out beds

When starting with an open piece of ground, the orientation of beds is your primary decision. It's said that they should run north-south to prevent plants shading one another, but this only applies if you grow mostly tall vegetables, such as runner beans, sweetcorn, and tomatoes. Where other lower-growing vegetables predominate in your plantings, shading will not be an issue, and I advise that your main focus should instead be on good access. Create pathways running away from the point where you enter the space, to allow you to reach beds, compost bays, and the water butt or tap as quickly and conveniently as possible.

If your site has a significant slope, this could be the overriding factor affecting the bed layout. Orientating beds up and down an incline works well for no dig soil (see pp.28–29). It's also far more comfortable to walk on a path which runs up and down a slope, because the level is the same for both of your feet. I successfully managed 2000m² (21,500ft²) of beds arranged in this way on the 10° slope of my previous garden, but on steeper hills you may need to consider terracing beds.

Bed and path width

I see no advantage in creating beds narrower than 1m (3ft), because this results in a high proportion of path to bed, and it's more work to look after a larger number of beds and paths. The width that I find easiest to manage is 1.2m (4ft). It is possible for no dig beds to be 2m (6½ft) wide or more, and I have a couple that large, but the widest ones I am happy with are 1.5m (5ft). This is partly because most crop covers (see pp.92–93) are 2m (6½ft) wide, so beds more than 1.5m (5ft) wide need larger covers, which are heavy and cumbersome to work with and store.

Open-sided no dig beds free up space to squat down comfortably while working and manoeuvre a wheelbarrow, and allow the paths between beds to be fairly narrow. In my garden

40cm (16in) path widths work well among the 1.2m (4ft) wide beds, while paths with a width of 30cm (12in) provide enough space among narrower beds.

The length of beds is not important, because several blocks of different vegetables can be planted in a long bed, as though it were actually a number of short beds. You can have beds as long as your plot to crop in segments like this or create an attractive mosaic of smaller beds, each planted with a distinct vegetable. One of my trial areas has this pattern of smaller beds, which I really like for its flexibility and easily identifiable areas of growth (see above).

A trial area at Homeacres with a mixture of bed widths, lengths, and orientations.

Construction method

Hold temporary wood sides for no dig beds in place using large stones, or hammer stakes into the ground and screw the wooden sides to them. Sides such as this are a template to contain the filling, and are lifted off once the compost has settled. This allows the wood to be reused, keeping costs down. If you use wooden sides when starting on weedy ground, it's vital that cardboard sits underneath them, to control the new growth of perennial weeds. Beds with permanent sides can be useful to delineate the growing space in a small area or where children play.

CONTROLLING WEEDS

No dig means less time weeding, largely thanks to careful and clever mulching in the first year, when new growing areas are often beset with weeds. Mulching can quickly eliminate established weeds, and massively reduces the amount of subsequent weeding required. Here I explain how my garden stays weed-free with minimal effort, giving me time to enjoy propagating, planting, and harvesting vegetables.

Initial cover to control weeds

When setting up new beds and paths on weedy soil, suppress weed growth with a layer of overlapped cardboard sheets, covered with 10–15cm (4–6in) compost (see pp.44–45). You don't need to remove soft-stemmed weeds, but use a sharp spade to slice through and remove the woody base of brambles (*Rubus fruticosus*) and the top 15cm (6in) of large dock tap roots (*Rumex* spp.) before laying your mulch. Perennial weeds also need to be controlled in pathways to prevent them spreading back into your beds. The first year is a blitz on all weeds in the entire growing area.

The deep parent roots of perennial weeds will regrow and push new growth up through a mulch. Pull or lever these shoots out from the loose compost layer with a trowel every week; without any leaves to photosynthesize, the parent roots will eventually be exhausted. This happens within four months for creeping buttercup (*Ranunculus repens*), six months for dandelions (*Taraxacum officinale*), a year for couch grass (*Elymus repens*), two years for bindweed (*Convolvulus arvensis* and *Calystegia sepium*) and longer for mare's tail (*Equisetum arvense*).

Using a black plastic mulch

Sometimes perennial weeds are so vigorous that a longer lasting mulch than cardboard and compost is required. Black plastic is a useful, durable mulch for clearing larger areas, and can be planted through. I have used it successfully on an area of old pasture where a mulch of card and compost was not enough to prevent regrowth of bindweed (*Convolvulus arvensis*). The area was covered with old black plastic (600 gauge), through which were transplanted winter squash, potatoes, and winter brassicas. It was necessary to remove bindweed that grew through these planting holes, but that was far easier than weeding the whole area. After harvesting the crops, the plastic was removed for reuse and the bindweed had been controlled.

Removing long, thick weed roots is easy in the soft surface of no dig beds.

Woven polypropylene weed control fabrics are expensive and shed polluting plastic threads into soil. It is important to remove any plastic mulch as soon as it has served its purpose. Do not use them for long-term "weed suppression" on beds or paths.

Maintaining weed-free beds and paths

Weeding little and often is the best way to control weeds and is easy thanks to no dig. This commitment to keep the ground clean saves time and work in the long run. Watch for weeds all the time, and hoe or pull them when tiny, especially in early spring when you notice a surface shimmer of green. Grasses have fibrous roots and are best pulled as seedlings.

Regularly mow and trim adjacent grass and weed areas, to reduce photosynthesis and root growth, and slow the entry of creeping weeds into beds. Check for weeds under the foliage of large vegetables, where limited space and light may prompt them to flower and drop seed when small. Stay vigilant in dry weather, when weed leaves become matt with a grey tinge, making them less visible.

Weedy pasture yielding harvests while covered with black plastic (top) and weed-free (above).

Manage compost heaps

If you add seeds to a cool compost heap, either from weeds or ornamental plants, these will germinate where the compost is spread. This need not be a problem in no dig beds where seedlings will be easy to hoe or pull from the soft compost. To avoid this however, try adding a larger volume of material to compost heaps so they become hot (see pp.52–57), or send seedheads to garden waste recycling.

BUILDING, PLANTING, AND MAINTAINING A NO DIG BED

Creating a no dig bed is an easy way to transform weedy ground into a productive garden in just a few hours, without disturbing the soil. Construction requires few materials, and you can modify the dimensions to suit any growing space. Plant up your new bed immediately in spring and summer, on the same day you make it, and you can be harvesting homegrown vegetables in as little as three weeks.

Tips for success

No dig beds can be made on any type of soil, including heavy clay, sites containing builders rubble, and even on top of concrete or slabs as long as the surface slopes to aid drainage. Remove any protruding rocks and dig out the main stems of woody plants, such as brambles. If the ground is uneven, fill hollows with new soil or compost, or use a sharp spade to shift the soil from ridges into any dips. Cut or strim down weed growth before beginning, so that mulches lie flat on the ground. You do not need to dig heavy soil beforehand, because soil life will aerate it for you, and all weed roots can be left in the soil.

Lay cardboard over the base of the bed to create a temporary barrier which suppresses weed growth during the eight to twelve weeks it takes for cardboard to decompose. Most weeds will be killed by this period of darkness, but the strong roots of perennial weeds will continue to push new growth up towards light, which needs to be removed regularly to weaken and eventually kill the roots (see p.40). Wooden edges are best as a temporary measure and aren't essential, but make it easier to create a bed and maintain weed-free edges initially.

Filling your bed with compost rather than soil will enable stronger, healthier plant growth for several years. Although I recommend a large quantity of compost for this initial stage, you will need much less in future. Use any well-decomposed compost (see pp.22–23) to fill the bulk of your bed, even if its texture is coarse. Just ensure that the top 5cm (2in) is soft and friable, with no large lumps. Firm the compost, to hold moisture and allow plants to anchor their roots. Have trays of young plants ready to transplant on the day you build your bed for quick crops while the weeds underneath gradually die.

Fill your no dig bed with module-raised plants for a quick and easy vegetable plot.

You will need

- Cardboard, brown rather than shiny, with plastic tape or metal staples removed

- Wooden planks x 4, new or reused to form edges of bed

- Large stones to support the planks for a few months

- Compost – 4–6 large barrowloads for 2.4m (8ft) x 1.2m (4ft) bed

- Peat-free multipurpose compost (optional) – about 3 x 40 litre bags

- Watering can with a fine rose

- Rake

- Wheelbarrow

- Trowel

- Dibber

- Young plants, seeds, seed potatoes for planting

1 Stake out the dimensions of your bed (here 2.4m/8ft x 1.2m/4ft) by pushing canes into the ground. Lay planks of wood flat to mark the bed edges, so that their corners meet, and remove the canes.

2 Lay cardboard over the base of the bed and underneath the planks so that it protrudes at least 15cm (6in) outside the bed's edge. Ensure that each piece of cardboard overlaps by 10–15cm (4–6in) so that the ground is completely covered. In dry conditions, water the cardboard thoroughly once it is laid.

3 Add the first layer of compost to make a mound in the centre. Place the wooden planks upright and keep them in position by pushing heavy stones against them on the outside of the bed, while pulling compost against them on the inside.

4 Top up the compost until it is at least 15cm (6in) deep and spread it out evenly with a rake to level the surface. Firm the compost by methodically treading the surface of the bed with your boots.

5 If the compost used to fill the bed has a coarse texture, add a final layer of peat-free multipurpose compost, with a fine texture suitable for transplanting and sowing. Level this layer with a rake and tread the surface of the bed lightly.

6 Finally, level the surface of the compost with the back of your rake, water thoroughly using a watering can fitted with a rose, and your bed is ready for seeds and plants.

7 Measure the spacing for each row of vegetables, dib holes for transplants, and push them in firmly – a little below surface level. Sow seeds, such as carrots, into drills made with your fingers or the back of a rake, and plant seed potatoes into slits made with a trowel. Water the bed after planting.

8 In spring, protect young plants from cold weather and pests by covering the whole bed with fleece after planting. Lay the fleece directly on top of plants and secure it at the edges with stones.

Alternative options

Laying cardboard to cover weedy soil, then adding a 15cm (6in) layer of compost is just one of many ways to create no dig beds. The exact method you use will depend on the condition of the ground and the amount of space you're dealing with. There is no need to lay cardboard on largely weed-free ground; simply rake soil level, spread a 5cm (2in) layer of compost, then sow and plant straight away. To make beds on a lawn, where grass and weed plants have weaker root systems thanks to regular mowing, cardboard with only a 5cm (2in) compost mulch can be enough to suppress weed growth. Wait a month for most of the lawn plants to die before planting, however, so that that they don't grow through where vegetable roots make holes in the cardboard. When preparing ground on a larger scale, especially where perennial weeds are persistent, plant vegetables through a black polythene mulch (see pp.40–41).

Plant potatoes through black plastic to produce a heavy crop while the weeds underneath die off.

Maintaining your bed

No dig methods reduce weed growth, but regular weeding is still essential to keep the soil clear.

New weeds from seeds that were in the surface compost are easily removed when they are very small by hoeing or pulling. The more difficult and ongoing weed growth is from roots of any strong perennial weeds underneath the cardboard, the new growth of which needs to be removed at weekly intervals using a trowel, so that the parent root is weakened and eventually dies (see p.40).

It's important to control perennial weeds at the edges of beds, to prevent them spreading. New weeds often push shoots through surface cardboard around bed edges as it decomposes, after about six weeks. When you see this happening, place more cardboard on top to suppress their growth further, and repeat a third and fourth time if necessary.

Watering depends on weather conditions, the consistency and maturity of compost, and how firmly you trod it down when the bed was made. Water new plantings every two days for their first week and after that you should not need to water often if your bed was thoroughly watered after construction (see pp.88–91). If fresh, hot compost was used to fill beds, they will need to be watered more frequently and with larger amounts for the first two or three months.

Making the most of your growing space

Plan successional planting for your bed so that you have seeds or young plants ready to go in as soon as space becomes available when your first planting is harvested and cleared (see pp.66–69). In this bed, for example, I planted leeks after potatoes, kale followed spinach, and lettuce filled the space left after

Remove wooden sides during the first growing season, along with growth from perennial weeds.

radishes and peas. You can also help maximize the productivity of your bed by interplanting or sowing new crops between vegetables which are still growing (see p.70).

Maximizing growth year after year

The temporary sides of your bed can be removed by its first autumn, because the initial 15cm (6in) depth of compost will measure less than 10cm (4in) deep within three months as a result of decomposition and consumption by soil organisms. With little left to hold, the sides become irrelevant and their removal allows plants to root into path soil (see p.29).

Firstly, lay fresh cardboard on the path, then remove the wooden edges of the bed and add a little extra compost along the newly exposed sides of the bed, before pushing them into a 45° slope. Finally, spread a little compost along the edge, then top with woodchip, to define the edge of the bed, reduce weed growth, and keep the soil fertile.

Add a new 3cm (1¼in) mulch of compost to the bed every year, from late autumn, whenever there is space to spread it, along with a similar depth of old wood chip or compost to the paths. This provides food for soil organisms and maintains fertility for plantings throughout the following year.

Perfecting paths

It's important to realize that when you have open-sided beds you need to create and maintain weed-free paths, because there is no barrier to prevent weeds rapidly spreading into your growing area. This is simple to achieve by covering fairly weed-free ground with a 3cm (1¼in) layer of wood chip. Where there are thick weeds, lay cardboard, topped with a little wood chip to suppress their growth and remove any shoots that grow through with a trowel. Alternatively, just lay bare cardboard, held in place by a few stones, and add more cardboard on top if bindweed or couch grass push up.

Using these methods, path soil can be as weed-free as your bed soil within a year or two and after that it's easy to keep them clean without using more cardboard, by removing any weeds that appear when they are tiny.

SOWING FOR SUCCESS

Rather than sowing seeds directly outdoors, I start almost all the vegetables I grow in modules under cover, for transplanting after three to five weeks (see p.84). I find that this has many advantages, and repays many times over the modest amount of time and effort required. The exceptions that I sow direct are carrots and parsnips, because their long tap roots are often broken during transplanting, along with garlic, onion sets, and potatoes, which contain sufficient stored energy to start growth without extra help.

More reliable germination

Sowing in warm, controlled conditions under cover gives precious seeds the best chance to germinate successfully, keeping losses to a minimum. Seeds sown outside, especially early in the growing season, are at the mercy of unpredictable weather, which means they are slow to germinate and have a higher failure rate. To compensate for this, you need more seeds to achieve a full stand of plants from direct sowings, and a full bed is less certain because of potential weather and pest damage. Sowing under cover gives more dependable results and reduces spending on seeds.

Protection from pests and bad weather

Raising plants under cover helps to protect them from pests and bad weather when they're small and at their most vulnerable. Think of it as a plant nursery or kindergarten, where delicate seedlings receive extra care and attention, in the same way that we look after young children. A clean propagating area with no pests in damp corners or under rotting wood, ensures that seeds have a healthy environment in which to germinate evenly and grow strongly. These sturdy little plants are then quick to establish outside, making them less likely to suffer pest damage.

Sowing seeds under cover gives them the best possible start and allows you to keep beds full.

Extend the growing season

Nights can still be very cold, even frosty, in a greenhouse during spring, which does not give seeds the consistent 24-hour warmth they need to germinate. Rather than heat my greenhouse in late winter and early spring, I get spring sowings off to an early start in the house, where nighttime temperatures are always around 12–15°C (54–59°F). After about a week, I move the more cold-tolerant seedlings out to the greenhouse, sometimes onto bottom heat for a week or two (see pp.79–81). You could also use a small electric heat mat to

germinate the first sowings. Providing this extra heat for your first sowings produces earlier harvests.

Efficient use of space

Modules or seed trays of young plants can be densely packed together under cover if you transplant seedlings young and small (see pp.84–85). Move plants on quickly to prevent overcrowding and leggy growth as plants compete for light. Together with multisowing (see pp.78–79), this allows hundreds or thousands of seedlings to be grown, even in limited propagation space, and stops valuable bed space being wasted while seedlings establish from direct sowings. These transplants can be raised while a preceding vegetable matures in a bed, so they are ready to go in as soon as that crop is cleared. This ability to overlap the growing periods of vegetables is one of the best ways to get the most from a small space. Increase productivity further by setting young plants among a maturing crop, a technique known as interplanting (see p.70), so that new plantings are well established by the time the first is removed. My 1.5 x 5m (5 x 16ft) no dig trial bed yields 100kg (220lb) of vegetables annually, because I produce two harvests from every part of the bed each year.

My greenhouse is packed with young vegetable plants throughout spring and summer.

DELVE DEEPER SOURCING SUCCESSFUL SEEDS

A growing ability to produce hybrid seeds and the low price of seeds in general has caused the quality of many traditional or "heirloom" open-pollinated varieties (OPs) to be eroded, as seed companies focus on the production of more profitable F1 hybrids. From the seed of poorly maintained varieties grow plants with low yields, poor colour, and even disappointing flavours, which gardeners may attribute to their own mistakes. I want to encourage an understanding of this issue that many gardeners are unaware of, to help you choose seeds that will set you on the path to successful harvests.

Choose reliable varieties and good quality seed to avoid disappointing results.

It is labour intensive to remove (rogue) any plants that are small, misshapen, or off-colour from a large field of plants growing for seed production. If farmers are not being paid to rogue the crop properly then these unwanted characteristics (traits) will be present in the seed harvest and affect gardeners' crops.

I have noticed the deterioration of a number of popular varieties over the years, sometimes to the point where their poor growth has forced me to find alternatives. Beetroot 'Boltardy' still resists bolting when sown early, but now often produces pale or small roots and thick, chard-like stems. I avoid growing most open-pollinated varieties of Brussels sprouts, tomato 'Gardener's Delight', and broccoli 'Late Purple Sprouting'.

In July 2021, I voiced my concerns about the performance of open-pollinated varieties to seed producers in the UK, through the Royal Horticultural Society (RHS). Brian Smith, who had a long career in plant breeding research at the National Vegetable Research Station at Wellesbourne, and is now Chair of RHS Vegetable Trials forum, explained to me that, "After the introduction and success

THE PROBLEM WITH CHEAP SEEDS

There is pressure on seed companies to offer popular vegetable varieties at prices so low that they in no way reflect the amount of work required to produce genuinely good seed. Therefore companies channel resources into more lucrative F1 hybrids, and some of the older or heritage varieties have not been maintained well enough to retain their desirable traits and qualities.

of F1 hybrids from the late 1960s, the effort to maintain OPs has diminished to the point where little maintenance is done on heirloom varieties".

USING F1 HYBRIDS

I grow F1 hybrids where there are no good open-pollinated alternatives, because it's such a maddening waste of space and time to grow a variety that gives poor results. Hybrid seed is more expensive, and does deliver what is described on the seed packet, which is a crucial first step to success. When I first grew broccoli 'Claret' F1 in place of 'Late Purple Sprouting', I could scarcely believe the increased size of head and cropping period. The alternative to beetroot 'Boltardy' is 'Pablo' F1, which grows lovely uniform, round roots with small stems.

SOURCING GOOD QUALITY SEED

There are thankfully still some brilliant open-pollinated varieties available and before you buy seed, do check each vegetable profile in this book for the varieties that my gardening experience gives me cause to recommend. It is also worth looking beyond the price of seed packets to find seed companies that care about the future of OP varieties and work hard to look after them, either by producing their own seed or subcontracting trusted gardeners and farmers to enable them to supply larger quantities (see p.286). Another option for many vegetables, although not all, is to save your own seed (see pp.104–107). I encourage you to give it a try, but only from OP varieties because seed from hybrids does not grow true.

Use beetroot 'Boltardy' for early sowings, but more consistent hybrid varieties for later crops.

MAKING YOUR OWN COMPOST

Compost heaps convert waste material into a valuable mulch and feed for your no dig soil. The process is fascinating, life-giving, and less precise than is sometimes suggested, because there are so many variations in every garden and season. You have scope to tailor your approach and be creative with your set-up. When this produces good results, making compost comes a close second to the fun of gardening. The first step is to understand the key principles.

The composting process

Composting harnesses and hastens the natural processes of decomposition, to transform organic waste into crumbly, brown material. Many organisms facilitate the decomposition, such as bacteria, fungi, brandling worms, and woodlice, and we need to create the right conditions in a heap for these to thrive. This means adding the best possible proportions of carbon-rich "brown" materials and nitrogen-rich "green" materials (see p.53) to feed the process, as well as to maintain a balance of air (oxygen) and moisture within the heap. Heat is generated when you add a mix of materials in decent quantities, and a heap's temperature provides an indication of the speed of decomposition within it.

Where to site a compost heap

Compost heaps should not smell and can be an attractive feature, rather than hidden away in a hard-to-reach corner. For larger spaces I recommend a central location, in order to save a lot of time transporting waste to the heaps (less so for spreading compost because of the decrease in volume). Site heaps in sun or shade, on soil preferably, but a hard surface will work if it's the only option, as long as there is good drainage. You can also place a compost heap on weedy ground, including where there are difficult perennial weeds, because they cannot grow up through a heap's thick layer of organic waste. Control weeds around the edges with a light-excluding cardboard mulch.

What type to choose?

Match the size of your heap or heaps to your growing area, because a small garden will not generate enough waste to fill a large bin, and bins make better compost when you fill them within two or three months. Most small and urban gardens will be well served by one or two plastic, cylindrical bins, because they are light and can be lifted off easily when you want to

The main row of large compost bays is positioned at the heart of my garden at Homeacres.

*Adding to the heap in thin layers makes it easier
to balance green and brown materials.*

spread the finished compost. For larger gardens and allotments I recommend creating compost bays from pallets to generate at least a half cubic metre (half cubic yard) of compost from each filling (see pp.56–57). It is possible to manage with one heap, but two makes things easier, because you can be filling the second one with waste while the first finishes decomposing. A third bay allows you to turn the first bay's contents while you continue to fill the second one.

Compostable materials

Almost all organic waste can be composted, and successful decomposition happens when you achieve a good balance of ingredients and moisture, for an end product that is neither soggy nor too dry. Waste can be divided into carbon-rich "brown" materials, which feed fungi and other decomposing organisms and maintain air pockets, and nitrogen-rich "green" materials, which feed the bacterial

decomposers. In terms of volume, you need to add 60–75 per cent mostly green materials to a heap to enable speedy work by decomposing organisms, whose numbers and activity will increase if the heap warms up.

Green materials are leafy, mostly green in colour, and often contain significant moisture, all of which means they decompose rapidly. Examples include grass mowings, weeds, and vegetable waste from the garden or kitchen, as well as brown-coloured coffee grounds and fresh horse manure (without bedding) which fall into this category because of their high nitrogen content. Brown materials are woody, fibrous, slow to decompose, and sometimes dry. Common sources of brown material are woody prunings, wood chip, sawdust, straw, paper, non-shiny cardboard, and dry autumn leaves. Many materials are not totally green or brown, but a combination of the two; for example, green tree leaves, green (new and unripe) wood, and tough vegetable stems have both green

Split tough brassica stems along their length and chop before adding to the heap.

The value of temperature

Heat is generated in a heap by the activity of bacteria, which feed on the recent additions of green material. It's possible to make good compost without a heap ever going above 30°C (86°F), but the two issues with this are that weeds seeds will survive (it takes 50–55°C/122–131°F to kill them), and the process takes longer. The volume and frequency of additions to a heap determine how much heat is generated: bigger heaps get hotter and retain heat for longer. Pallet heaps of at least 1m² (11ft²) can temporarily generate temperatures that kill weed seeds and speed up decomposition. But they generate and hold much less heat than my large main heaps of 3m² (32ft²), which can maintain 60°C (140°F), even three weeks after we finish adding materials. The internal temperature of heaps can easily be monitored using a compost thermometer, with a 30–40cm (12–16in)-long probe.

and brown characteristics. During summer there is considerably more green waste than brown, so remember in winter to save dry leaves and chipped wood to mix with summer greens.

Smaller pieces of any material decompose more quickly, because there is more surface area available to microbes, so chop and/or crush stems and fibrous materials so that they are less than 10cm (4in) long before adding them to the heap. Invest in a shredder if the garden generates large amounts of woody waste, or you can run a rotary lawnmower over fibrous (but not woody) materials laid on the ground, which chops then catches the shredded waste in the grass collection box.

It's easy to be put off by negative advice suggesting that you shouldn't compost weeds, lemon peel, rhubarb leaves, diseased material, and many other wastes. I would like to reassure gardeners that you can add all of these, and free yourself from these concerns. This saves much time spent in separating out "uncompostable" waste, and allows you to enjoy filling heaps. To my heaps I regularly add bindweed roots and the leaves of tomato plants with late blight, always without any adverse effects, and the same applies to heaps with little heat. The only thing I wouldn't compost is Japanese knotweed.

Balancing air and moisture

Air is vital for making sweet-smelling, aerobic compost. Without sufficient air, the bacteria that facilitate aerobic decomposition die and anaerobic bacteria take over, resulting in soggy compost and a sulphurous smell. An excess of green waste can add too much moisture, especially in a wet climate, which pushes out the air and causes anaerobic conditions. Fibrous brown materials, such as woody prunings and wood chips, add volume and hold air in a heap. It may be necessary to water compost heap materials in hot, dry climates, but this is rarely good advice in the UK, where it's often best to add dry cardboard or paper to soak up the moisture held in lots of green leaves. It is also worth keeping a lid or cover over compost heaps to keep out the rain and prevent waterlogging. That's why I have a roof over my main compost bays, and use corrugated iron covers over pallet heaps that are not currently being filled (see image opposite).

Turning the heap

Turning speeds up decomposition by introducing oxygen for aerobic bacteria, and ensures a more even end product from your compost heap. It is also a chance to discover that trowel you lost a few months before! A heap needs turning only once, from five to eight weeks after making the last additions, when the contents have cooled and are no longer subsiding fast. There is no hard and fast method, but it's easiest to move all the contents of a heap into an adjacent empty bay, using a manure fork to mix soggy and dry materials and shake out the lumps as you lift them, which mixes materials and introduces air. If half-finished compost looks wet, check the moisture level by squeezing a handful. If more than two droplets of water fall out then it's too wet, probably from too much green material or rain. Add dry paper while turning to soak up the excess moisture.

When is compost ready?

Ready does not mean perfect and don't wait for or expect your homemade compost to be as finely textured as bagged composts you buy. For spreading on beds, as opposed to using for propagation, small woody pieces are good because they contribute to a lovely, fungi-rich soil surface. Break up larger lumps with a fork and pick out more substantial woody bits to put back on the current heap. Look to have finished compost within a year of starting to fill a heap, and if your heap reaches 55°C (131°F) for a decent amount of time, you can have excellent compost within six months. Aim to produce something that's reasonably dark brown, with a soft, fairly dry texture, so that when lifted and shaken it falls through a fork. Soggy, black compost suggests anaerobic decomposition, which isn't ideal, but it can still be used, spread onto a bed as a mulch to allow it to dry out, so that decomposition can continue.

Use a fork to extract crumbly finished compost from the heap and break up any lumps.

Create a pallet compost heap

Pallets made from untreated wood make excellent sides for a compost heap because they are cheap or free, and will serve for between three and five years. They are quick to assemble using only wire, which makes the bays easy to open, to move, or repair if needed. I knock the bottoms off the pallets and enclose heaps with just the top frame, because full-depth pallets need extra space, are heavier to handle, and are more difficult to keep weed-free at the base.

You will need

· Wooden pallets x 4

· Wire 3mm ($^1/_8$in) thick

· Pliers

· Cardboard – brown with plastic tape and metal staples removed

· Drawing pins

1 Lay out four pallets on the ground around a square base of at least 1m² (11ft²).

2 Lift two pallets to make a 90° angle at their corner and attach them at this corner by wrapping 3mm ($^1/_8$in)-thick wire around the uprights, one wire near the top and one near the bottom. Twist the wire ends with pliers or by hand to fasten securely.

3 Use the same technique to attach each remaining side and form a rigid, square bay.

4 Lay cardboard around the edge of the heap, tucked under the sides and not covering the base, to reduce regrowth of any perennial weeds and stop them spreading into the heap.

5 Line the inside of the heap with cardboard, to retain warmth and moisture. Attach it to the pallets with drawing pins. In windy locations,

Pallet heaps hold waste from larger gardens (top) and are home to toads and other wildlife (above).

add the cardboard a little at a time from the base, pushing it back into place as the heap is filled with waste.

6 Add organic waste from your garden and kitchen (see p.53). Tread down any bulky materials, at the beginning especially, to prevent large gaps and air pockets. You could fill the heap in anything from six weeks to six months.

TOOLS

No dig needs fewer tools, and they are used less, as there is so little work to do with the soil. Keeping the number of tools to a minimum means they are always to hand and makes it more affordable to buy the best quality. It's vital that you feel comfortable using them, so try tools before buying if possible or study reviews online carefully, paying as much attention to the handle as the tool's working end. I use copper tools, which minimize soil disturbance because the blades don't rust and stay sharp and smooth. This also means they rarely need to be cleaned after use. If you have steel tools, brush any soil from their blades before putting them away.

Long-handled dibber

This is a key planting tool that keeps soil disturbance to a minimum and can be made from an old wooden tool handle or bought. I've used one since the 1980s, because the 60cm (2ft)-long handle makes it easy to use, with less bending, a better overview of the planting area, and more leverage to make slightly deeper holes when necessary. Its 5cm (2in) diameter makes holes the perfect size for the rootballs of module-raised plants – you do not need a hole any larger – while the rounded tip pushes easily into soft no dig soil without leaving a cavity below the rootball.

Trowel

A trowel is so useful for removing new growth of perennial weeds, as well as planting potatoes and plants that have been raised in pots. It needs to slide in and out of the soil easily and have a sharp blade, and I find that a copper trowel retains those qualities with little maintenance. There is a choice of blade shapes, but I find that one about 16.5cm (6½in) long and 6.5cm (2½in) wide does everything well.

Knife

A small pocket knife with a folding blade that's easy to open and shut is invaluable for so many little jobs, including harvesting, trimming vegetables, cutting string, and cutting up plants to put on the compost heap. Make the size comfortable for you and something that will fit easily in your pocket, so you will always have it handy. Buy a good quality knife that stays sharp and learn how to use a sharpening stone to sharpen the blade. Over many years I've found that the blades of Opinel knives stay sharp for longer than most other knives.

Long-handled dibber, knife, and copper trowel.

My galvanized metal wheelbarrow is now 30 years old and has moved hundreds of tons of material.

Wheelbarrow

This is the workhorse in a busy garden, so avoid cheap flimsy models and invest in a robust one, made of galvanized metal, with a simple pneumatic tyre. Size is an important consideration and I would suggest opting for a larger one than you think you'll need, because most materials you move around the garden will be light and it's efficient to transport a bigger quantity in one go.

Rake

I use a rake for levelling the surface of beds that have been disturbed by harvesting or where compost has been applied and it's a bit uneven. Choose a rake with a short, solid blade, about 30cm (12in) wide, rather than a wiry spring-tine rake. You will use it for light work only, levelling soft compost when filling beds or before planting.

Spade

Don't laugh! This is a no dig book, but it's worth having a good spade even if you are a no-digger. Spades are useful for planting larger trees and shrubs, removing bramble or dock roots, chopping large plants, and levering out parsnips. Although it seems counterintuitive, choose a large spade with a heavy handle, since this will actually make it easier to do heavy work. Copper blades slide into soil easily and retain their sharp edge.

Copper rake, spade, manure fork, and swivel oscillating hoe.

Manure fork

With curved prongs that are longer and thinner than those of a digging fork, this is an absolute must for turning, moving, and spreading compost. It slides effortlessly past fibrous and woody material in a heap, unlike the blade of a spade, allowing you to lift up a lump of material and move it to wherever it's going. I often use it to spread compost too.

Hoe

This tool is only appropriate where there is a large surface area of soil and won't be needed for one or two beds. Hoeing disturbs only the top 1cm ($^1/_2$in) of soil and is a fantastic quick way to kill tiny weeds. I use an oscillating or swivel hoe, which has a pivoted head and a thin blade that is sharp on both edges, to cut weeds on both the push and pull stroke.

Watering cans

My watering cans and roses are made of plastic. Quality plastic cans are durable; the can in my greenhouse is 17 years old and I really value it. In my experience, steel cans and metal roses don't perform as well. A large can could hold up to 12 litres (2½ gallons), which is obviously heavy. Use the biggest one your strength allows to enable you to water beds efficiently. Usually larger cans come with a larger rose that produces bigger water droplets, which is fine for watering beds containing established plants, but a smaller can (7–10 litres/1½–2 gallons) with a finer rose is better for watering young plants and seedlings in modules.

There's a certain dynamic to a good watering can, which means they are not all equal and should be chosen carefully. Keep cans and roses clean so that they can function well. Roses are easily clogged up with debris from dirty water butts.

Long-handled edging shears and half-moon edger.

Long-handled edging shears and half-moon edger

These tools are used to keep the edge of turf neat and prevent grasses and weeds spreading into beds. The half-moon edger has a thin, straight blade that is useful to cut a clean new edge twice a year, a little back from its current position, to stop the lawn creeping forwards. A copper half-moon edger stays sharp, but a steel edger will benefit from sharpening. Long-handled shears are designed to tightly trim grass edges. Do this about once a month to maintain a tidy perimeter to the plot. Sharpen them every two or three months, depending on how much you use them.

Watering using large (left) and fine (right) roses.

CHAPTER 3

The principles of growing vegetables

TIMING SOWINGS

Finding the best time to sow each vegetable makes success more likely. Temperature is a key factor, so check before you sow that conditions will be warm enough for germination and transplanting (see pp.79 and 84). It is also possible to time sowings to avoid potential pests, and the natural flowering time of leaf vegetables. I have condensed the knowledge you need to do this into sowing times given in the vegetable and herb directory. They are a starting point for you to discover the timings for sowing that work best in your garden and climate.

Two categories of hardiness

Vegetables fall into two broad categories: hardy, cold-resistant plants and tender, warmth-loving ones. Hardy plants are not killed by frost, which means they can be sown early in the year. I recommend making your first sowings in mid-February rather than January, so they have less chance of meeting extreme cold when transplanted, and can grow more strongly in the all-important, improved light levels. From mid-February to mid-March under cover, you can sow a good third of all the vegetables you're going to grow.

The second phase of sowing is tender plants, such as cucumbers and climbing beans, that would be killed by frost and also need warmth to grow successfully. Many of these are fast growing, and do best when sown under cover between one and four weeks before your last frost date (see p.34). This allows them to

Hardy peas (left) grow in cold conditions, while tender sweet peppers (right) must have warmth.

Pak choi sown in August avoids insect pests.

grow steadily in sufficient warmth and avoids having plants stuck under cover when it's too cold to transplant them. Wait until after the last frost date to make sowings outdoors; in the UK, it could be early June before the soil is warm enough. One exception to this is the warmth-loving vegetables that are slow growers, especially capsicums, aubergines, and to some extent tomatoes, which are best sown earlier under cover to extend their growing season and produce plants that are already large when planted out.

Avoid the natural flowering time

Many leafy vegetables, salad crops, and annual herbs rise to flower in spring or late summer, bringing your harvest to an end even if it's only recently begun. This is known as bolting, and you rarely find information about these important flowering times on seed packets. A common example is salad leaves of the brassica family, including pak choi, salad rocket, and mizuna, which rise to flower in late spring. Seed packets say to sow in March and April, but this means the plants soon flower without many leaves to pick. A far better alternative is to make sowings in late summer, from which these plants are all highly productive over a long period.

Outwit pests

Pests tend to be prevalent at particular times of year and carefully timed sowings can sometimes allow plants to grow with minimal damage. This is another reason to delay sowing brassica salad crops until late summer, because the young leaves of spring and early summer sowings are often eaten by flea beetles, which pepper young leaves with holes. For peas and broad beans it's the other way around: early sowings are more likely to escape the insect pests which arrive in early summer and cause more damage to later sowings.

Coriander rushes to flower in summer.

SUCCESSION PLANTING

The idea of succession is that you keep your ground planted all the time, at least until winter. Soil doesn't need a rest and is, in fact, healthier with plants rooting into it (see pp.30–31). With your beds filled in this way, no sunlight is wasted because there are always leaves converting solar energy into organic carbon, which plants make available to the soil food web (see pp.16–17). Succession plantings also reduce the amount of space you need to grow vegetables. It's often assumed that each vegetable takes a whole year to reach maturity, but most grow from seed to harvest within half a year (half-season crops), which gives you time to grow a second, or even a third, follow-on or second planting for autumn and winter harvests (see p.69).

Raising transplants buys you time

Rather than sowing direct into the soil once you've cleared a vegetable, you can add significant time to the growing season by sowing under cover three or four weeks earlier, to overlap the growth periods of first and second plantings. Doing this will give you new transplants ready to pop in on the day that the soil is cleared, preventing valuable growing time being wasted.

No dig means that you don't need to "prepare" soil or spread compost for these summer plantings, which makes the process quick and easy at a busy time in the garden. You've already done your soil feeding and preparation by spreading compost in late autumn or early winter, making the ground ready for the rest of the year (see p.47).

Succession planting keeps beds productive. By 25th August these beds are filled with second crops. Top to bottom: spring broccoli after broad beans; brassica salads under mesh follow onions; lettuce and beetroot replace spring onions; broccoli follows lettuce; lettuce is newly interplanted with spinach; and endive and radicchio follow cauliflower and cabbage.

Organizing follow-on crops

Timing is key in order to have transplants of second follow-on vegetables ready at the best moment. To enable you to do this, it's important to work out the approximate last harvest date for a first crop so that you can sow the follow-on crop three or four weeks beforehand. Check the lists of crops for the first and second halves of the year on p.69, alongside a list of what you want to grow, so you can create your own planting sequences. Consult each vegetable and herb profile for precise timings.

Many vegetables that grow through the first half of the year are harvested and cleared by the middle of July, and often earlier, so it's good to be thinking about making most sowings for follow-on crops through May and June, with a few in July to follow later harvests. For the second half crops, choose vegetables that succeed when sown in summer: beetroot, carrots, and calabrese are great for both first and second plantings, but not all vegetables are. Plants grown outside their natural season will have more problems with pests and diseases, and deliver a lower yield. I don't recommend potatoes for summer planting because of the risk of late blight, and the fact that they will only produce a small harvest if they do manage to grow.

Keep records of the dates that you sow and clear each variety of each vegetable, to build up knowledge of the sowing dates that work best in your climate, and when crops are usually cleared after the last harvest. This is the route to rewarding succession plantings, for a whole year of growth and harvests.

Careful planning is needed to have seedlings ready when space becomes available.

Watering leeks planted in June, after cabbages were cleared.

FIRST HALF CROPS

Vegetables whose final harvest is before the end of the summer, and often earlier.

Radish (ip/is)

Early turnips (ip/is)

Spring cabbage

Spinach (ipb)

Early Florence fennel

Garlic (planted previous autumn) (ipb)

Beetroot

Lettuce (ipb esp. leaf lettuce)

Broad beans

Peas

Carrots (ipb)

Salad onions (ipb)

Early calabrese

Early cabbage

Early cauliflower

First and second early potatoes

Bulb onions and shallots (ipb)

Celery

Maincrop potatoes

Dwarf French beans (ip)

Ridge cucumbers (ip)

Basil

Outdoor tomatoes (ip)

Winter squash

SECOND HALF CROPS

Vegetables which have time to crop before or during winter, from a summer sowing.

Leeks

Celery

Courgette

Salad onions (ip)

Lettuce (ip and ipb)

Climbing and dwarf beans

Carrots (is)

Swede (ipb)

Brussels sprouts (ip)

Savoy/winter cabbage

Purple sprouting broccoli

Beetroot (ip)

Chard

Chicory/radicchio (ip)

Endive (ip)

Autumn calabrese

Romanesco and autumn cauliflower

Kale (ip)

Winter radish and turnips

Florence fennel (ip)

Salad rocket and mustards

Coriander, dill, chervil, parsley (ip)

Spinach (ip)

Pak choi

Chinese cabbage

Ridge cucumber (ip and ipb)

Onion, salad onion, cabbage, and garlic to overwinter

Corn salad (ip)

KEY   ip/is – interplant and intersow as succession plantings (see p.70)

ipb – vegetables that you can interplant or intersow between (see p.70)

Interplanting and intersowing

The next progression from succession is to notice vegetables still in the ground that are approaching their final harvest, and to transplant or sow among them. This is known as interplanting, or intersowing if seeds are sown direct, and it gains even more growing time for your follow-on plantings, because they are in the ground three or four weeks before the first vegetable is cleared. It's satisfying to feel that beds can be more than one hundred per cent full!

This is especially useful in summer and early autumn, when plants you've raised need to go into the ground promptly in order to have enough growing time before winter. Beds are often full, but interplanting allows you to find the small amount of space needed by transplants or newly sown seeds. Two combinations I particularly like and plant every year are Brussels sprouts among carrots

and spinach between lettuce. Interplanting can maximize space in spring and early summer too, when you can interplant fast-growing radish and turnips between early potatoes, and pick them before the potatoes need that space. Or you could finish harvesting a few lettuce or clumps of beetroot a couple of weeks early, to make space for ridge cucumber or outdoor tomato plants.

In my experience, small transplants thrive in the companionship of other plants - and grow better than they would if there were large open spaces around them. Gardeners worry about competition, but as long as you don't try to plant among crops that cover the ground completely, and ensure that the existing vegetable will finish within a month, this will afford the new plantings enough light and space just to become established. Growth is subsequently rapid, as soon as the plants that have finished cropping are removed. There is a notion that some plants don't grow well alongside other plants, but I have never found this to happen. You are free to try many combinations and will notice how successful interplanting is in healthy, no dig soil. I believe this is because young plants have access to an established fungal network (see pp.16–17) and profit from being part of an existing community of plants.

Interplanting also creates beautiful combinations of foliage colours and textures, and these possibilities are fun to explore. A lovely example is the red, frilled foliage of summer-sown lettuce 'Lollo Rossa' interplanted with bright green spinach, before the lettuce plants are twisted out in September.

Winter purslane thriving alongside lettuce (left). Other interplanting combinations include (clockwise from top left): Florence fennel among ridge cucumber, chervil between lettuce, spinach between lettuce, Brussels sprouts with carrots.

Relax about crop rotation

A four-year rotation, which involves grouping related vegetable plants together and growing each family in a different area of the garden in successive years, has long been presented as an essential practice to achieve strong growth and prevent a build-up of pests and diseases in the soil. However, this system stems from agricultural rotations, which are impractical to implement on a garden scale and don't take into account the range of vegetables often grown in gardens. They also discourage gardeners from planting follow-on crops.

I don't practise formal crop rotation, because I find it restrictive and unnecessary to prevent disease on plants growing in healthy no dig soil. I am conducting trials where broad beans and potatoes have been grown in the same piece of ground for the last seven years. So far good, disease-free harvests have been recorded each year. Having said that, I don't advocate growing the same vegetable in the same place every year; it's healthy to move plants around, but without formal rules, so that you can fit the vegetables that you want to eat into your space.

Flexibility is valuable, because although we all start with an idea or plan of what's going where, things don't always work out and growth varies with the weather. You may be popping in plants somewhere entirely different to the original plan, and it is developing this ability to respond that allows you to get the most from a growing space. For example, I would usually follow calabrese with vegetables from a different family, such as beetroot, but I'm not rigid about it. Sometimes, and very successfully, I have followed calabrese with another crop of calabrese, because circumstances meant that was the only place available for them to be transplanted. Succession planting and interplanting are good for mixing things up within a single growing season, creating mini-rotations that have the

added benefit of providing a varied diet to soil microbes. Rather than occupying soil with maincrop potatoes for a whole growing season, grow second early potatoes as a half-season crop to be harvested in summer and follow

with a planting of leeks for winter. This not only rotates crops around the garden quickly, but also yields two harvests where otherwise there might only have been one.

An attractive patchwork of crops without formal rotation.

PROPAGATION

Good propagation skills are important to achieve reliable germination and raise strong young plants that will thrive when transplanted. Looking after seedlings carefully when they are at their most fragile has incredible benefits. The keys to success are selecting the right containers, good compost to fill them, and a suitable growing space, so that your seedlings start strongly.

Choosing containers

The four types of container that I use for propagation are seed trays, module trays, and small pots in two sizes (7cm/2¾in and 9cm/3½in diameter). My recommendation is to sow into small containers to avoid an excess of compost around seeds. This helps to prevent waterlogging and saves valuable space in your propagation area. Small seed trays allow you to germinate a large number of seeds in surprisingly little space, and they fit easily onto a windowsill. Module trays with 3cm (1¼in) diameter cells require little compost and enable you to sow many seeds in a small area. Cells that taper towards the bottom work well for almost all vegetables, with the exception of beans with large seeds, which grow best in trays with 5cm (2in) cells. Drainage is vital and any container must have large enough holes in the base to allow excess water to pass through.

PLASTIC USE

Plastic remains the most practical material for pots and trays, and sadly it's possible to generate a lot of plastic waste when flimsy products disintegrate after one or two uses. To avoid this, invest in durable polypropylene containers, which can be reused for many years and even over a lifetime if treated with care. I became so fed up with throwing poor quality plastic away that I had a module tray manufactured to my own design (see p.286). Also watch out for pots being given away for reuse outside garden centres, or reuse plastic food pots and trays for sowing, after making drainage holes in the base. Making your own soil blocks with a special machine is one way to avoid plastic entirely, but this time consuming process is unlikely to be practical for all gardeners.

Finding the right compost

Good quality compost is key for propagation, because seeds need free-draining conditions and sufficient nutrients to allow them to grow into surprisingly large young plants in proportion to their root balls. Choose carefully because not all compost on sale is suitable for seed-sowing, and quality varies between brands, over time, and even between batches of compost with the same label. Look for the

Select the right container for each sowing to save space and encourage good germination.

words "potting", "potting and container", "multipurpose", or "all-purpose" compost, all of which suggest that the product will contain sufficient nutrients to grow seedlings in small cells and pots.

Once you purchase compost and open the bag, there are clues to its quality. For propagation, the texture needs to be fine enough to fill module cells evenly. It also shouldn't contain too much undecomposed wood, which will deprive plants of nitrogen – but this may be in small pieces and difficult to see. Dark or black compost is not necessarily a sign of good quality and a paler brown colour can also be good. Homemade compost works well, but needs to be sufficiently dry to pass through a 4mm (⅛in) sieve, to remove large pieces. The word "organic" can be used to describe any compost and does not indicate that it is free from synthetic chemical residues or fertilizers. Composts may be contaminated with pyralid weedkiller which will harm susceptible seedlings (see p.21).

Check that compost for sowing has a fine texture and contains plenty of nutrients.

Peas and broad beans sown into four different composts show how quality can affect growth.

HOW TO SOW

To maximize the likelihood of germination, you need to know how best to sow each type of seed. Advice for individual crops can be found in the vegetable and herb directory, which will enable you to choose whether to sow into modules or a seed tray, singly or in groups, and at what depth to place the seeds. Then you need to provide the correct amount of moisture, warmth, and occasionally light, to stimulate germination.

Sowing into modules

Trays of small module cells are ideal for making quick sowings of seeds that are large enough to handle, such as onions, leeks, beetroot, chard, peas, and beans, because they can be dropped in accurately. Seeds can either be sown individually or multisown to make clumps of particular number (see pp.78–79). You can transplant many vegetables as small, module-raised seedlings directly to their final growing position, or pot them on to grow larger before planting.

You will need

- Module tray
- Potting compost
- Seeds – here borlotti beans and runner bean 'Czar'
- Watering can fitted with a fine rose

1 Fill a module tray generously with compost, pushing the compost down quite firmly so that there is a decent amount in each cell to provide nutrients for growth. This also ensures that the root ball holds together when you pop the young plant out of the module.

2 Push down gently with your finger to make a little indent in the compost at the centre of each cell.

3 Drop the seed or seeds into each indent. It's easier to lay larger seeds, like courgettes, on their side than to push them in vertically, and they will germinate just as well.

4 Drop or push compost into the cells to refill the indent. A rule of thumb is to add a depth of compost roughly equivalent to the thickness of the seed. Lift up the tray to feel its weight before watering.

5 Use a can fitted with a fine rose to water generously at this stage, to be certain that the compost is fully moist in every cell, giving all seeds the opportunity to germinate.

6 Lift up the tray to see if water is coming out of the drainage holes and to feel the weight of the tray: wet compost feels remarkably heavy. Dry compost will need to be watered a few times, allowing time for the water to soak in between each watering.

Keep labels to reuse repeatedly.

Seed trays

Tiny seeds, such as celery, celeriac, and even lettuce, are difficult to handle with any precision and are best sown into a seed tray. Seedlings can then be pricked out individually into modules (see p.83) to give them more space to grow on.

Fill the seed tray with compost and push down only gently to give a loose fill. This aids the drainage of water from the trays, which often drain slowly, and also makes it easier to lift out seedlings. Water the compost with a fine rose before sowing, because small seeds may float away if you water after sowing. Failure is often the result of sowing too deep, so sow onto the surface and cover with compost as lightly as you dare. Celery and celeriac need light to germinate and should not be covered with any compost; instead, cover the tray with a sheet of glass or slide it inside a clear plastic bag, to keep compost moist during germination.

Multisowing optimizes your growing space. I've reused this polystyrene tray for 35 years.

Labelling

Label trays immediately to keep track of each sowing. You can reuse plastic labels many times; check that alternatives such as wooden labels are strong, otherwise they rot in the moist compost and you lose useful information before transplanting. I recommend writing in permanent marker pen, because pencil or biro can wash off labels when you water. There is limited space on labels and the two most important things that I record are the variety and sowing date, which immediately tells me what I need to know. The variety is important to label because it's often difficult to distinguish between young plants of varieties that need to be treated differently, such as tomatoes destined for growing under cover or outside.

Multisowing

Sowing several seeds together to develop into a cluster of plants is a wonderful way to sow quickly and raise large numbers of seedlings in a small space, using less compost. Another remarkable benefit is that seedlings actually grow better when they're close to one another, both in modules and after transplanting; there is no diminution of growth through what people might think of as competition. For many vegetables, multisowing gives a higher overall yield than single plants and means that you can grow more food in a small space.

The important thing is to work out which vegetables to multisow and with how many seeds, because one result is a larger harvest of medium-sized vegetables, so this would not be the right option if, for example, you want large swedes or celeriac to store. Check the vegetable and herb directory to find the suitability of individual crops and the recommended number of seeds to multisow into each module.

BEST VEGETABLES TO MULTISOW

Radish, turnip, salad onions, onions, leeks, beetroot, peas, spinach, and many salad plants to harvest for smaller leaves.

Achieving good germination

A key condition for successful germination once seeds are sown is warmth, and that means 24-hour warmth until you see that first tiny leaf appear. During late winter and much of spring this is difficult to achieve in a greenhouse or other garden structure, where nighttime temperatures can easily fall low enough to stop the germination process. To avoid this, I germinate all of these early sowings in the warmth of the house and then quickly move the hardier seedlings into the

Germinate seeds on a windowsill in the warmth of the house during spring.

greenhouse, because germination needs more warmth than subsequent growth. Germination can occur in darkness, except for celery and celeriac, so module trays can even be stacked on top of each other or kept in a warm cupboard until the first shoots appear. Check trays regularly, because the first shoots can emerge from three days after sowing and will usually appear within a week.

Before or straight after sowing, I advise watering trays so that the compost is fully moist. Then they are unlikely to need watering for several days, because germinating seeds and the first tiny leaves are not pulling much moisture from the compost. You could also cover trays with plastic or a sheet of glass to retain moisture.

In late spring and early summer, once nights warm in your climate, seeds will germinate evenly in any garden structure, and outside in summer. Sometimes trays may need to be kept in shade, perhaps under staging, to keep direct sun off the compost and prevent it drying – I find that this helps with summer sowings of lettuce. One last consideration is that rodents may eat larger seeds like peas, beans, and sweetcorn, so keep a mousetrap nearby when they are germinating in an outdoor space.

Hardy seedlings grow well in the greenhouse during early spring.

THE PRINCIPLES OF GROWING VEGETABLES

CARING FOR SEEDLINGS

Once seeds have germinated, seedlings need full light to avoid them becoming drawn upwards with long, spindly stems. This will be an issue anywhere with restricted light and especially if you plan to raise plants on a windowsill for a week or more after germination: I suggest using LED grow lights to provide additional light and ensure you grow sturdy plants. All seedlings do best in full light but many need less warmth than for germination. Check the requirements of each vegetable and herb in the directory. Be careful at this stage not to overwater, and to have bed space ready for transplanting seedlings.

Moving seedlings out of the house

Unless you use indoor lights, seedlings need to be moved out of the house into the fuller light of a garden structure as soon as possible, but before you do this check the vegetable and herb profiles to find out how hardy each crop is and whether the temperature will be suitable. Hardy seedlings, like peas, lettuce, and spinach will tolerate some spring frosts, but tender vegetables, such as cucumbers, will be killed. This links back to timing sowings correctly, so that tender plants do not get too big before it's warm enough for them to move out of the house (see pp.64–65).

You could also provide a heat source in your structure outside, which can make all the difference, especially when nights are cold. I use a traditional hotbed to give heat from below, and likewise an electric propagation mat is ideal to warm plants from underneath, rather than trying to heat the whole space. Alternatively, move tender seedlings indoors before any frosty nights that are forecast.

Common problems

It is essential to avoid overwatering young plants, and the frequency of watering will depend on the weather, plus where your plants are. In cloudy conditions during early spring I may water seedlings every two or three days, compared to every day or sometimes twice a day when the weather is bright and sunny.

It's best to water in the morning rather than the evening, to allow leaves to dry more quickly and reduce the likelihood of fungal diseases. Also make sure your greenhouse is clean and uncluttered, to reduce places for pests like snails to hide.

Thinning

The most wasteful thing in propagation is an empty cell or pot, so sometimes you sow two seeds when you want only one plant to ensure that a module tray is full. Individual beetroot and chard seeds often produce more than one

Thin brassicas by removing the weaker plant in each cell. I should've thinned these sooner!

seedling, which may also result in more than you need. Where you have too many seedlings, remove the excess (thin), to allow the best seedlings to grow into sturdy plants. Thin when seedlings are small, even before they have a true leaf, by gently pulling the weaker ones upwards and out, so that no stem is left behind.

When to move plants on

On average plants can stay in modules for three or four weeks before they start to run short of space and nutrients. Ideally you will transplant them or pot them on (see right) before they look stressed in any way. Check for maturity by popping out a module root ball from the base, using your finger or a pen, and look for plenty of roots but also a little compost that's unfilled. Transplant at this stage and you'll see much better growth than if you wait another week, when roots may become congested, leaves turn pale or discoloured, and plants draw up and become leggy from lack of light due to overcrowding.

Module-raised brassicas of this size can be planted out or potted on.

Potting on

This process simply moves growing plants into a larger amount of compost and growing space so that their development can continue unchecked. It's a way to keep plants growing under cover when space isn't yet available outdoors, or to extend the growing season for plants that are both warmth-loving and frost sensitive, to give them more time to ripen a harvest where summers are shorter. Best results come from potting into only slightly larger pots, to save propagation space and to reduce any risk of roots becoming waterlogged. Pot modules into 7cm (2¾in) pots, then later into a 9cm (3½in) pot if necessary. Half-fill the pot loosely with compost, make a deep hole with one or two fingers and pop the plant in. Bury as much of the stem as is feasible, to provide support and produce sturdy plants. Push the root ball down firmly and fill around roots with compost. Water plants thoroughly.

Chard seedlings left in modules for too long have overcrowded roots and dark, discoloured leaves.

Pricking out

Pricking out means transferring seedlings from a seed tray into individual containers – preferably module cells – and is most successful when seedlings are very small. I prick out seedlings that have only their first two cotyledons (seed leaves), before they develop too much root, so the transference process is quick and simple.

Fill the module tray (or small pots) firmly with compost and water with a fine rose, so that the compost is soft and it's easy to push in a mini dibber, such as a blunt pencil. Tease out a group of seedlings from the tray with your tool, lift each seedling by one leaf and drop the root into a small hole dibbed in the compost. Bury the stem as much as possible, so that the leaves are just above compost level. Push compost firmly around the seedling and repeat to fill the module tray. Water again using a can fitted with a fine rose to help settle compost around the seedlings. Growth will restart a couple of days after pricking out and will continue quickly after that. You can prick out several different vegetables into a single module tray.

Gently lift groups of seedlings from a tray, before planting them individually, and watering in.

TRANSPLANTING

I transplant small seedlings, often as little as two or three weeks after sowing, with only one or two true leaves. This is easy, hugely successful, and more efficient than growing transplants to a larger size. People worry that little seedlings are vulnerable to pests and setbacks. However, there is every reason for them to thrive when you have raised sturdy transplants in full light and good quality compost, each planting is made at its best time, and beds provide minimum habitat for slugs and other pests.

Transplant small

Seedlings are ready to transplant when they are big enough to handle and pop into a pre-made hole, with the root system intact. There are several significant benefits of transplanting small. Firstly, young plants establish quickly, making new growth in just two or three days when it's warm, compared to a week for larger plants. Moving plants to their final positions quickly also allows many seedlings to be raised in a small propagating area and means that there is no need to pot on most plants, saving time and reducing compost use. Little transplants need only one watering with a fine rose after planting, whereas bigger transplants need watering repeatedly while their roots establish.

Avoid hardening off

Traditionally, plants raised under cover are gradually acclimatized to outdoor conditions using a process called hardening off. I find this is unnecessary, and instead use fleece to soften the transition for plantings in cold weather. Plants raised in an unheated greenhouse or polytunnel are surprisingly tough, because at night these structures are nearly as cold as outside. From early spring, plants from my greenhouse go straight into open ground,

and are then covered with fleece to provide warmth and wind protection (see pp.92–94). When the weather warms, and the last frost date passes, fleece covers become unnecessary. In autumn, use mesh covers to protect new plantings. Only plants raised in the house with artificial light need hardening off, because they won't be at all used to outdoor conditions: move them outdoors by day and indoors at night, for three days before planting.

Small plants are tough, quick to establish, and do well when transplanted outdoors.

A long-handled dibber is the perfect tool for planting module-raised seedlings.

Transplanting techniques

Water trays of module-raised seedlings before transplanting so that their root balls are moist. Plant deep to shelter young plants from wind, and stabilize any long, slender stems. Before transplanting, check the stem length of plants, and make holes deep enough to keep them largely below surface level.

A wooden long-handled dibber (see p.58) reduces soil disturbance, because it creates a precise hole just bigger and deeper than a seedling's root ball. Push the dibber in and rotate a little so it comes out cleanly. It's quick to pre-dib all the holes first, then slide a root ball into each and push down on it on either side of the stem to ensure contact between module compost and the surrounding soil. Don't fill in the holes, as they channel water to roots, and soon refill with surface compost.

Use a trowel to plant larger transplants that have been potted on. Push the blade down vertically on four sides to make a hole deeper

Strings for aubergines have knotted ends under the root ball and are tied to a wire above.

and slightly wider than the root ball. Slot the root ball in and push it down with most of the stem below surface level. To plant through a black plastic mulch (see p.40), cut two slits in the sheet to make a cross, fold the triangles of plastic underneath, and plant in the same way, folding the plastic back out to cover the soil after planting. Cut slits rather than holes when planting seed potatoes (see p.250) to keep the plastic as intact as possible for reuse.

Supports

If you plan to use string supports for tall plants under cover, place the knotted end of each string at the bottom of the hole, before your transplant goes in (see p.173). All other types of supports can be added later, once plants are more established. This will barely damage their roots, and allows new transplants to be protected with fleece or netting if necessary.

SPACING

Planting distances for the same vegetable can be varied according to the size and regularity of the harvests required, and you can manipulate spacing to achieve the returns you want from your garden. The information below describes the effects of varying the distance between plants and different planting patterns, but check individual vegetable and herb profiles to find the spacings that I use and recommend.

Factors to consider

Before starting, be clear what you hope to harvest from each planting: do you want to grow large lettuce heads that need lots of room to develop, or plants to pick for outer leaves that stay more compact? General advice on seed packets doesn't always explain these differences, or that you can use spacing to influence the size of vegetables, for example by planting closer together for more small onions, or further apart for fewer large ones. My rule of thumb is to plant as close as possible without overcrowding. I find time and again that seedlings benefit from being planted close

to one another, because they seem to like contact with neighbouring plants – think of it as a form of companion planting.

Specific growing conditions can influence your chosen spacing. For example, it may be necessary to grow plants further apart in a dry climate to allow them sufficient moisture. Wider spacings are also useful in damp climates to increase air circulation around leaves, helping them to dry after rain, which reduces their susceptibility to fungal diseases. The relative absence of new weeds in no dig soil makes close spacing considerably easier. Larger distances between plants are often recommended to enable hoeing between them, but as undisturbed soil grows few weeds and it's quick to pull them by hand, closer spacings are easy to manage.

Equidistant spacing vs rows

Just 50 years ago, it was revolutionary to grow on a bed system in gardens, but gardeners now appreciate the advantages of growing in clearly defined beds, with access from paths, over growing vegetables in rows with space left between to walk on the soil. Beds allow vegetables to be grown closer together, arranged in blocks with equal space between each plant, creating a series of triangles and staggered rows. This is an efficient use of space that gives plants equal access to moisture and soil, reducing competition, and increasing the

Multisown spring onions accurately planted at an equidistant spacing will deliver a large harvest.

Careful spacing keeps beds full, maximizes yields, and creates some striking patterns.

yield from your bed. A single planting distance is all you need for equidistant spacing, while growing in rows requires two spacings, within and between rows.

Laying out plants

I lay out plants by eye, but there are many ways to achieve even spacing. You can use a tape measure or a stick cut to length to check planting distances. A string tied tightly between two sticks serves as a guide to plant straight lines, which is helpful when there are no wooden sides to beds. Keeping the edge lines straight and defined when you spread compost

and wood chip on beds and paths respectively is also worthwhile, although with no dig there is no significant difference between the underlying soil in beds and paths, because in both cases the structure is firm while being open to roots (see p.29). Plants grow well, and sometimes even larger, when they are close to pathways, as they can access extra moisture from path soil. Closely spaced vegetables can be planted very near the edge of a bed, while larger, spreading vegetables are best set further into the middle, so that they don't block pathways.

WATERING

Watering brings you into close contact with your plants and is a wonderful way to gain a better understanding of their growth. You can use your observations to work out when and how much to water at each stage of development. Watering requirements vary widely among different vegetables and will also differ depending on whether plants are in open soil, outdoors, under cover, or in containers. It's also important to know when not to water, because overwatering can be more damaging than under-watering.

Judging when to water

The frequency of watering depends on the weather, the type of plant, and above all on its stage of growth. Always water each plant individually after transplanting, to help settle its roots into the hole, ensuring contact between the root ball and surrounding soil or compost. If it's hot and sunny check new plantings every two days for the first week, and water until you see the first signs of new growth. Established plants growing outdoors in open soil may need watering twice a week in warm, dry weather, but focus on the vegetables that are currently cropping. Advice for each crop is given in the vegetable and herb directory, but generally any plants being picked for leaves will need more frequent watering than those grown for their roots. Fruiting and podding crops grow fast during summer, and need regular watering once you see flowers, to help fruit and pods set.

Plants growing under cover experience higher temperatures, which means they need to be watered more often than plants outdoors, although I still would not water plants in open soil under cover every day. During autumn and winter, when the air is cool and moist, most plants under cover need watering perhaps once a week. From December to February, salads growing under cover in my polytunnel are watered as little as once or twice a month.

Observe plants closely so that you develop the ability to notice changes in their appearance when water is in short supply. You will see how leaves turn a darker shade of green (or even slightly blue for brassicas) and their surface develops a dull, matt appearance. A plant showing these symptoms won't die, but is under stress and its growth has shut down. This may not matter during summer for a vegetable that will be harvested in autumn or winter, but plants nearing harvest need to be watered immediately.

Moisture-loving celery needs frequent watering to produce lush growth and a good harvest.

How to water

I water with a can and rose, or with a hose if the water butts are empty, so that water can be used efficiently and directed precisely to where it's needed. Ensuring that the rose points downwards makes this easier and does not damage even the tender leaves of young plants and salads. Apply water to soil at the roots of wider-spaced plants, to reduce evaporation and save water, but where dense foliage covers a bed it is fine to water from above. I water in the morning rather than the evening, so that leaves and the soil surface are dry before nightfall, which reduces damage from slugs and fungal disease.

It's more efficient to apply a larger amount of water less frequently, rather than watering little and often, so that water soaks deeper into soil where it can be accessed by roots, and with less evaporation. Dry soil needs more water than you might think to be moist to a depth of at least 5cm (2in): check after watering by dibbing a small hole. Avoid using sprinklers that throw water up in a way that is hard to control, as this wastes water on empty soil, on plants that may not need it, and to evaporation.

Watering with cans delivers water precisely to where it's needed.

WETTING DRY SOIL AND COMPOST

In hot weather, compost and soil can become so dry that water simply runs off the surface without soaking in and wetting the layers below. This can be counteracted by watering in stages. Apply a little water and stop when you see surface run-off. Leave it for a minute so that some moisture soaks in, then water lightly again. Pause and repeat this five or six times until the soil is more receptive to water and it soaks in better. Once this happens you can water as normal.

Plants in pots

Plants growing in containers have a restricted root run, and need to be monitored and watered frequently in order to flourish. This is especially true for those in porous clay pots, which dry out faster than plastic containers. Even so, it is possible to overwater plants in containers – best let the compost dry out a little between waterings rather than keep it fully moist all the time. The simplest way to check whether watering is required is to lift the pot, and give water only if it's light and therefore dry. Apply a good dose at each watering, which will be at least every day during sunny summer weather, and perhaps every two days when it's overcast. Pay attention to the requirements of different plants, because established plants will need more water than recent transplants. You can even control fruit and root sweetness by varying the amount of water given. Reduce watering in cooler spring and autumn weather.

Automatic watering systems are useful if you're going on holiday and have nobody to care for your plants, but otherwise I would not recommend them. They are expensive, tricky to set up, use a lot of plastic, and crucially cannot adapt the amount of water given to each plant, which can easily lead to over- or under-watering.

Collecting rainwater

Use water butts to collect and store rainwater from the downpipes of any roof. Diverter devices are available that slot into existing downpipes from buildings so that water can be directed into butts for storage. Collecting rainwater is particularly useful in large gardens and on allotments, where mains water isn't available. Unfortunately, water butts are not the total solution because they empty quickly in dry weather, which is exactly when you need the water most. I have installed two 1000 litre (220 gallon) intermediate bulk containers, to collect a larger amount of rainwater and help prevent summer shortages.

The taps on most water butts are too small to be useful, and I enlarge the hole at the top so it's possible to fill a watering can by submerging it in the water. The downside of this is that the lid no longer fits, so algae are able to grow in daylight and the water becomes smelly. I take the opportunity to clean water butts when they are almost empty, at least four times a year, by brushing the insides and rinsing. This prevents the water becoming putrid and makes it sweeter for watering plants, especially seedlings.

Cleaning removes algae from water butts (top). A diverter directs rainwater for collection (right).

USING CROP COVERS

Crop covers include fleece, netting, and mesh, and their judicious use can be the difference between success and failure. Inform yourself about the activity of pests that might damage each vegetable (see pp.108–279), in order to choose the right cover to protect your plantings and produce healthy harvests, without any need for synthetic pesticides. Fleece covers provide pest protection, but mostly serve to insulate young plants from cold weather in early spring. Invest in good quality covers because they can be used repeatedly over many growing seasons.

General considerations

Crop covers allow rain and air through, with no need for extra watering or ventilation while they are in place. The most effective stage for use is when plants are young and vulnerable. They are quick to lay, then need occasional lifting to remove weeds, take harvests, and carry out any plant maintenance. I find that covers with a 2m (6½ft) width are ideal for 1.2m (4ft) wide beds, because there is enough spare width to anchor the cover with large stones along each side, whether it is supported on wire hoops, or laid directly on plants so that it will be pushed upwards as they grow.

Fleece

Fleece is the best cover from early to mid-spring, for warmth and to protect plants from wind. It filters air rather than blocking it, which makes it less prone to blowing away or suffering damage in high wind. It is especially effective in windy conditions when laid directly on top of plants, where it holds valuable warmth at soil level. Fleece also protects plants from pigeons, rabbits, and even insect pests if well secured. I lay a fleece cover over every new sowing and planting during March, and usually continue to use it until the end of April. It is less useful later in the year, because in late

spring and summer it retains too much heat, and in autumn plants tend to lack daylight rather than warmth. Thin 17gsm ($^3/_5$oz/yd²) fleece shreds easily and will not last more than one growing season, so check that what you purchase is 25–30gsm (1oz/yd²) – anything more than this will be too thick and heavy for vegetable seedlings.

Mesh

As the weather warms in late spring I transition to covering susceptible plants with mesh. This allows more airflow and keeps the temperature underneath the cover lower than fleece, while also excluding pests. Buy the finest grade available (ideally around 1mm/$^1/_{16}$in) so that it will exclude even small pests like flea beetles. Check which pests are likely to affect each vegetable and when, so that mesh can be used preventatively, before pests arrive. It is a heavier fabric than fleece, particularly if wet, and is best supported on hoops that span the bed, but its strength and ability to let air pass through make mesh better than fleece for wind reduction and pest protection during winter. Mesh is also easy to see through, which is useful for keeping an eye on the plants underneath.

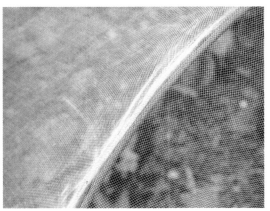

Thermacrop

A hybrid cover, thermacrop holds more heat than mesh, but has larger holes so it is possible for insects to wriggle through. It offers wind protection, with good ventilation, throughout the year, shade against strong sun in a heatwave, and will protect against all but the smallest insects. A disadvantage is that you can't see through it, and if I had only two covers, I would use fleece and mesh.

Fleece is used extensively in early spring, to protect young plants from the weather.

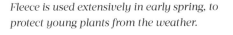

Crop covers (top to bottom): fleece, mesh, thermacrop, and bird netting.

*Crop covers supported on galvanized wires
(left) and anchored with large stones (right).*

Bird netting

Black bird netting with 12mm (½in) squares
provides a protective, but almost invisible,
shield against large pests. Buy UV-treated
polypropylene and it will last for many years.
Support netting on hoops spanning a bed,
or for taller winter brassicas create a wooden
structure with posts to hold the netting mainly
as a roof, which deters birds from feeding
underneath because they can't take off quickly.
This allows access from the sides without
having to lift the netting, which is a chore
when you want to pick a few Brussels sprouts.

Supporting hoops

For 1.2m (4ft)-wide beds, I use 2.5m (8ft)
lengths of 4mm (⅛in), high tensile, galvanized
wire to support crop covers. The strong wires
are easy to push into soil on each side of a
bed, exclude little light, and are simple to
store when bought in straightened lengths.
Supports of slim wire look and perform better
than plastic alkathene pipe. Find a supplier to
cut and straighten the wire for you (see p.286),
otherwise it will be in a coil that is springy
and awkward to handle.

Plastic use

These crop covers are all made of plastic, and
I find that the best quality products can be
reused for many years. Thicker grades of fleece
should last four years, while mesh and bird
netting can last for 15 years, provided you
use and store them carefully. Prevent rips by
securing the sides well in windy weather, and
hang covers over a wood batten in the shed
when not in use. Mice may chew through to
nest in covers left on the floor, leaving holes
which render them useless. You can use a
single cover on multiple crops through the
growing season, increasing the quality and
quantity of your harvest, and reducing the
amount of imported or plastic-wrapped food
you need to buy, which means that the careful
use of suitable covers can reduce plastic waste.

I have trialled cotton muslin and a sheep's
wool cover as plastic-free alternatives to fleece,
but so far have found that they are expensive,
heavy, less permeable to light, and degrade
when in contact with soil. They don't match
fleece's ease of use and boost to early growth.

CONTROLLING SLUGS AND SNAILS

No dig soil grows stronger plants that tend to suffer less damage, but Dr Elaine Ingham has also discovered that compacted layers in cultivated soil, where anaerobic fermentations of organic matter produce alcohol, actually attract slugs. Leaving soil undisturbed helps to establish a balance between the populations of pests and beneficial organisms, including ground beetles, which eat slugs, snails, and their eggs. Such predation controls rather than eliminates pests, and where slug numbers remain significant, you can take action to reduce them.

Remove habitat and reduce numbers

Reducing slug and snail habitat dramatically improves the chances of survival for plants. The biggest potential hiding places are the wooden sides of raised beds, where colonies of slugs lurk in cavities formed as the softwood sides decay when in contact with the soil. This happens after three or four years and makes it easy for slugs to emerge and feed on plants by night. Open-sided beds (see pp.38–39) are free of this problem.

Avoid growing vegetables close to slug habitats, such as overgrown and shady areas. Keep your plot edges neat and nearby grass mown short. If there's an overgrown area nearby, such as on a neighbouring allotment, lay a strip of black polythene between it and your plot to lift regularly and remove slugs sheltering underneath. Keeping the garden tidy means it has a beautiful sense of order, as well as reducing pest problems. Weed regularly and remove fading lower leaves from plants to minimize potential slug habitat.

Another way to reduce the slug and snail population is by going out regularly at dusk with a torch, picking up any that you find, and dealing with them as you see fit. Barriers of wool and copper may protect individual plants, but do nothing to reduce slug numbers and are not guaranteed to be effective.

Pick yellowing and damaged lower leaves regularly to reduce food and hiding places.

GROWING UNDER COVER

The term "under cover" applies to any structure made of glass, polythene, or polycarbonate, which admits sufficient light for plant growth. This includes greenhouses, polytunnels, cold frames, and also the house, where the light from windows needs to be augmented with electric grow lights. A greenhouse or polytunnel can be expensive, but is a worthwhile investment to extend your growing season in both spring and autumn.

The value of under cover growing space

At all times of year, under cover spaces provide extra warmth as well as protection from wind and extreme weather. In summer, they enable you to grow more exotic vegetables, such as melons and aubergines, while keeping tomato foliage dry and free of late blight. Growing leaf vegetables under cover in winter increases harvests substantially compared to outdoors, and provides a pleasant space to work through the colder months.

Growing under cover also makes it possible to raise young plants almost year-round, and with the added advantage of fewer pests (see pp.48–49). Starting in late winter extends the growing season to produce earlier harvests,

A polytunnel provides ample space to raise young plants and grow a range of heat-loving crops.

giving more time for planting second crops in summer (see pp.66–69).

What are the options?

Glass and polycarbonate hold a little more warmth than polythene, which is of particular benefit on cold nights during springtime. Greenhouses are expensive new, but can sometimes be obtained secondhand. It is usually necessary to anchor and stabilize a greenhouse frame on stone or concrete. Polytunnels are a more cost-effective option and need no concrete to hold their frame, but their cover of UV-treated polythene needs to be replaced at least every 15 years.

If space or budget are limited, ground-level cold frames of glass or plastic are a more compact and cheaper option, along with plastic-covered metal frames, which can be attached to a wall. Both are a good way to start raising plants under cover.

It is practical to germinate seeds in the warmth of the house because most don't need light (see p.79), although growing plants on in the restricted light on a windowsill is not easy without LED grow lights. It's possible to grow salad leaves and pea shoots in a tray on a windowsill, along with dwarf varieties of heat-loving vegetables, but watering plants may cause a mess.

No dig under cover

It's much easier to grow plants in soil than in containers, because the extensive root systems in soil mean that plants need less feeding and watering. I add compost to the soil in my greenhouse and polytunnels once a year in May at the changeover between winter and summer vegetables, but with an extra 2cm (³/₄in) depth compared to outdoor beds, because they are cropped more intensively.

If you cannot access the soil under cover, fill the largest containers available with your best compost, which can serve for two years or more. Plastic pots are lighter and retain

September-sown salads can be picked regularly of larger leaves all winter with no extra heat.

moisture better than clay, but ensure that there are drainage holes underneath. Grow bags are another option, but be careful not to over-plant them: even large bags are better with two tomato plants rather than three.

Caring for plants under cover

The lack of rainfall and higher temperatures under cover mean that plants need more frequent attention than those outside, especially in summer. Regular watering is vital, although the need for this is reduced where plants are growing in soil (see p.90–91). Ventilation is essential to circulate air around plants and reduce summer temperatures. Open doors and greenhouse vents daily and, if in doubt, provide more air rather than less. Polythene retains very little warmth at night and during frosty weather. Closing polytunnel doors will only keep in warmth in windy conditions. To maximize light levels, clean glass and polythene annually using water (with no added products) and a cloth. Keep the space tidy and uncluttered to leave the maximum space for plant growth, and fewer hiding places for slugs, snails, and woodlice.

HARVESTING

Harvesting is a result of good growth and, when done carefully, also enables further growth and productivity. Many vegetables are picked repeatedly, so it makes sense to look after their growth and health as you harvest, to enable them to remain prolific over a long period. This is also an opportunity to remove weeds, pests, and fading leaves, and maintain the garden at a top level.

Timing is key

There is no single perfect moment to harvest, but there will be a stage when each vegetable's flavour and texture reaches its peak, which becomes easier to recognize with experience. After this, some vegetable harvests lose flavour and quality, or develop a texture you may not like. To get the best from my crops, I check maturing plants every day or two in summer, and maybe once a week in cooler conditions, when development slows.

Knowing what to look for is important, so check each profile in the vegetable and herb directory (see pp.108–279) for my harvesting advice and read the characteristics of each variety on seed packets. When to harvest is also down to personal preference; some like small broad beans, while I prefer them larger because of the higher proportion of sweet flesh to bitter skin. When winter arrives, delaying some harvests allows frost to increase sweetness (see p.100).

Maximize productivity

Specific techniques can prolong the productive period of many vegetables, which increases total yield and allows you to make fewer sowings. My method of harvesting lettuce by picking outer leaves so that the central rosette continues to grow (see pp.224–225), produces a steady supply of leaves for two months or more, from just one sowing. Pick fruits and pods promptly so plants continue flowering.

Gently twist the largest beetroot from multisown clumps to avoid disturbing nearby roots.

Carefully twist only the largest roots from multisown clumps, to create more space for the rest to continue growing and prolong the harvest period from each sowing. Sweet vegetables harvested when they're small are a treat, but eating them all at this stage would dramatically reduce yields. For more to eat, enjoy few a baby vegetables and leave the rest to swell. You have many options.

Plant care

Cut or push down on pod stalks gently, to avoid ripping and weakening the main stems. Twist and push down on leaves such as lettuce, leaving the main stem clean and free of rotting stalks, where slugs could hide. Picking by hand may seem slow, but you will increase speed with practice, and it causes less damage than cutting across plants to harvest leaves, giving faster regrowth and longer-lived plants.

Repeated picking leaves lettuces with long, bare stems so that they resemble little trees.

DELVE DEEPER HOW GROWING CONDITIONS INFLUENCE FLAVOUR

Weather conditions and watering have an impact on the taste of vegetables. It's fascinating to notice the flavour changes through a season of growth in harvests from the same plants. Sometimes it's worth accepting a smaller harvest as pay-off for maximizing flavour, and an understanding of the processes involved allows you to decide whether this is worthwhile.

Water chilli plants in containers minimally to concentrate the spicy heat of their fruit.

Soil moisture affects both flavour and yield, because lower moisture levels limit growth which increases sweetness in fruiting crops, such as tomatoes and sweet peppers, and root crops, like carrots and beetroot. It's easy to influence the moisture available to plants grown under cover and in containers by watering sparingly. Similarly, I rarely water carrots and beetroot growing outdoors during summer, to avoid diluting their sugary flavour. In trials where I have grown the same variety of cherry tomato in outdoor containers and in soil in the polytunnel, the harvest from the drier containers was significantly sweeter than fruit from moister polytunnel soil. Watering less also speeds up the ripening of fruit.

Winter conditions affect flavour in a different way, because plants defend themselves from freezing by converting starches in their leaves and roots into sugars. These act as an antifreeze in plant tissues and they make Brussels sprouts, kale, and cabbages sweeter after frost, along with overwintering roots such as parsnips and swedes. When harvesting leaves from overwintered spinach in March and April, I find incredible sweetness in some of them – as though they had been sprinkled with sugar. This is a great advantage of winter gardening and is a fantastic reason for growing hardy vegetables through winter.

STORAGE

Storage is not a complicated process and you will be successful, because vegetables grown in healthy no dig soil keep much better than those you buy. Storing vegetables allows you to eat much more food from one planting, especially through winter and early spring, and harvesting to store also frees up space to plant a succeeding vegetable. Here I summarize the quickest and most convenient methods of storage and highlight some of the most rewarding vegetables to store, but check each vegetable profile for further detail.

Where to store your harvest

I keep very few vegetables in my tiny fridge and don't have any kind of cold store. A perfect place to store vegetables all year is an outbuilding of stone or brick with a tiled roof, similar to my shed, all of which helps to mitigate large fluctuations in temperature. A cellar would also be perfect if you have one, for a constant temperature of around 10–12°C (50–54°F), while my shed is often 20°C (68°F) or more in summer. Buildings with a metal roof and wood or tin sheds may get too cold in winter and too hot in summer to keep produce in good condition. A few vegetables store well in the dry warmth of a house.

Root vegetables

Roots store nicely in two- or three-ply paper sacks – I use old flour sacks from the local bakery. Harvest beetroot, celeriac, and carrots as late as possible, so that they're fresh going into store and will keep until early spring. Leave some soil on most roots and cut or twist off leaves at harvest, to retain moisture in the roots. An exception is potatoes, which need to be dry going into storage and kept in the dark. Fold over the top of a potato sack, to prevent them going green.

About halfway through winter, empty the sack and remove any roots that are rotting. Root vegetables are living storage organs and will sprout to grow again in mild temperatures; just rub off the sprouts and the roots are still good to eat. Again potatoes are different, because they need 20–25°C (68–77°F) warmth after harvest to cure, and then remain dormant for a long time, before sprouting in early winter.

Twist leaves off maincrop carrots 'Oxhella' and 'Berlicum' before storing in a paper sack.

Garlic bulbs with plaited stems keep for ten to eleven months when hung in my conservatory.

Onions, garlic, and winter squash

These vegetables are easy to keep for long periods and store best in the dry warmth of a house. Winter squash have a strong skin to retain moisture and will keep on a sunny windowsill for months, whereas in the dampness of a shed, mould develops on their stalks and spreads down into the flesh. Onions and garlic are similar and when kept indoors, mostly remain in good condition until late spring. They are convenient to use and look attractive hanging in the kitchen with their stems plaited, while squashes make a pleasing display anywhere in the house.

Leaf crops

Keeping moisture in freshly picked leaves is the key to successful storage. I wash freshly harvested salad leaves and don't dry them, so that the residual humidity enables them to stay alive and in good condition for several days. To retain this moisture they either need to be sealed in a polythene bag or in a covered plastic box; paper bags and other non-plastic containers are not as effective at retaining humidity. Wash and reuse any plastic used for storage to minimize plastic use and waste. In plastic crates, covered with a sheet of reusable

polythene, salad leaves store for a week in winter and three days in summer at ambient temperature in my shed. Brassica leaves and broccoli store best in a fridge, especially salads like rocket and mustard, which often go yellow after three days at room temperature.

Tight heads of cabbage and chicory retain moisture well and can store for two to three months over winter, in cool and damp conditions. They start to go mouldy on the outside, but carefully peel away that protective layer of unappealing leaves and you'll be amazed to find a beautiful heart inside.

Processing vegetables for storage

You can process gluts of vegetables that wouldn't otherwise store well. I cut tomatoes into 5mm (¼in) thick slices and dry them in a food dehydrator. This concentrates the flavour into something special, and once dry, they store in a jar for two or three years. Dry beans and peas store for more than a year in jars, paper sacks, or buckets with lids. Freezing adversely affects the flavour of many vegetables, but is an option for peas, broad beans, sweetcorn, and whole cherry tomatoes, if you harvest more than you can eat fresh.

Producing your own fermented pickles is a fantastic way to store leaves from hearted vegetables, roots, and fruits. It's easy to shred gluts of cabbage hearts, Chinese cabbage, carrots, and cucumbers to pickle, so that they ferment and store in jars. I've only done it for the last three years and love the results.

Clockwise from top left: dehydrated tomato, dried borlotti beans, fermented Chinese cabbage with carrot, and sauerkraut with dill.

SAVING SEED

Saving and sowing your own seed is empowering, not only for you, but also for your plants, which often grow more strongly from home-saved seed. Start with the four simplest vegetables, then progress to those that need a year of growth before they flower and set seed, as well as neighbouring plants for cross-pollination. Seed matures best in dry weather, so saving seed can be difficult in wet climates, where rain in late summer may cause seeds to rot before ripening.

Simple seed saving

There are four vegetables that it's easiest to save seed from, because they rarely cross-pollinate with other varieties of the same vegetable nearby, and only a single plant is required to provide a strong pool of genes. Peas are an ideal first vegetable to try, because you need only leave pods of mature peas on one plant for three to four weeks after they reach eating stage. Pick them when they dry and turn brown, and shell them for seeds. French bean seeds are saved in a similar way, but pods need more time to mature and dry on the plant. Ripe tomatoes already contain seeds that are easy to collect and process (see p.261) for sowing the following spring. Ensure you are not saving seed from an F1 hybrid variety (see p.105). Lettuce needs a long season to mature and your seed crop can be spoiled by summer rain, therefore it's more reliable to grow for seed under cover. It's also simple to save harvested potatoes and garlic to plant for your next crop, just be sure they came from healthy plants.

Creating a larger gene pool

Some vegetables need to be grown in a group with other plants of the same variety to provide sufficient genetic diversity for the production of healthy seed. This applies to broad beans, runner beans, beetroot, carrots, onions, corn salad, and brassicas, all of which I've saved seed from successfully (see directory entries). Saving seed from single plants of these crops results in inbreeding and seed that either doesn't germinate, or grows weakly.

Potential problems

It pays to be aware of some of the pitfalls that commonly affect gardeners trying to save their own seed. If you don't collect seed at the right moment, seeds will fall onto the soil and result

Stored onions and beetroot, replanted in spring for seed production, come into flower in June.

Once leek flowers fade, globe-shaped seedheads form during summer.

in a lot of extra weeding. Plants grown for seed also take up valuable space, as they need longer in the ground and become larger than when grown as a vegetable crop. One way to save space, and produce good quality seed, is to select the best beetroot, carrots, and onions from a stored harvest and replant them in spring in an area devoted to seed production. Seed saving often works well in community gardens, where as few as eight beetroot plants could yield seed for 100 people to share.

Cross-pollination occurs when pollen is transferred from the flowers of one plant to those of another in the same species. This helps to ensure healthy growth thanks to the genetic diversity in new seeds, but can have undesirable results for gardeners, including the introduction of unwanted traits from closely related wild plants or other varieties of the same vegetable growing nearby.

Cross-pollination between varieties means that some otherwise easy seeds, such as winter squash or broad beans, are better not saved where more than one variety is grown. The only way to avoid this is to isolate plants, which is often impractical in gardens.

Seed saved from F1 hybrids won't produce offspring the same as the parent plant. An F1 hybrid is the result of controlled pollination between two inbred and "pure" plant lines, each of which has uniform and desired characteristics. Only open-pollinated varieties, naturally pollinated by insects or the wind, will come true from home-saved seed.

Seed needs to be dry to enable it to be rubbed out from seedheads and stored successfully. It often helps to lift plants and hang them up to dry under cover. Bean and pea seeds may be damaged if they remain too moist when pods are left to dry on plants: peas can germinate in pods before they dry, which reduces the germination rate of saved seed.

Extracting seed

How do you know when seed is ripe and ready to harvest? Pods will have turned yellow or brown and need to feel dry, but not yet crackling. Tomatoes and melons should be ripe to eat, but cucumbers need to have hard yellow skin and be almost inedible. All squash seeds must come from ripe fruits with hard skins. A rule of thumb for lettuce, umbellifers, and brassicas is to gather plants before the seeds are completely dry. Often there is only a short period between seed coming ready to gather and it falling to the ground, so it's best to pull these plants a little early and hang them under cover for about two weeks, before you rub the stalks or seedheads over a sheet to extract the seed.

Clean seed by winnowing in a light breeze, pouring it slowly and steadily from one container to another. The breeze blows away any small bits of pods and dust, leaving you with a satisfying quantity of seed.

Clockwise from top: cutting ripe tomatoes to extract seed; winnowing carrot seeds to remove lighter debris; rubbing beetroot seeds onto a sheet for collection.

Seed storage

I use old seed packets for storing my harvests, with new labels stuck on to record the variety and the date seed was saved. Larger amounts keep well in old yogurt pots, jam jars, or food storage boxes; an airtight seal isn't necessary. Dryness is important to keep seed in good condition and including a small pack of silica gel reduces moisture levels. Temperature is not critical, but cool is best, so keep seed in the least heated room in the house.

Seeds of tomato, cucumber, and melon store the longest – for up to ten years – while parsnips lose vigour within two years, and beetroot and chard keep for only a little longer. All other vegetable seeds keep well for around three to four years, which I would suggest is the maximum time they should be stored before sowing.

Clockwise from top: dry borlotti beans popped from their pods; pea seeds stored in a glass jar; seedheads of bulb onions hung up to dry in the shed.

CHAPTER 4

Vegetable and herb directory

LEGUMES – PEA AND BEAN FAMILY

Broad beans

Climbing beans

Dwarf French beans

Peas

Plants from the legume family are grown almost exclusively for their pods, which are either eaten whole or shelled for their fabulous peas and beans. Legume plants have the ability to fix nitrogen from the air, thanks to nodules on their roots containing beneficial bacteria. Almost all of this nitrogen is utilized for their own growth, especially when grown to maturity for pods such that, contrary to popular belief, little is left for use by the next crop.

Choosing what to grow

Peas and broad beans are hardy enough to tolerate frost: sow them early and they thrive in cooler conditions, to harvest in late spring and early summer. Choose from shelling peas or varieties of mangetout and sugarsnap peas with edible pods. You can also grow succulent pea shoots to add to spring salads. French, runner, and other types of dwarf and climbing beans are summer crops that need warmth to flourish and are killed by even a slight frost. Freshly picked pods have a fine flavour, but can also be allowed to mature for a store of dry beans to enjoy in winter. Dwarf and climbing varieties of peas and beans are available to suit every growing space. Choose compact varieties for containers and windy gardens.

Sowing, growing, and harvesting

Legume seeds are easy to sow, into 3cm (1¼in) modules for peas and dwarf French beans, and wider 5cm (2in) modules for the large seeds of climbing beans. You don't need to use the deep root-trainers marketed for sowing beans. Success comes most easily when you follow each vegetable's natural growth pattern and flowering time. Broad beans and peas sown early will suffer fewer pests and diseases than later sowings. In contrast, it's important to respect dwarf French and climbing beans's need for warmth. Sow them under cover no earlier than the last frost in your area, for fast-growing transplants ready to go out when the soil is warming up. No dig soil mulched annually with compost retains the plentiful

CROP		JAN	FEB	MAR	APR	MAY	JUN	JUL	AUG	SEP	OCT	NOV	DEC
Broad beans	Sow		▬▬▬▬▬▬▬									▬▬▬	
	Harvest						▬▬▬▬▬▬▬						
Dwarf French beans	Sow					▬▬▬▬▬▬							
	Harvest							▬▬▬▬▬▬▬					
Climbing beans	Sow					▬▬▬▬							
	Harvest								▬▬▬▬▬				
Peas	Sow		▬▬▬▬▬▬▬▬				▬▬▬					▬▬▬	
	Harvest						▬▬▬▬▬			▬▬▬▬			

▬▬ Outdoors   ▬▬ Under cover

moisture that legumes need, without the need to fill deep trenches with organic matter the winter before planting.

Supports are essential for all peas and beans, except dwarf varieties and peas grown for shoots. Check how high your chosen variety will grow and provide a suitable framework for it. The stems of climbing beans readily twine themselves around smooth canes. Growing the 2m (6½ft)-tall plants up conical teepees rather than along lines of canes allows the wind to flow through and results in less damage. Peas need a denser structure of netting, string, or twiggy pea sticks to grasp with their coiling tendrils. This allows growth to spread out, and makes finding and picking pods easier among the dense foliage.

Harvest pea and bean pods at different stages of development according to your taste, sampling them every few days to find the stage you like. Picking young pods regularly should increase the proportion of later flowers that develop pods, but won't extend your harvest for a long period.

Common problems

Dry soil conditions can prevent pods setting. Misting flowers is often recommended as a remedy for this, but makes little difference to yields, because plants need moisture at the roots. Dry soil can also weaken plants, making them susceptible to blackfly. These aphids suck the sap from soft new growth and are particularly common on later sowings of broad beans. Sow early to avoid this pest, and once the main stems are full of flowers, pinch out the growing tips of broad bean plants to remove the aphids' favourite landing point. Late summer and autumn peas often develop powdery mildew, which is visible as a white dust of fungal growth; peas sown in early

Pick speckled borlotti bean pods in early autumn, once they begin to dry and the leaves have faded.

Peas flower in early summer alongside a vibrant Oriental poppy.

spring are much less susceptible. Pigeons and rabbits may devour young transplants, and peck or nibble new growth such that plants cannot develop. A remedy is to delay adding supports until three to four weeks after transplanting, which allows you to cover seedlings easily while they establish. Once supports are added, plants may then need protection with mesh or bird netting while they continue to grow.

Pea and bean weevils eat semi-circular notches into leaf edges, particularly on seedlings and near the base of plants. Strong plants growing in moist, mulched soil will grow away from this damage. Weevils also burrow out of saved seed, so check for damage and remove weevils from home-saved seed in mid-autumn. If you find small maggots feeding on peas inside the pods, pea moth is the culprit, but usually only a few peas are affected. This pest is more common by midsummer and I find that the pods of early spring sowings are picked before moth caterpillars cause too much damage.

BROAD BEANS

Broad beans are suited to cool climates because, unlike other beans, they are frost hardy. Sow them either in late autumn or late winter for a crop of fat pods, starting in early summer. They grow less well in the heat of high summer. Once picked, the plants can be cleared in time for planting another vegetable; perhaps beetroot or kale to harvest in autumn, or sprouting broccoli to pick the following spring. Early sown broad beans are a wonderful half-season vegetable (see p.66) for keeping your plot productive year-round.

Sowing and transplanting

Sow under cover if possible, where it's easier to protect the seeds and young plants. Mice love to eat the fat seeds (set a mousetrap near to your sowing), and birds may pull up seedlings of outdoor sowings to eat the germinating seeds. Raise plants in 5cm (2in) modules rather than deep root-trainers; it's fine for the tap root to coil around in the module compost before they go in the ground. Sow from late October to early November if your climate is not too cold in winter, or from January to February under cover to transplant in March. You can also sow in March and April outdoors.

Transplant seedlings after four to six weeks, when they are about 5–7cm (2–2¾in) tall. Dib a hole 3cm (1¼in) deeper than the root ball, push the module in so that its top is about 2cm (¾in) below the surface, and water in if the weather is dry. Space plants 20–25cm (8–10in) apart in all directions or with 15cm (6in) between them in rows 45cm (18in) apart.

Care and protection

A mesh cover on overwintering plants gives wind protection, or netting can be used to protect seedlings from birds. Broad beans grow early in the year when watering often isn't needed, but once flowering commences it is worth watering in dry conditions to help pod development.

Support is not essential, but tall plants do recline on the ground after wind, and pods are easier to harvest when plants stay upright. Two levels of strong string secured around posts at the end of rows, or the corners of blocks, will be enough to support plants bearing the weight of swelling pods. Blackfly are a common pest during May or June, especially on later sowings,

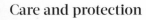

Flowers are frequently visited by pollinating insects, but are also able to self-pollinate.

Keep the flexible stems upright with simple supporting strings around blocks or along rows.

whose softer or drought-stressed growth is more attractive to these sap-sucking insects. Prevent damage through earlier sowing and by pinching off the tops of plants once their main stem is full of flowers. It also helps to water in dry weather and to squirt plants with a hose to wash the insects off.

Harvesting and storage

When to harvest is your call. You can pick finger-sized pods to eat whole as mangetout, but this means fewer larger beans to harvest later. Watch how the pods swell, squeeze a little to check for beans inside, and taste them at different stages. Small beans have a higher ratio of bitter skin to bean. I prefer them larger and fatter, when they develop a creamy taste and texture, but if you leave them to mature for too long, the pods darken and beans turn dry and starchy. Harvest by pushing pods downwards where they meet the main stem, often two pods at a time because they usually grow in pairs. Broad beans are best eaten freshly picked, but will keep in their pods for a few days if necessary.

You can also allow pods to mature and turn dark brown on the plant, for harvesting dry or almost dry. Shell the beans and place on a tray in a sunny window until completely hard. They store well in an airtight jar in the kitchen. Soak them overnight before cooking and rub off the outer skins prior to using them in dishes such as hummus.

Clear plants by cutting the main roots just below the stem. Contrary to popular belief there are not many nitrogen nodules on roots after harvest, because by this stage the plants have used most of them, but it's still good to leave roots in the soil as food for microbes. Your dry beans are also seed, which is

For the best flavour, harvest and pop open the fat pods just before you plan to eat the beans.

good to sow for up to three years when stored at room temperature. However, if other varieties were flowering nearby at the same time they will have cross-pollinated, causing saved seed to grow differently.

VARIETIES

'Aquadulce Claudia' Ideal for autumn and winter sowings as it's hardy. Long pods contain up to seven tasty beans.

'Monica' (or 'De Monica') A smaller plant, good for windier gardens, with shorter pods containing up to six beans.

'Saturn' A good dwarf variety well suited to growing in containers.

KEY INFORMATION

Seed to harvest: 4 months (from late winter and spring sowings) **Sowing to transplanting:** 4–6 weeks
Position: Adaptable, will tolerate some shade **Spacing:** 20–25cm (8–10in) equidistant or 15cm (6in) apart with 45cm (18in) between rows **Hardiness:** Fully hardy, but can be adversely affected by a long cold spell

	JAN	FEB	MAR	APR	MAY	JUN	JUL	AUG	SEP	OCT	NOV	DEC
Sowing		▬	▬	▬	▬					▬		
Transplanting			▬	▬	▬	▬						▬
Harvesting						▬	▬	▬				

DWARF FRENCH BEANS

Freshly picked French beans are a fine taste of summer. The compact plants are easy to grow when it's warm, need no supports, and crop continuously for two months. They flourish in containers on a sunny patio or in a greenhouse where summers are cool. Many colourful varieties are available, as well as dwarf borlotti beans with their creamy, freckled seeds.

Sowing and transplanting

Dwarf French beans are heat-loving plants that will be killed by frost, so there is no advantage in sowing them too early. Sow seeds individually into 3cm (1¼in) modules under cover, where the warmth results in better germination, especially for early sowings in late April or early May. Make the first sowing three weeks before your last frost date, so seedlings aren't ready to transplant too early. I sow early for a summer crop, followed by a second sowing in mid-June or early July to keep harvests going from late August into early autumn. Summer sowings can be made outside into dibbed holes, 3cm (1¼in) deep.

Transplant seedlings about three weeks after sowing, when they are sturdy but still small, with the first true leaf just emerging. Ideally, wait until a week after your last frost date to ensure that plants have enough warmth by night. You can also grow dwarf French beans in a polytunnel in cooler climates or simply for earlier harvests than plants growing outdoors. Space plants a minimum of 30cm (12in) apart each way, or 35cm (14in) apart to make it easier to find and pick pods. For modules, use a dibber or trowel to make holes just a little wider than the root balls, and about 2cm (¾in) deeper. Push the root ball into the hole, leave it unfilled, and water plants in well.

Care and protection

Cover early plantings made in late May or early June with fleece, to insulate the seedlings and protect them from cool or blustery weather. Leaves turn yellow if the soil is too cool, not from a shortage of nitrogen, but because they cannot photosynthesize at low temperatures. Their colour returns and growth resumes once the weather warms.

Plants need little water when young, but once flowers and pods start to develop water twice a week if the weather is dry. Plants growing under cover and in pots will need frequent watering. Pods often fail to set after flowering when plants are too dry at the roots and this is easily remedied by watering.

Transplant dwarf French beans under cover for harvests two weeks earlier.

Dwarf French beans are sometimes troubled by black fly, but keeping plants well watered makes them less vulnerable to attack. Slugs may feed on pods that hang down to the ground, creating holes and shortened pods. Pick frequently while they are young to prevent most of them reaching soil level.

Harvesting and storage

When to harvest depends how you like your pods; they can be picked small and tender or fatter and longer, for varied flavour and texture. Pull gently to snap the stalk, when pods are 10–15cm (4–6in) long and starting to swell, but before you see bean seeds starting to show. Harvesting at least twice a week encourages plants to grow plenty of new pods for up to eight weeks. Plants tend to produce shorter, fatter pods as they get older. Pods have the best flavour and texture when freshly picked, but can be stored in a polythene bag (see p.102) in the fridge for up to five days.

Saving seed

Saving your own seed from dwarf French beans is easy because the plants don't cross-pollinate, which means that you can grow different varieties next to each other and the seeds they produce will grow true to the variety. Leave a few pods on any plant to develop fully and dry to yellow-brown. Pick the pods at the end of summer, shell the beans, and ensure they are dry before storing them in a packet to sow the following year, or in jars for eating if you have a lot. Borlotti beans can be harvested and stored in the same way.

Harvest fine pods, before the beans inside develop, for a tender texture.

VARIETIES

'Cupidon' A reliable variety producing tasty long, green beans.

'Orinoco' Yellow, slightly waxy pods with a buttery flavour and good texture.

'Safari' A prolific variety bearing fine green pods, starting a week after 'Cupidon'.

Borlotti Dwarf varieties of 'Lingua di Fuoco' and 'Borlotto' are available to harvest for pods of fresh or dried beans.

KEY INFORMATION

Seed to harvest: 2½ months   **Sowing to transplanting:** 3 weeks   **Position:** Full sun and warmth
Spacing: 30–35cm (12–14in) apart each way   **Hardiness:** Not hardy. They will be killed by frost

	JAN	FEB	MAR	APR	MAY	JUN	JUL	AUG	SEP	OCT	NOV	DEC
Sowing					▬	▬						
Transplanting					▬	▬						
Harvesting						▬	▬	▬	▬	▬		

CLIMBING BEANS

These vigorous beans are prolific croppers and staples of the summer garden. You will find a diverse range of varieties in seed catalogues, from runner beans with beautiful red or bicoloured flowers, to round or flat-podded French beans, and the pink-flecked pods of borlotti that can also be grown for seed harvests. Grow them all in the same way, trained up tall, strong supports.

Sowing and transplanting

All these beans need warmth to succeed and will die if exposed to frost, so avoid sowing them too early, which is often tempting when April is warm. I sow into modules under cover from mid-May to June and sow outdoors from the end of May. The large seeds need a good-sized 5cm (2in) module, but the deep root-trainers marketed for sowing beans are unnecessary. Lay one seed flat on the compost in each module, push it in gently, cover with compost equivalent to twice the thickness of the seed, and water thoroughly. There is no need to pre-soak seeds as they swell easily when in contact with moist compost.

Transplant seedlings no earlier than a week after your last frost date – around two weeks after sowing – when they have long stems, but just one true leaf. It isn't necessary to prepare soil by making a trench filled with organic matter: no dig beds retain moisture and have plenty of fertility. There is also no need to push in supports before you plant out, and this means you can cover early plantings with fleece should the weather be cold.

Space plants according to the support you plan to construct. A teepee, made of a circle of canes tied together at the top, is strong and stands well in wind. Make it 90–120cm (3–4ft) in diameter, with each cane spaced 30cm (1ft) apart. My teepees have six canes for a 1.2m (4ft)-wide bed or eight for a 1.5m (5ft)-wide

bed. A double line of supporting sticks can also be built across a bed, with their tops leaning together and secured along a horizontal cane. Space the two lines 60cm (2ft) apart, with 30cm (1ft) between each plant along the lines. Any sticks around 2.5m (8ft) long can be used, including bamboo or hazel, but they must be stout enough to support the weight of plants laden with pods.

This 'Cobra' climbing French bean can produce heavy crops of long pods for more than two months.

Store the seed from dried borlotti bean pods for soups and stews during winter.

the weather stays dry. It's moisture at the roots that will help pods set once the flowers have faded, rather than misting water onto the flowers as some gardeners claim. Watering also helps to prevent and resolve attacks on the young growth by black fly.

Harvesting and storage

The length and thickness of the pods you pick is a matter of personal taste, but both runner and French beans tend to get stringy once the pods become swollen. It's best to catch them when their profile is even, without the shape of the beans inside showing through. Pick pods by lifting and twisting to snap the stalk, every two days in warm weather and for as long as two months. Pods are best eaten fresh but keep well in the fridge for four or five days in a polythene bag (see p.102).

If you want to harvest the beans, either to eat fresh or to dry for storage, then leave pods unpicked so their beans swell. Pick fat, green pods to shell the fresh beans inside or let the pods dry to a pale yellow-brown on the plant to harvest dry beans. Remove dry beans from pods and ensure they are completely dry before storing in a jar, where they will keep well for a year or more. Dry beans are delicious when cooked after being rehydrated in cold water overnight.

Care and protection

Watch the new stem growth and once they are quite long check that they are wrapping around their supports. No tying in is needed, just twist each stem around its cane at first and the plants will be self-supporting. Usually there is no need to protect climbing beans from pests, but deer or rabbits may bite the top off a stem, and if you expect that, wrap a cover of mesh around young plants.

Climbing beans are vigorous plants with lots of leaves, which makes them a thirsty crop. Start watering in dry conditions when you see the first flowers, and once plants are in full flower, give them a good soak twice a week if

Seed saving

Runner beans planted within 50m (164ft) of each other will cross-pollinate, so if you or a neighbouring allotmenteer grow more than one variety, the seeds you save probably won't grow true to your original variety. Save seed by leaving some pods unpicked, until they go pale yellow and then brown, which shows that they are about 90 per cent dry. Shell them, lay them out on paper indoors, and let them finish drying before storing in a paper bag or jar for sowing the following year.

VARIETIES

My preference is to grow 'Czar' for dry beans, and 'Cobra', 'Golden Gate', and 'Scarlet Emperor' for pods.

FRENCH BEANS

'Cobra' A popular variety with long, green pods.

'Neckargold' Plants laden with slightly flattened, golden pods look really attractive.

'Golden Gate' Prolific quantities of flat yellow pods.

Borlotti Pink-flecked pods filled with freckled beans that can be harvested fresh or dried.

RUNNER BEANS

'Scarlet Emperor' Striking red flowers and good crops, but pods aren't as long and tender as they used to be.

'Czar' A white-flowered variety that makes tasty large, white beans for drying.

'Stardust' A hybrid between French and runner beans, which some gardeners find sets pods more readily than standard runner bean varieties.

'Hestia' Dwarf variety is good for container growing.

KEY INFORMATION   ▬ Outdoors   ▬ Under cover

Seed to harvest: 3 months for pods, 4–5 for beans   **Sowing to transplanting:** 2–3 weeks   **Position:** Full sun, can tolerate some shade. Avoid a windy position   **Spacing:** 30cm (1ft) apart, 60cm (2ft) between rows
Hardiness: Killed by frost and need warmth to thrive

	JAN	FEB	MAR	APR	MAY	JUN	JUL	AUG	SEP	OCT	NOV	DEC
Sowing					▬	▬						
Transplanting					▬	▬						
Harvesting							▬	▬	▬	▬		

Foliage-covered teepees of borlotti beans.

PEAS

By the time you've sown, transplanted, supported, harvested, and podded peas you probably don't get the greatest return for your time. What makes it all worthwhile is the unique, sweet flavour of freshly picked peas which far surpasses any that you can buy. Plus you can choose between podding peas, or mangetout and snap varieties with edible pods, dwarf varieties just 60cm (2ft) high, or tall varieties that rapidly reach 2m (6½ft) high. Know the varieties you grow in order to provide suitable supports and to harvest at the best time.

Sowing and transplanting

Peas work best as a half-season vegetable, sown early and finishing before midsummer. It's possible to sow dwarf varieties in November to transplant in February, but is simpler and more effective to make first sowings in mid-February under cover, and the last ones in April. If you sow in May and June, plants are more likely to suffer mildew on the leaves and caterpillars in the pods, with reduced harvests. Another advantage of early sowing is that cropping finishes by the middle of summer, leaving ground free for a second planting of beetroot, broccoli, and many other vegetables, whereas options are more limited after clearing later sowings.

Pea seeds are adored by rodents and birds and outdoor sowings are difficult to protect. It's easier to prevent rodents damaging sowings under cover because you can set a mousetrap close to the newly sown trays. Sow into 3–5cm (1¼–2in) modules, with two or three seeds per cell, which you then plant as a little clump. Germination should be rapid but may be erratic, and the age of seed is more likely to be a problem than growing conditions or pests. Try saving your own pea seeds to sow the following year (see p.124) and you will find that germination rates improve.

Transplant peas at three weeks old and no more than 5cm (2in) high. Dib a hole deep enough for the root ball to be 3cm (1¼in) below ground level, and leave the hole unfilled so that plants sit in a dip. Cover early plantings with fleece to keep them warm, and protected from rabbits and pigeons. The spacing and planting pattern depends on the size of the variety (see p.125). You can grow dwarf peas in short lines across beds and taller varieties in double rows along their length.

Care and protection

For all but the shortest varieties, support is important to give curling tendrils something to grasp and make it easier to harvest pods. Wait until early May, when the fleece cover is removed, before adding supports. For medium varieties, 75–120cm (2½–4ft) tall, hammer a stout stake into the ground at each end of the row and add some twiggy pea sticks between them to help plants climb. Tie strings between the posts, from 15cm (6in) above soil level and at 15cm (6in) intervals thereafter, to support to the mass of growth. Plastic netting held between two posts is an option, but is more work to disentangle from plants when clearing. For tall varieties, bang in 2.5m (8ft) fence posts at either end of the row and at 1.5m (5ft) intervals along it, with strong strings tied between them every 15–20cm (6–8in) up their height.

Create sturdy supports, using both stakes and pea sticks, to keep plants upright and easy to pick.

VEGETABLE AND HERB DIRECTORY

If pigeons eat the leaves, use bird netting to keep them off plants after you remove the fleece. Pea weevils chomp a jagged pattern into leaf edges. They are common in dry springs, but nothing to worry about where a well-mulched, moist soil allows plants to grow away from damage. Early sowings are usually harvested before pea moths become active in late June, but from July you may find their maggots in peas you shell. Powdery mildew is common on the foliage of older plants from early summer onwards, but is mostly a problem on late sowings, when the mildew resistant variety 'Terrain' is useful.

GROWING PEA SHOOTS

Young, tender pea shoots are a delicious addition to salads and work well from dedicated sowings grown at a 25cm (10in) equidistant spacing. Any variety of garden pea will serve, as will marrowfat peas from the supermarket, although the latter have many tendrils. Sow from mid-February to April in the same way as peas for pods, then transplant in a block, like a salad crop. When each plant is 20–25cm (8–10in) high, pinch out its main shoot at the top between thumb and forefinger for your first harvest. New sideshoots appear within a week or two in spring and harvests of new shoots continue for up to eight weeks from one sowing. As peas are hardy, you can also sow in October to grow under cover in the soil or containers, for a steady harvest of shoots until early May.

Watering is not usually necessary for the early growth of peas transplanted in spring, when there are good moisture levels in the soil. If it doesn't rain once they start to flower, water regularly to ensure a full harvest.

Harvesting and storage

Know what type of pea you have and at what stage you're looking to harvest: shelling peas will have fat, glossy, dark green pods; mangetout varieties are picked when pods are thin and flat; sugarsnaps have swollen edible pods filled with juicy peas. After you see flowers, start watching the pods develop so that you catch them at the best stage. There's an element of personal preference, as shelling peas can be harvested when pods are still thin for fewer small but extra-sweet peas, or left to grow larger for a bigger crop of fatter peas that are still sweet, or allowed to dry for eating during winter and to use as seed. For maximum sweetness, pick at least every two or three days, because it's easy to miss a few that will then go starchy. Peas lose sweetness after harvest, so it's best to harvest on the day you want to eat them.

You can save seed from a single pea plant and there is only an extra month or so of growing time from harvesting green pods to picking them dry for seed. They don't cross-pollinate, so you could save seed from two or three varieties planted close together. I grow a few pea plants purely for seed, separately from the rows for eating. Gather pods in mid- to late summer, when they are quite dry and have turned more brown than yellow. Shell them out straight away and leave the seeds on a plate or tray on a sunny windowsill for a few days, to dry fully before storing in a jar or envelope. Check for small round holes made by pea moth maggots and compost any damaged seeds.

VARIETIES

DWARF PEAS

The earliest to mature on compact plants that don't need support, but the harvest is usually small and over a short period.

'Meteor' Productive, early shelling pea; 60cm (2ft)

'Sugar Ann' A compact sugarsnap pea; 60cm (2ft)

'Nairobi' A sugarsnap that can also be shelled for peas; 75cm (2½ft)

MEDIUM PEAS

This category includes most of the classic peas and plants require support.

'Hurst Green Shaft' Long, thin pods containing up to ten fat peas; 90cm (3ft)

'Starlight' Smaller pods packed with up to seven sweet peas; 90cm (3ft)

'Terrain' Shelling pea with mildew resistance, for sowing late June to early July for an autumn harvest; 90cm (3ft)

'Oregon Sugar Pod' A mangetout with sweetness in the pods. Best picked thin; 1.2m (4ft)

'Cascadia' A sweet-podded sugarsnap; 1.2m (4ft)

TALL PEAS

Can reach more than 2m (6½ft) tall and need sturdy supports. Produce generous harvests.

'Alderman' Reliably produces heavy crops of big fat pods for shelling; 2m (6½ft)

'Sugar Snap' Tall sugarsnap variety; 1.8m (6ft)

'Ne Plus Ultra' Large yields of long, fat, green pods for shelling; up to 2.2m (7ft)

'Carouby de Maussane' A mangetout with purple flowers and pods to 12cm (4¾in) long; up to 1.8m (6ft)

Pods of sugarsnap pea 'Cascadia' start to swell as they approach maturity.

KEY INFORMATION

Seed to harvest: 3–3½ months **Sowing to transplanting:** 3 weeks **Position:** Full sun, moist soil, align rows at 90° to prevailing wind **Spacing:** Dwarf varieties: 15cm (6in) apart with 30cm (12in) between rows across bed. Medium varieties: Double row 30cm (12in) apart along length of bed, with plants 20cm (8in) apart, or single rows across bed 45cm (18in) apart with 20cm (8in) between plants. Tall varieties: Single row along length of bed with plants 15cm (6in) apart **Hardiness:** Hardy, to around -5°C (23°F) **Suitable for multisowing and saving seed**

	JAN	FEB	MAR	APR	MAY	JUN	JUL	AUG	SEP	OCT	NOV	DEC
Sowing			▬	▬	▬		▬				▬	
Transplanting		▬	▬	▬	▬		▬					
Harvesting						▬	▬	▬		▬	▬	

BRASSICAS - CABBAGE FAMILY

Broccoli

Brussels sprouts

Cabbage

Cauliflower

Kale

Radish

Swede

Turnip

Healthy brassicas are a decorative feature in my garden throughout the year.

The huge, exciting family of brassica plants offers possibilities for year-round harvests of leaves, flower stems, and roots, but they are susceptible to an array of common pests. Brassicas are frost hardy to varying degrees, which offers scope to produce valuable fresh and stored vegetables to help see you through the cold months of winter and early spring.

Choosing what to grow

There are many brassica vegetables to choose from, each with a host of varieties, giving options for different cropping seasons, plant sizes, colours, and many other characteristics.

For quick harvests, grow radish in spring and turnips from late summer sowings. Kale is a reliable choice for regular pickings of leaves over a long season, and has dwarf varieties that are well suited to small growing spaces. Summer and autumn are the main season for harvesting broccoli, cauliflower, and cabbage hearts, but select varieties carefully so that you know when to look for the harvest. Brussels sprouts, kale, winter radish, and swede all

come into their own during winter, because they are so hardy to frost and develop a sweeter flavour when exposed to low temperatures.

Sowing, growing, and harvesting

To maximize chances of success, I avoid insect pests as much as possible by timing sowings carefully and sowing under cover. All brassicas germinate fast and the strong seedlings transplant successfully with their long, slender stems below soil level. Radish and turnips can be multisown, but the rest are best grown as single plants. All brassicas grow exceptionally well in no dig soil, because annual mulching with compost means it is

CROP		JAN	FEB	MAR	APR	MAY	JUN	JUL	AUG	SEP	OCT	NOV	DEC
Broccoli	Sow		▬	▬	▬	▬	▬	▬	▬				
	Harvest			▬	▬	▬	▬	▬	▬	▬	▬	▬	
Brussels sprouts	Sow				▬	▬	▬						
	Harvest	▬	▬	▬							▬	▬	▬
Cabbage	Sow		▬	▬	▬	▬	▬	▬	▬				
	Harvest	▬	▬	▬	▬	▬	▬	▬	▬	▬	▬	▬	▬
Cauliflower	Sow		▬	▬	▬	▬	▬	▬	▬				
	Harvest			▬	▬	▬	▬	▬	▬	▬	▬	▬	▬
Kale	Sow			▬	▬	▬	▬	▬	▬				
	Harvest	▬	▬	▬	▬	▬		▬	▬	▬	▬	▬	▬
Radish (spring)	Sow		▬	▬	▬								
	Harvest				▬	▬	▬						
Radish (winter)	Sow							▬					
	Harvest	▬	▬								▬	▬	▬
Swede	Sow					▬	▬						
	Harvest	▬	▬	▬							▬	▬	▬
Turnip	Sow		▬	▬					▬				
	Harvest				▬	▬	▬				▬	▬	

fertile and retains the moisture that allows rapid, leafy growth. You may see advice to firm the soil before transplanting, but this is unnecessary in no dig beds, where soil already has a stable structure. The use of crop covers is essential to protect plants from pests at crucial times and achieve a healthy harvest.

Broccoli, Brussels sprouts, and kale give repeat harvests of delicious greens, often from winter to early spring when you appreciate them the most. Watch fast-growing radishes and turnips, as well as heads of cabbage and cauliflower, to catch them at their best. Swedes and winter radish can be harvested from the soil or stored over a longer period.

Common problems

The key with brassicas is to know your enemies, especially the insect pests. Using crop covers is an almost miraculous way to prevent damage, to small plants especially (see pp.92–94). Familiarity with pests and individual crops means you put covers in place only during vulnerable periods of growth and they don't need to be used all the time.

Flea beetles are tiny, black insects that eat small, circular holes in young leaves during spring and summer, often weakening young plants. Sowing under cover helps to avoid them. In summer and autumn, caterpillars devour leaves, hearts, and flowering stems and can quickly decimate crops. Prevent this by covering beds before adult butterflies have a chance to lay their eggs. In spring and autumn, cabbage root flies lay their eggs at the base of plants so that their maggots can burrow down to feed on the roots. Unexplained wilting is often the first visible symptom. Use mesh covers to keep adult flies away from plants. Sap-sucking insects such as cabbage whitefly

Brussels sprouts 'Brendan' F1 with buttons ready for picking through winter.

and mealy cabbage aphid can be prolific on the underside of leaves in winter, but applying an annual compost mulch promotes healthy plant growth, which reduces their presence. Larger pests, such as pigeons and rabbits, also love brassicas and are best kept off with a covering of bird netting.

Brassica plants have a beautiful appearance and a great way to enhance this is to regularly remove any yellowing leaves near ground level. This also helps to reduce slug numbers by minimizing their habitat.

Covering young spring cabbages with mesh protects them from pests and strong winds.

Calabrese is delicious when freshly picked and easy to grow given protection from insect pests.

BROCCOLI

The various types of broccoli crop at different times of the year, which gives you a range of harvest options to choose from. There is large-headed, green calabrese to harvest in summer and autumn, and hardier purple sprouting broccoli to overwinter and pick in spring. A third type is a cross between Chinese kale and European calabrese called kaibroc, which is also known as Tenderstem or Broccolini. It quickly grows smaller heads with longer stems than calabrese, and crops in cool conditions. All types of broccoli are easy to grow, but are susceptible to many pests, particularly when plants are small, which makes protection with crop covers worthwhile.

Sowing and transplanting

Sow calabrese from mid-February until the second half of June. Purple sprouting broccoli can be sown in April, but I recommend early June because that allows you to grow another crop beforehand in the same space. Sow kaibroc from April for picking through summer and autumn, and again in July for late autumn and winter harvests.

Sow under cover, because young seedlings are much more vulnerable to insect pests, such as flea beetle, than older and stronger plants. The germination and growth of brassica seeds is erratic and I get the best results from sowing all broccoli in a seed tray, then selecting the strongest seedlings to grow on. Scatter seeds thinly over the compost, cover with only a thin layer of compost, water, and keep under cover. Within a week, prick out sturdy seedlings into 3–5cm (1¼–2in) modules (see p.83), to grow a batch of strong plants. To raise only a few plants – for example of purple sprouting broccoli, where six large plants can be enough to feed a family – sow into modules rather than a seed tray. Sow two seeds into each cell and thin to the strongest seedling.

Transplant after three to five weeks. If space isn't available when transplants are ready, pot them on into 7cm (2¾in) pots (see p.82) to continue growing for two more weeks. Transplant with the long stems below ground level, to provide support in windy conditions. Space calabrese and kaibroc 30–40cm (12–16in) apart, adjusting the distance according to the size of heads you want to produce. Purple sprouting broccoli plants grow large and need a minimum of 50cm (20in) between them.

Care and protection

These tough plants generally flourish with little attention. Water transplants until established, perhaps twice a week in dry weather. After that there is usually no need to water until they start to make heads, when it is worth watering if conditions are dry. Tall purple sprouting broccoli sometimes blows over in late summer or autumn. Generally their roots are fine and, rather than trying to add supports, stems can be left lying on the soil and allowed to grow upwards at 90°. Snap to remove the lowest leaves from large plants as they yellow.

Crop covers are necessary at specific times to grow reliably good broccoli. Transplants are vulnerable to flea beetles in spring and caterpillars in summer, while plants can be decimated by pigeons at any stage, but especially in winter. Lay fleece over transplants in cold spring weather, to keep out pests and provide extra warmth, for an early harvest. In summer, I use mesh to protect plants against insects, for at least the first four to six weeks after transplanting. Fleece and mesh covers prevent adult cabbage root flies laying eggs at the base of transplants, better than collars in my experience. Covers may not always be needed, but where pigeons are a problem protect plants with bird netting when mesh or fleece is removed.

Where you only have a few plants, squash caterpillars on leaves, but you're likely to find a few caterpillars hidden in calabrese heads during late summer and autumn. Aphids multiply on plants struggling in poor, dry soil and I rarely see them on brassicas in my healthy soil. If they do appear, wash them off with a spray of water, water plants, and spread another 3cm (1¼in) of compost around them. Clubroot is a disease that causes swollen, deformed roots and poor growth, but I have not experienced it in no dig beds.

Harvesting and storage

All broccoli grows tight, domed heads of flower buds, which gradually elongate and need to be harvested before they open into yellow flowers. Harvest young heads to ensure that the delicious stems remain tender and don't become fibrous. Cut the first central head before it's too advanced and a second crop of smaller sideshoots will soon develop lower down. Each plant can produce multiple pickings over a period of two to four months, depending on the variety. Fatter stems are best cut with a sharp knife, while thinner ones snap off quite easily. Frequency of picking depends on the temperature; check summer calabrese every two days, and spring purple sprouting broccoli twice a week. Broccoli is always best freshly picked and goes yellow quickly in warm conditions. Heads will store for up to five days if kept cool, below 10ºC (50ºF).

Harvest 15cm (6in) of tender, sweet stem with purple sprouting broccoli to discover why it's called "poor man's asparagus".

VARIETIES

CALABRESE

'Belstar' F1, **'Marathon' F1** Reliable large, green heads.

'Stemia' F1 Smaller heads and shoots, on longer stems.

'Green Sprouting' Open-pollinated (see p.37), producing smaller heads over a longer period.

PURPLE SPROUTING

'Late Purple Sprouting' An open-pollinated variety (see p.37) that may only yield small, thin shoots.

'Claret' F1 Amazing modern hybrid yielding a large central head, followed by shoots over a long period.

'Rudolph' F1 Crops from mid-winter if the weather is not too cold.

'Summer Purple' Gives harvests from midsummer through autumn.

KAIBROC

'Apollo' F1 Fast to crop from a sowing in mid-July.

'Green Inspiration' F1 Produces sturdy stems for many months from a May sowing.

Kaibroc broccoli 'Green Inspiration' F1 yields pickings of sturdy, sweet shoots over an exceptionally long period.

KEY INFORMATION (All suitable as a second follow-on crop)

CALABRESE

Seed to harvest: 3 months **Sowing to transplanting:** 3–5 weeks **Position:** Adaptable, tolerates shade
Spacing: 30–40cm (12–16in) **Hardiness:** Hardy to approx. -3°C (27°F)

	JAN	FEB	MAR	APR	MAY	JUN	JUL	AUG	SEP	OCT	NOV	DEC
Sowing		▬	▬	▬	▬	▬						
Transplanting			▬	▬	▬	▬	▬	▬				
Harvesting						▬	▬	▬	▬	▬		

PURPLE SPROUTING

Seed to harvest: 9 months **Sowing to transplanting:** 3–5 weeks **Position:** Adaptable, tolerates shade

Spacing: 50–60cm (20–24in) **Hardiness:** Very hardy to approx. -10°C (14°F)

	JAN	FEB	MAR	APR	MAY	JUN	JUL	AUG	SEP	OCT	NOV	DEC
Sowing				▬	▬	▬						
Transplanting					▬	▬	▬					
Harvesting	▬	▬	▬	▬					▬	▬	▬	▬

KAIBROC

Seed to harvest: 2½ months **Sowing to transplanting:** 3–5 weeks **Position:** Adaptable, tolerates shade

Spacing: 30–40cm (12–16in) **Hardiness:** Shoots hardy to approx. -3°C (27°F), plants to -6°C (21°F)

	JAN	FEB	MAR	APR	MAY	JUN	JUL	AUG	SEP	OCT	NOV	DEC
Sowing				▬	▬		▬	▬				
Transplanting				▬				▬	▬			
Harvesting							▬	▬	▬	▬	▬	

BRUSSELS SPROUTS

Brussels sprout plants are easy to grow, but achieving a good harvest of tight buttons can be a challenge. They need good, fertile soil and make large plants that take up a lot of room during autumn and winter, but for me this is worthwhile for a steady harvest of homegrown Brussels that are full of flavour and less bitter than their shop-bought counterparts. Choose varieties carefully to crop at the time you want them, in autumn or deep winter. I always grow F1 hybrids because open-pollinated varieties (see p.37) often produce "blown" sprouts with loose leaves.

Sowing and transplanting

Seed packets say to sow from February to April, but I sow in early May, because I find that plants sown earlier can get too big and give harvests before you want them. In addition, sowing slightly later allows time to grow another vegetable first (see below).

Most households should have plenty to harvest from six to ten plants. Either sow thinly into a small seed tray and prick the seedlings out individually into 3cm (1¼in) modules, or sow two seeds into each module cell and thin to the strongest once they have germinated. After about a month, pot them on into a 7cm (2¾in) pot to give you a decent-sized transplant by mid-June. It's really worth looking after them to give them a good start.

While you're doing all this propagation, grow a crop of lettuce, carrots, spring onions, or anything that finishes cropping by mid-July. I find that young Brussels sprouts do better interplanted (see pp.70–71) between these earlier vegetables, spaced the necessary 60cm (2ft) apart, because when they are small they don't thrive in bare ground and far from their nearest neighbour. Harvest a few carrots to make a gap for each Brussels sprout plant. Make a neat hole with a trowel and pop the root ball in deep, so that its top is about 5cm (2in) below soil level, to provide support for the seedling's long stem.

Care and protection

Water plants well at transplanting, when the weather is often dry. Ensure there is sufficient water for summer growth, but don't water lavishly at this stage. You may need to water more in September, but by the time the first sprouts form in autumn it's usually cool and wet enough to make watering unnecessary.

Immediately after transplanting, cover the bed with mesh supported on wire hoops, because during summer there will be flea beetles, cabbage root flies, and swede midges ready to strike the small plants. By July, butterflies will also be laying eggs that will hatch into caterpillars. Keep the cover in place for six to eight weeks, until the mesh sides rise above ground level, when you can remove it. Watch out for caterpillars in late summer and squash them, particularly in the head of the plant where they do most damage. If there are pigeons, replace mesh with bird netting supported on a frame above plants, to allow height for growth and prevent birds sitting on plants to peck through the netting.

Add a sturdy stake next to each plant in late summer and tie in the stem, if you want to keep it upright and make picking easier. Around this time, plants start to shed lower leaves, which you can pull off as soon they yellow. This avoids decaying leaves creating hiding places for slugs.

Aphids and whiteflies can be a problem from autumn into winter. I find adding sufficient compost to beds each year and keeping plants well watered reduces these insect numbers.

Harvesting and storage

Picking usually begins in October, especially for the early varieties. Buttons mature from the base to the top of the stem and need to be picked in that order. The first buttons at the bottom stay small, so don't wait for them to get bigger or they they will just go yellow. If the buttons are blowing open into mini cabbage-like shoots they will never form a tight button, but are still edible and best picked promptly. To harvest, push down with your thumb on top of a button and it will snap off the main stem cleanly. Harvest firm, round sprouts weekly over eight to ten weeks as they mature. Late varieties will be sweeter once they have experienced cold weather (see p.100) and can be picked until early spring. Even sprouts that have elongated and started to flower in spring, are still edible. The leafy plant top is probably

Plants reach an impressive size (top). Transplants thrive interplanted among a carrot crop under mesh (bottom).

Snap sprouts off the main stem regularly to catch them at their best.

the most delicious harvest and can be cut, together with the last few sprouts, from late December to March. Brussels sprouts are so hardy that they can stand in the ground all winter ready to be picked, but can also be kept for two weeks in a cool shed or fridge.

Twist harvested plants from the soil and chop up their tough stems before adding to the compost heap, to help them break down faster. Slice lengthways along the fibres first, so they can be cut into 15cm (6in) lengths more easily.

VARIETIES

'Brendan' F1 Small to medium buttons from October to January.

'Ruby Crunch' F1 Dark colour and firm, small sprouts that can be harvested from November to February.

'Trafalgar' F1 Medium to large sprouts from November to March, sweeter than some varieties.

'Igor' F1 Sweet sprouts that are ready to harvest from December to March.

KEY INFORMATION

Seed to harvest: 5–7 months **Sowing to transplanting:** 6–8 weeks **Position:** Any position, including shade. Will tolerate wind **Spacing:** 60cm (2ft) equidistant spacing **Hardiness:** Very hardy **Suitable for interplanting**

	JAN	FEB	MAR	APR	MAY	JUN	JUL	AUG	SEP	OCT	NOV	DEC
Sowing				▬	▬							
Transplanting						▬	▬					
Harvesting (early)	▬	▬								▬	▬	▬
Harvesting (late)	▬	▬	▬									▬

CABBAGE

Success with cabbage is all about varietal choice and timing, to produce harvests throughout the year. Sow spring cabbage in late summer to overwinter as small plants, for a welcome crop during mid-spring, when other fresh greens are in short supply. Sow summer varieties in late winter to produce tight heads by early summer, before caterpillars become a problem. Autumn cabbages from spring sowings make the biggest heads that stand and store well. Tough winter varieties provide valuable greens through the coldest months. Savoys are particularly hardy, because they don't make a tight head which allows them to stand frost really well.

Sowing and transplanting

Read seed packets to find out when each variety matures and how long plants will stand in the ground in good condition, to work out how many of each to grow. All types of cabbage can either be sown thinly into a seed tray to prick out into modules, or two seeds into each module cell, to be thinned to a single plant if both germinate. Grow them in 3cm (1¼in), or better still in 5cm (2in) modules, because they are greedy young plants. I always sow under cover to protect seedlings from flea beetles, other insect pests, and slugs. Time your sowings to have plants ready as soon another vegetable finishes – winter and spring cabbages are useful second plantings to follow summer harvests like beetroot and onions.

Seedlings are ready to transplant after about four weeks. Set spring cabbages in the ground at this stage in September, while the soil is still warm. Summer and autumn varieties are transplanted in April–May and May–June respectively. They could also be potted on into 7cm (2¾in) pots to continue growing under cover if the weather is really cold in April, or if you are waiting for a spring crop like spinach, radish, or broad beans to finish. Winter cabbages are ready to transplant in July, when the weather is warm and space is more available. No dig soil hasn't been fluffed up by digging so there is no need to firm the soil before planting, contrary to the dictate of gardening tradition, which tells you to firm the soil because it assumes prior loosening.

Transplant deeply, burying as much stem as you can to give plants the best anchorage and wind protection. It's fine to bury the small seed leaves if they are still present. Push the root ball in firmly and water each plant well. Spacings vary for different cabbage types and also influence the size, and even the type, of heads produced; spring cabbages are more likely to heart-up when planted 30cm (12in) apart, and to form loose heads of spring greens at a 20cm (8in) spacing. Some varieties of autumn cabbage make heavy heads when spaced at 60cm (2ft).

Care and protection

Continue to water newly transplanted cabbages regularly until you see them begin to grow. Only summer and autumn cabbages may need watering after that stage, when the weather is dry and they are starting to make a heart.

I cover newly planted cabbage at all times of year, because they are prone to damage by many pests and there is a real risk of losing all of your small plants just like that. In spring, protect transplants of summer cabbage with fleece until early May on average. Fleece shields plants from wind and cold weather, plus it keeps out flea beetles, cabbage root flies, birds, and rabbits. Fine insect mesh is the best choice to protect small plants from late spring into autumn, as it's less warm than fleece and excellent protection against insects. Leave a mesh cover on overwintering spring cabbage to keep birds off and provide protection from the weather, which benefits growth in spring. After protecting spring and summer plantings for the first six to eight weeks, they may be grown on without a cover, but where pigeons are present, cover cabbages with bird netting throughout their growth.

Remove yellowing lower leaves to keep plants tidy, which also enables you to spot and pull any weeds and keep slug numbers low. Add the leaves you remove to the compost heap, along with weeds, and any slugs that were feeding on them.

Harvesting and storage

A strong knife is required to cut through the woody stem of a big cabbage. It's up to you how many of the less tender, but entirely edible, outer leaves you eat with the sweet central heart. It can be tricky to judge when to harvest, because the size and density of hearts vary according to the type and variety you are growing. Spring cabbages are ready from mid- to late spring: harvest when you see a nice folding of paler central leaves, rather than waiting for a tight head. Left too long they will flower. Summer cabbages make tighter hearts and it's best to cut the first one as soon as it feels firm, because they quickly lose quality in summer heat and insect damage will start to occur. Look for good tight heads before cutting autumn cabbages, which will stand in

You may need a covering of bird netting to keep hungry pigeons off cabbages.

VEGETABLE AND HERB DIRECTORY

the ground for up to two months in the cool of autumn. Winter cabbages are leafier, with looser central hearts, and remain in good condition in the ground for two or three months. The dark green outer leaves of a Savoy cabbage are delicious, so cut low on the main stem to use as many as you can.

You can leave the cut stems to re-sprout for a second harvest, but the benefits are small. To try it, cut off the existing leaves after harvest, cut a cross in the central part of the stem, and leave it for four to six weeks to regrow small heads. Usually this time would be better used to plant another vegetable, such as leeks after your spring cabbage.

Autumn and winter cabbages with firm hearts can be cut and stored in a cool shed for up to two months. Leave them in the ground for as long as possible, because the later you harvest, the cooler it will be and the better they will store. The outer leaves go mouldy in store, but can normally be peeled away carefully to reveal a sound cabbage heart underneath. Hearted cabbages can also be processed to store as sauerkraut, pickles, or fermented cabbage.

'Granat' is a beautiful red cabbage.

VARIETIES

SPRING

'Wheeler's Imperial' An old classic, for a bigger, leafy plant without much heart. Ideal for spring greens.

'Advantage' F1 or **'Duncan' F1** Both are compact with a pointed heart in mid-spring.

SUMMER

'Cabbice' F1 Excellent for producing quite large, round, tight heads of sweet leaves.

'Cape Horn' F1 A small variety yielding pointed heads of less than 1kg (2lb), earlier than 'Cabbice'.

I no longer grow traditional open-pollinated varieties like 'Greyhound' as they are not well maintained (see pp.50–51) and often don't make a heart.

AUTUMN

'Filderkraut' A German variety with large pointed heads of green leaves, sweet and ideal for sauerkraut.

'Granat' My favourite red cabbage variety, for dense, burgundy heads that store well.

WINTER

'January King' Half Savoy and half plain cabbage, this classic has pretty, ruffled leaves tinged with red. Crops in late autumn or early winter.

'Tundra' F1 A hardy hybrid that forms quite open, pale hearts to cut in late autumn and winter.

'Paresa' F1 A tough Savoy hybrid with medium-sized heads of deep green, puckered leaves.

'Ormskirk' This old-fashioned Savoy variety may not heart up reliably, but is still a valuable source of delicious winter greens.

KEY INFORMATION

SPRING VARIETIES

Seed to harvest: 7–8 months **Sowing to transplanting:** 4–6 weeks **Position:** Tolerates some shade
Spacing: 20–30cm (8–12in) (closer for loose greens, further for hearts) **Hardiness:** Cabbages are fully hardy.
Tight hearts can split below about -5°C (23°F) **Suitable for second follow-on planting**

	JAN	FEB	MAR	APR	MAY	JUN	JUL	AUG	SEP	OCT	NOV	DEC
Sowing								▬				
Transplanting									▬			
Harvesting			▬	▬	▬							

SUMMER VARIETIES

Seed to harvest: 4 months **Sowing to transplanting:** 4–6 weeks **Position:** Tolerates some shade
Spacing: 35–40cm (14–16in) **Hardiness:** Cabbages are fully hardy

	JAN	FEB	MAR	APR	MAY	JUN	JUL	AUG	SEP	OCT	NOV	DEC
Sowing		▬	▬									
Transplanting				▬	▬							
Harvesting							▬	▬				

AUTUMN VARIETIES

Seed to harvest: 4 months **Sowing to transplanting:** 4–6 weeks **Position:** Tolerates some shade
Spacing: 45–60cm (18–24in) **Hardiness:** Cabbages are fully hardy. Tight hearts can split below -5°C (23°F)

	JAN	FEB	MAR	APR	MAY	JUN	JUL	AUG	SEP	OCT	NOV	DEC
Sowing				▬	▬							
Transplanting					▬	▬						
Harvesting									▬	▬	▬	

WINTER VARIETIES

Seed to harvest: 5 months **Sowing to transplanting:** 4–6 weeks **Position:** Tolerates some shade
Spacing: 40cm (16in) **Hardiness:** Cabbages are fully hardy **Suitable for second follow-on planting**

	JAN	FEB	MAR	APR	MAY	JUN	JUL	AUG	SEP	OCT	NOV	DEC
Sowing						▬						
Transplanting							▬					
Harvesting	▬	▬	▬								▬	▬

Cut tough cabbage stems above the lowest leaves with a sharp knife.

CAULIFLOWER

Success with cauliflower is not easy, so you must ensure that everything is right by choosing a variety suited to the season you want to harvest, sowing at its best time, and protecting plants from pests. To keep things simple, I suggest three sowing options: the first in warmth in very early spring for a midsummer harvest in time to plant a follow-on crop; the second in early summer for an autumn harvest; the third in midsummer to harvest in early spring.

Sowing and transplanting

Make the first sowing from mid-February to mid-March under cover with warmth to trigger germination, which may mean starting them in the house. You can also sow in June for transplanting in July as a follow-on crop after clearing earlier vegetables like beetroot, carrots, or salad onions. This works well to produce beautifully geometric heads (curds) of Romanesco in autumn. For an early spring crop, sow hardy varieties in late July, under cover to protect them from pests. Cauliflower curds from any one sowing mature over a short period of two or three weeks, so there is no point growing too many. Sow a small number of seeds in a seed tray to prick out into 3–5cm (1¼–2in) modules or sow two seeds per module and thin to the strongest seedling.

Transplant about four to six weeks after sowing, spacing plants according to the size of curd you want. Plant 40cm (16in) apart for small cauliflowers, 55cm (22in) apart for large specimens, or in the middle of this range for good-sized curds. Make a straight-sided planting hole with a dibber or trowel and transplant up to 5cm (2in) below soil level to help support the long stem. Water in well.

Finding space to transplant cauliflowers to overwinter can be a challenge, but they do well interplanted between summer crops that are a few weeks from finishing, such as lettuce, carrots, or dwarf French beans. Interplanting may distract pigeons, which sometimes don't spot brassicas among other plants.

Care and protection

Water new transplants while they establish, especially in summer. Plants need little extra watering once they are growing strongly, but water in dry weather when curds start to swell for a summer harvest.

Cover spring transplants with fleece or mesh from day one, to insulate them from the weather and keep out flea beetles and cabbage root flies, which could ruin unprotected young plants. Prevent problems with caterpillars, which are a major pest through summer and early autumn, by protecting plants with mesh.

Cauliflower 'Medallion' F1 is hardy enough to overwinter.

The beauty of transplanting in late summer is that there are few damaging insects during the spring cropping period, but keep pigeons off with bird netting.

While plants are growing, snap off any yellowing outer leaves by pushing down on their stalks, to keep plants clean and reduce problems with slugs. This is also a chance to pull any weeds and see what's going on; you might notice caterpillars that need squashing or a baby cauliflower forming.

Harvesting and storage

Once the leaves of neighbouring plants touch, curds will soon be starting to develop. Look among the central leaves and if you see a little curd then watch it closely; in summer it will mature within one or two weeks, while it may take a month in early spring. Pick a few curds before they reach full size to avoid a glut, because mature curds quickly lose their even, domed top as broccoli-like stalks push up to flower. Harvest by cutting the main stem below a few of the enfolding outer leaves. The small central leaves are tasty and tender when plants are freshly cut. Cauliflowers keep in a cool place for a week or so, but quickly discolour if kept at room temperature. After harvest, twist out plant stems and add them to the compost heap.

Romanesco curds form exquisite fractal patterns.

VARIETIES

'Purple Graffiti' F1 Lovely violet curds to harvest in early summer or autumn, depending on when you sow.

'All The Year Round' An old variety that is a bit variable but lives up to its name and can be used for any of the sowing options.

Romanesco 'Navona' F1 Produces reliable and beautiful autumn harvests.

'Medallion' F1 Medium-sized white curds in early spring from summer sowing.

'Aalsmeer' Forms creamy-white curds to harvest in early to mid-spring.

KEY INFORMATION

Seed to harvest: 4 months (summer and autumn crop), 8 months (early spring crop) **Sowing to transplanting:** 4–6 weeks **Position:** Any position, tolerates some shade **Spacing:** 40–55cm (16–22in) equidistant
Hardiness: Hardy to -10°C (14°F) in leaf and -5°C (23°F) for curds **Suitable for interplanting in late summer**

	JAN	FEB	MAR	APR	MAY	JUN	JUL	AUG	SEP	OCT	NOV	DEC
Sowing (midsummer crop)		▬	▬									
Sowing (autumn crop)						▬						
Sowing (early spring crop)							▬					
Transplanting				▬					▬			
Harvesting			▬	▬	▬	▬	▬			▬	▬	

KALE

Kale is one of the best green leaves to grow for steady harvests through the colder months and into spring. It tolerates really cold, harsh conditions and, when you pick lower leaves only, growth continues for repeat harvests. The varied colours and leaf textures of different varieties look decorative in the garden. Red kale is extremely attractive, but green varieties are easier to grow, hardier, and more productive. Choose between flat-leaved varieties with softer leaves that are good in salads, and curly kale which is a little tougher and best for cooking. There are also compact dwarf varieties, ideal for smaller spaces and containers.

Sowing and transplanting

A range of sowing dates can provide you with kale for most of the year. Sow as early as March for harvests through summer, autumn, and possibly in winter too. Sowings from mid–May to June provide autumn harvests and are the best option for overwintering, as the slightly younger plants are more resistant to winter weather. Transplants come ready at a brilliant time to follow early crops of peas, broad beans, early potatoes, or spinach. Aim to tailor your kale sowing to produce transplants that are ready to go when ground becomes available. Another option is to sow in late July, for smaller plants to pick for salad leaves over winter. These can either be planted outdoors or under cover after tomato plants are cleared.

Either sow two seeds into a 3cm (1¼in) module and thin to the strongest seedling or sow thinly in a seed tray to prick out into 3cm (1¼in) modules. Multisow kale into modules to produce smaller plants for salad leaves.

Thin out the weaker seedling in each module.

Curly kale is hardy enough to crop through winter.

If your ground is ready, transplant kale from just three weeks after sowing. Where it's necessary to wait for space to become available you can allow up to six weeks from sowing, by potting on into 7cm (2¾in) pots to produce strong young plants (see p.82). Raising plants in this way gains time, because your six-week-old kale plant will have been growing while an earlier crop is in the soil. This adds weeks to the growing season, compared to sowing directly. Plant kale deep, with the top of the module roughly 5cm (2in) below soil level, because young plants have long stems that will benefit from this extra support. Water in well.

Care and protection

Water newly transplanted kale until it has established. After that they need water only in very dry weather. Pests are the main issue and it's best to cover all new plantings with mesh or thermacrop for at least six weeks to keep off insects, pigeons, and rabbits through that critical phase of establishment. After that, plants tolerate some damage, but each garden is different and longer term protection may

be necessary. Support bird netting on hoops so that pigeons cannot land on plants and peck through the net. Most varieties are tall, so you may need a wooden structure to support the netting as plants mature. Taller varieties in windy gardens may need to be tied to sturdy 2.5cm (1in) square stakes. About a month after planting, the lowest leaves will begin to yellow and are best removed to keep plants tidy, make picking easier, and reduce slug numbers.

Harvesting and storage

It's worth allowing plants to establish before picking too many leaves. Push downwards on the stalk of the lowest leaf to snap it off the main stem. Harvest all of each leaf stalk even if you're not going to eat it, because that keeps the plant tidy and makes ongoing picking easier. Spread each picking over several plants. Try to keep up with each plant's production to prevent the lowest leaves yellowing, but avoid over-picking a single plant to leave just a few small leaves at the top, as regrowth then takes longer. As the season progresses plants end up with a mini trunk and leaves clustered at the top, like a palm tree. Flowering can initiate in late winter, especially for 'Cavolo Nero', and these flowering stems can be picked as tender, broccoli-like shoots, before their buds open into yellow flowers, to extend the harvest into spring. With each pick the new flowering shoots become thinner and stringier. Finally, when they are no longer tender, that's the end of your harvest and the main stem of each plant should be twisted out of the ground to compost. Harvest for salad leaves in the same way, just at a smaller leaf size.

Kale is easy to pick as and when you need it. The leaves are quite high in dry matter, which means they keep well in a polythene bag (see p.102) in the fridge for about a week.

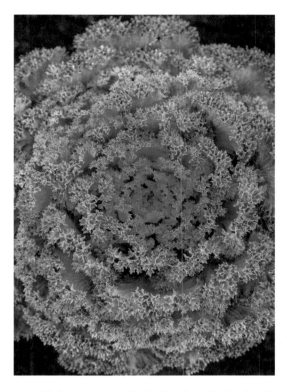

Highly ornamental kale 'Rainbow Candy Crush'.

VARIETIES

'Red Russian' A classic kale, with a purple hue to leaves, which are tender at all stages, but especially when picked small to eat raw.

'Pentland Brig' This old-fashioned green curly kale is tall and very cold hardy.

'Hungry Gap' A green variety that produces leaves for a long period before it flowers in spring.

'Dwarf Green Curled' A compact variety perfect for smaller gardens.

'Curly Scarlet' An attractive dwarf kale with purple-tinged stems and leaves.

'Redbor' Dramatically dark red, curly leaves on tall plants. Highly ornamental.

'Cavolo Nero' Black Tuscan kale with beautiful deep green, blistered foliage and pale stalks. There can be considerable variation between seed packets; some

selections grow tall with long, thin, drooping leaves, while those with a compact habit and fleshy leaves are more productive.

'Black Magic' F1 A 'Cavolo Nero' hybrid with fatter leaves and shorter stems.

'Red Devil' A purple-stalked version of 'Cavolo Nero' on compact stems.

'Rainbow Candy Crush' Ruffled leaves, vivid violet when young, look attractive both in the garden and on your plate.

For perennial kales see p.271.

KEY INFORMATION

Seed to first harvest: 2–3 months   **Sowing to transplanting:** 3–6 weeks   **Position:** Full sun is ideal, but will tolerate some shade   **Spacing:** 45–50cm (18–20in) for large varieties, 35cm (14in) for dwarf varieties, 22cm (8¾in) for salad leaves   **Hardiness:** Very hardy, down to at least -10°C (14°F)   **Suitable as a follow-on crop**

	JAN	FEB	MAR	APR	MAY	JUN	JUL	AUG	SEP	OCT	NOV	DEC
Sowing			▬	▬	▬	▬						
Sowing (salad leaves over winter)							▬	▬				
Transplanting					▬	▬	▬	▬	▬			
Harvesting (large)	▬	▬	▬			▬	▬	▬	▬	▬	▬	▬
Harvesting (salad)	▬	▬	▬	▬						▬	▬	▬

RADISH

Their rapid growth means that radishes are often the first spring-sown harvest on your table. April's roots offer a mild flavour and crisp texture, then become hotter and more pungent as the weather warms. Larger winter radishes are sown in late summer to enjoy through autumn and winter, so be sure to know which type you're sowing and when to expect the harvest.

Sowing and transplanting

Multisowing five spring radish seeds to each 3cm (1¼in) module gives them an early start under cover and avoids the insect pests that trouble direct-sown seedlings in spring. Make the first sowing by mid-February and keep them warm in the house, to ensure rapid germination. Seedlings can stand frost, so move them into a cold greenhouse for two weeks, before transplanting in early March in temperate climates. A second sowing in late March and a third in mid-April prolong the harvest, while sowings from May to August give spicy radishes. Spring radish can also be sown in early September for a late autumn crop. Larger winter radish are best grown singly or in pairs: sow two seeds per module from mid-July into the first week of August.

Twist out the larger roots from radish sown in rows or multisown in clumps.

Transplant as little as three weeks after sowing. Dib holes deep enough to shelter the long stems below soil level. Plant multisown spring radish 15cm (6in) apart, and leave 25cm (10in) between winter radishes.

Care and protection

Cover early transplants with fleece during March and April, for protection from cold winds. Once temperatures rise, swap the fleece for fine mesh to keep out the flea beetles and cabbage root flies that are active by mid-spring. Winter radishes benefit from fine mesh covers until late September, when established plants are more resistant to damage.

Watering spring radishes every two days during dry weather will produce a bigger, tastier harvest. Winter radishes need little watering once established, unless it is dry in early autumn when roots start to swell.

Harvesting and storage

Spring radishes have a short harvest period, so twist out the vibrant roots while young and tender. Left in the ground for too long, their texture will quickly turn fluffy or woody as a flower stem forms. Remove leaves after harvest to prevent them drawing moisture out of the roots – the leaves are edible, although hairy.

Harvest winter radishes from October as required. Once temperatures drop below about -6°C (21°F) or colder, twist out the remaining roots with a little soil attached and they will keep in a box in the shed until February.

Hardy winter radish 'Shawo Fruit'.

VARIETIES

SPRING

'Rudi' My favourite red, spherical variety. Grows strongly and stands for three weeks in damp weather.

'French Breakfast' An old-fashioned variety, with pretty, long, cylindrical, red and white roots. Harvest young because roots rapidly turn soft and hollow.

WINTER

'Black Spanish Round' A round variety for winter salads with dark skin and crisp, white flesh.

'Long White Icicle' Harvest in autumn for large, white, cylindrical roots, more turnip-like in flavour.

'Shawo Fruit' A Chinese variety with green and white skin and striking green flesh. The long roots can be eaten raw or cooked, and sweeten after freezing.

'Dragon' F1 One of several red- or partly red-skinned winter radish. Crisp and pretty, with a long shape.

KEY INFORMATION

SPRING VARIETIES

Seed to first harvest: 6 weeks   **Sowing to transplanting:** 3–4 weeks   **Position:** Full sun or some shade
Spacing: Multisown 15cm (6in) equidistant   **Hardiness:** Moderately hardy   **Suitable for multisowing and as a second or third crop**

	JAN	FEB	MAR	APR	MAY	JUN	JUL	AUG	SEP	OCT	NOV	DEC
Sowing			▬	▬								
Transplanting				▬	▬							
Harvesting					▬	▬						

WINTER VARIETIES

Seed to first harvest: 3 months   **Sowing to transplanting:** 3–4 weeks   **Position:** Full sun or some shade
Spacing: 20cm (8in) equidistant   **Hardiness:** Moderately hardy, down to -4°C (25°F)
Suitable as a follow-on crop

	JAN	FEB	MAR	APR	MAY	JUN	JUL	AUG	SEP	OCT	NOV	DEC
Sowing							▬					
Transplanting								▬	▬			
Harvesting	▬	▬								▬	▬	▬

SWEDE

Swedes stand in the ground through the hardest winter weather, untroubled by frosts or pests, and their dense, sweet, nutritious roots are a valuable vegetable in the coldest months. Although called a root vegetable, the part we eat is a swelling above the tap root, which means swede can be sown in modules and successfully transplanted. And swedes do come from Sweden, where they were discovered in the 15th century, probably in fields of turnip or radish.

Sowing and transplanting

Sow from mid-May in cold regions to early June in warmer areas, under cover to protect vulnerable seedlings from flea beetles. Seed packets may suggest sowing earlier, but swedes don't need the whole growing season to get to a good size and sowing later leaves time to grow an early crop of spinach, beetroot, or carrots before transplanting the swede. Sow two seeds per 4cm (1½in) module and thin to the strongest seedling, or sow in a seed tray and then select the strongest seedlings to prick out into modules.

Transplant about four weeks after sowing, spaced 30–35cm (12–14in) apart each way, using the wider spacing if you're looking to grow larger swedes. Dib deep holes so that the stems are below soil level to the first true leaf and water plants in well because the soil is often dry after a first harvest.

Care and protection

If it doesn't rain after planting, continue to water young plants until they are established and growing well. They tolerate dry spells during summer, but keep an eye on the weather in early autumn, when swedes really begin to swell, and water if there is no rain.

I protect young plants with enviromesh for the first six to eight weeks after transplanting, because keeping them sheltered at this stage

and free of insect pests, like flea beetle and cabbage root fly, can make the difference between a reliable harvest and one that might fail. Swede or gall midge is the most damaging insect pest, because it eats the new leaves and halts growth until plants initiate a new growing point, resulting in smaller swedes. Covers can be removed by mid-August, when the plants are established and able to resist pest damage. The leaves are enjoyed by pigeons, however, so cover with bird netting for the remainder of the growing season where they are a pest.

Lower leaves naturally yellow as they age and can become a habitat for slugs and other pests as they die. Twisting them off the plant before they are too yellow improves the appearance of the crop and reduces slug numbers and damage. Compost all the leaves you remove.

Remove yellowing leaves regularly.

Mature swedes can be harvested from late September until March.

Harvesting and storage

There is no rush to harvest as swedes stand well in the soil right through winter. Just pull them gently from the soil as you cut the roots underneath with a trowel, as required. Finish harvesting before the weather warms in spring, when roots toughen as new leaves start to take the energy stored within them. You can also harvest swedes during December to store in a box in the shed, until March.

VARIETIES

'Marian' and **'Gowrie'** Two old open-pollinated varieties (see p.37) that have stood the test of time and grow consistently fine roots.

'Tweed' F1 A newer hybrid variety that has some resistance to club root. In other respects it's no improvement compared to the older varieties.

KEY INFORMATION

Seed to first harvest: 4 months   **Sowing to transplanting:** 4 weeks   **Position:** Full sun or a little shade
Spacing: 30–35cm (12–14in) equidistant   **Hardiness:** Extremely hardy, to at least -10°C (14°F)
Suitable as a second follow-on crop

	JAN	FEB	MAR	APR	MAY	JUN	JUL	AUG	SEP	OCT	NOV	DEC
Sowing					▬							
Transplanting						▬						
Harvesting	▬	▬	▬	▬						▬	▬	▬
Storage	▬	▬	▬									▬

TURNIP

Turnips are best grown fast and either early or late in the growing season, for small, sweet roots. There are new varieties that are far better suited to this method (see opposite) than traditional turnips, which tend to be watery with a strong, somewhat bitter, mustard flavour. Rapid growth makes turnips useful for interplanting among slow-growing vegetables and they grow well in multisown clumps.

Sowing and transplanting

I make two sowings either side of turnips' summer flowering time, which you must avoid to prevent plants bolting before their roots have a chance to swell. Turnips thrive in multisown clumps and I sow five or six seeds into each 3cm (1¼in) module cell, aiming for clusters of three or four plants. Make your first sowing in late winter or early spring for a spring crop. Keep early sowings in the warmth of the house to germinate seeds, but move the tough seedlings out into a cold greenhouse once they emerge. For an autumn harvest, sow in the first ten days of August. There is more risk of bolting and damage by insect pests if turnips are sown in July.

Young turnip plants are robust and will grow quickly after you transplant them small. This is usually after three or four weeks for early sowings, but seedlings can be just two weeks old when transplanted in August. Dib a hole and pop the root ball in so that it sits just below soil level, spacing multisown clumps 25–30cm (10–12in) apart.

Multisown turnip 'Sweet Marble' F1 with mushrooms, showing the fungal life in no dig soil.

Care and protection

Cover early plantings with fleece for at least a month, not only for warmth, but also protection from pests including flea beetles, cabbage root fly, and pigeons. If pigeons or rabbits are present, protect autumn turnips with mesh, because the weather will be too warm for fleece. A mesh cover in late summer and autumn also helps keep out the second generation of cabbage root flies looking to lay their eggs.

Water newly transplanted turnips until they begin to grow. There is often enough moisture in the soil for growth during spring and autumn, but during dry spells it is worth watering when the roots start to swell.

Turnip seedlings multisown in small modules.

Harvesting and storage

Exactly when to harvest varies according to your taste, so try harvesting roots at different stages to see what you prefer. Cherry-sized turnips are tender and sweet, but by the time they are the size of an apricot that sweetness is diminishing and the texture becomes more watery. Look for the largest turnip in each multisown clump, grasp the leaf stalks, and rotate until the roots at the base snap off, to leave the remaining turnips undisturbed. The leaves are edible and good to eat if you harvest baby turnips, after which they become a little coarse. There is no point trying to store baby turnips, but if you grow traditional larger roots they will keep well in a box in a cool shed for two or three months. Ensure they are harvested before any hard frosts, twist off all leaves, and don't wash roots before storing so that the soil can help retain moisture.

VARIETIES

'Sweet Bell' F1 Spherical, purple-topped roots, ideal for quick harvests of baby turnips.

'Sweet Marble' F1 Attractive purple skin on white turnips. Firm and sweet when harvested small, and in autumn they are still juicy when larger.

'Purple Top Milan' A classic old variety with less sweetness but a pretty purple top to the slightly flattened roots.

'Petrowski' Globe-shaped, yellow roots with a good mild flavour.

KEY INFORMATION

Seed to first harvest: 2 months **Sowing to transplanting:** 2–4 weeks **Position:** Full sun **Spacing:** 25–30cm (10–12in) equidistant **Hardiness:** Hardy to approx. -5°C (23°F) **Suitable for multisowing and interplanting**

	JAN	FEB	MAR	APR	MAY	JUN	JUL	AUG	SEP	OCT	NOV	DEC
Sowing			▬					▬				
Transplanting				▬				▬				
Harvesting					▬	▬				▬	▬	

*Laying harvested red onion
'Lilia' out in the sun to dry and
cure the bulbs for storage.*

ALLIUMS – ONION FAMILY

Garlic

Leeks

Onions

These fantastic staple crops are full of flavour, easy to grow, and extremely frost hardy. Slender allium leaves do not shade the surrounding soil, which makes alliums good for interplanting between, but also provides an opportunity for weeds. This is where the reduced weed growth of no dig soil is a big advantage, saving you time and reducing possible damage to allium leaves when pulling out weeds.

Choosing what to grow

Thanks to their upright habit and thin leaves, you can fit a good quantity of these vegetables into small areas. Where growing space is really at a premium, closely planted multisown salad onions are my recommendation, because they are quick to grow, and can be harvested over many months from just two or three sowings. Garlic and onions take longer to mature and have a single period of harvest, after which they are easy to store for many months of use, and can be available almost year-round when you grow enough. Sowing two or three different leek varieties at the same time in April, can produce harvests over nine months of the year. Many leeks are hardy enough to stand in the ground through winter.

Sowing, growing, and harvesting

Onions can be grown either from seeds or sets, which are small, immature onion bulbs that come to harvest more quickly than onions grown from seed. Just don't plant sets too early, as this may cause them to flower. Multisow onions, salad onions, and leeks to save time and space. Garlic plants are raised by planting individual cloves. Initially you need to buy bulbs of your chosen variety to split into cloves for planting, but after that you can use your own harvest for new seed garlic. Leeks grow particularly well in moisture-retentive no dig soil, because they respond to continual dampness around their roots. Weed control is vital, but the few weeds that grow in no dig beds pull easily from the soft surface.

CROP		JAN	FEB	MAR	APR	MAY	JUN	JUL	AUG	SEP	OCT	NOV	DEC
Garlic	Sow									▬	▬	▬	▬
	Harvest						▬	▬					
Leeks	Sow			▬									
	Harvest	▬	▬	▬	▬			▬	▬	▬	▬	▬	▬
Salad onions	Sow		▬	▬	▬	▬	▬	▬		▬			
	Harvest				▬	▬	▬	▬	▬	▬	▬	▬	
Bulb onions & shallots (seeds)	Sow		▬	▬									
	Harvest								▬				
Bulb onions & shallots (sets)	Sow			▬	▬								
	Harvest								▬				
Overwintering onions (seeds)	Sow								▬				
	Harvest						▬						
Overwintering onions (sets)	Sow										▬		
	Harvest						▬						

Harvest by cutting under plants and bulbs with a trowel, to sever roots and minimize soil disturbance, while taking care not to damage garlic and onion bulbs that are destined for storage. Watch for the signs that onions and garlic are ready, given in each vegetable profile, then lift all of each variety at the same time and dry thoroughly before storage.

Common problems

Several pests and diseases have the potential to affect alliums, but they can mostly be prevented or controlled. Allium leaf miner is the worst pest in both spring and autumn, when white maggots tunnel into all parts of plants, leaving pale lines on foliage and allowing rot to set in. The small, brown pupae can be found within affected stems and bulbs. A cover of mesh is some help, from February to mid-June and again from September to November, depending which allium crop is growing. Leek moths fly from midsummer and their caterpillars eat the heart leaves of leeks, but damage often only becomes noticeable in autumn, when plants begin to fail and sometimes collapse completely. The best remedy is to cover new plantings with mesh until mid-September, to prevent adult moths laying eggs.

Onion white rot is a fungal disease that destroys the roots of plants, and is usually only apparent too late, when leaves suddenly turn yellow in spring. White fungal growth appears around the roots of affected plants, which should be removed, but not composted. It's common on over-cultivated soil that lacks organic matter, and no dig methods reduce its occurrence. Orange pustules on leaves are a symptom of rust. This fungal disease is not usually too damaging on leeks, but if it strikes garlic during May and June it can significantly reduce the harvest. It helps to remove and compost rusty leaves. Garlic grown under cover suffers little rust. Downy mildew causes onion leaves to yellow and develop patches of dark fungal growth in wet weather during early summer. This halts bulb growth and causes them to rot before autumn. Reduce damage by sowing mildew-resistant varieties and by planting overwintering onions in autumn, for earlier maturity in June.

Freshly picked salad onions are succulent and full-flavoured from their bulb to their leaf tips.

GARLIC

Garlic is easy to grow, tolerant of winter cold and summer heat, and stores easily in the house, so that one harvest can last for up to ten months. Autumn planting allows garlic to grow over winter and mature around midsummer, giving time to plant other crops after it's harvested. Choose from hardneck varieties that form flower stems in late spring and fatter, delicately flavoured cloves, or high-yielding softnecks with bigger bulbs of smaller, more pungent cloves.

Sowing

Plant cloves of garlic directly into the soil outdoors. The best time to do this is October, but anytime from mid-September to late December can produce a good crop. Another option is to plant under cover, perhaps in a polytunnel, at the same time, for larger and earlier harvests. It's possible to plant in early spring, but this yields smaller harvests and the bulbs may not differentiate into cloves if they are not exposed to some frost.

Before planting, gently break up each bulb (whether bought from a seed company or one that you've saved) and select the bigger cloves to plant, leaving little ones for the kitchen. Make holes with a dibber spaced 10–15cm (4–6in) apart equidistantly, or 8–10cm (3–4in) apart in rows with 25cm (10in) between them. Ensure that each hole is deep enough that the tip of the clove sits a little below ground level, and pop in each clove with its flat base at the bottom of the hole and tapered top pointing upwards. Spread compost on top after planting to provide a bit of cover for the cloves and to feed soil life for the coming year. If planting later, after the bed has been mulched (see p.47), make slightly deeper holes for cloves.

Planting in rows makes it easier to interplant garlic with other vegetables in spring. In the polytunnel, I grow garlic between winter salads, in a line up the middle of a bed: the salad plants finish in April, just before the garlic's main phase of growth.

Care and protection

Plants need little attention through the growing season, apart from regular weeding, which should be easy in a no dig bed. Watering is unnecessary during winter and early spring, but in a really dry spring, watering in late May and early June will produce fatter bulbs. In late spring, hardneck varieties start to grow looping flower stems. Snap off these edible "scapes" before the flowers open to focus the plants' energy on swelling their bulbs, and eat them sautéed or steamed. From mid-May you can intersow garlic with carrots or beetroot, or interplant with kale or lettuce. Interplants readily establish in the space between the tall, slender garlic plants.

Garlic cloves are easy to plant in soft no dig soil.

*Snap off scapes and cook them
for a late spring delicacy.*

Garlic is usually healthy, but plants can be damaged by allium leaf miner and leek moth in spring. Cover garlic with mesh to keep these pests out if you suspect they are present. Raised orange pustules on leaves are a symptom of the common fungal disease rust. Plants can tolerate mild infections, but if leaves are covered in pustules growth will stop and it's best to harvest a smaller crop of bulbs immediately. Garlic grown under cover suffers less rust. Onion white rot may be a problem on allotment sites; the roots of affected plants decay, causing leaves to turn bright yellow and even plants to collapse. Pull out infected plants straight away and do not compost.

Harvesting and storage

In late spring, you have the option to harvest some of your crop as green garlic. Pull up plants and use as you would a spring onion, but stronger in flavour. Harvesting mature garlic bulbs is not the same as for onions; don't wait for the necks to fall over or for the leaves to go yellow. Harvest time is governed by day length with bulbs swelling and differentiating into cloves during the weeks before and after the summer solstice. Most softneck varieties mature from mid- to late June, while hardneck varieties are ready from early to mid-July. Garlic under cover is ready two weeks earlier. Harvest before the bulb's outer skin has degraded, as this reduces quality for storage.

Use a trowel or your fingers to pull away soil from around the bulb, and if you see it has swollen with cloves making bumps in the surface then that's a sign it's ready. Slip a trowel under bulbs at 45° to cut the roots, which can be quite strong, and lift the bulb by pulling its stem upwards. Harvesting slightly immature is good, so that you can peel off the outer skin to reveal a nice clean bulb that's in peak condition to dry and store.

Hardneck bulbs laid to dry in a crate under cover.

Keep bulbs somewhere well ventilated for about a month after lifting, until the tops go yellow and fairly dry – shelves in a garage would work well. Avoid direct sunlight as this can turn cloves bright pink and even damage them when it's hot. Plait the leaves before they go brittle to create attractive clusters of bulbs to hang up. Garlic stores for many months in warm, dry indoor conditions.

VARIETIES

SOFTNECK

'Provence Wight' Grows large bulbs made up of decent-sized cloves with purple-striped skin.

'Solent Wight' Smaller, bright white bulbs are ready to harvest a little later than other softnecks, in early July. Stores well.

HARDNECK

'Carcassonne Wight' A high-yielding garlic with fat purple-skinned cloves.

'Doocot' A hardy Canadian variety that's less prone to rust and grows well in cold conditions.

'Red Duke' The pink-skinned cloves are a good, even size and not too pungent.

KEY INFORMATION

Seed to first harvest: 8 months when sown in October   **Sowing to transplanting:** Not applicable
Position: Adaptable; likes sun and warmth in spring and summer   **Spacing:** 10–15cm (4–6in) equidistant
or 8–10cm (3–4in) apart in rows 25cm (10in) apart   **Hardiness:** Hardy to at least -12°C (10°F)
Suitable for interplanting or intersowing in May or June

	JAN	FEB	MAR	APR	MAY	JUN	JUL	AUG	SEP	OCT	NOV	DEC
Sowing									▬	▬	▬	▬
Harvesting						▬	▬					
Storage	▬	▬	▬	▬	▬		▬	▬	▬	▬	▬	▬

LEEKS

Leeks can be harvested from July until April, but their real value is in winter, when they are hardy enough to stand in the soil through the coldest months and to grow larger in any mild winter weather. The stems are sweeter and gentler in flavour than other alliums, and a sautéed leek in winter is an absolute delicacy. Varieties mature at different rates, so it is important to be clear which variety you're growing for which season, and to harvest at the appropriate time.

Sowing and transplanting

I sow all varieties of leeks under cover in the second week of April. This is a safe date, which is not too early, and therefore avoids exposing these biennial plants to any cold conditions that simulate winter and trigger flowering in summer. This sowing date also allows plenty of time for slower-growing winter leeks to make a large harvest.

The seeds are large enough to count as you sow and I multisow four or five per module. Multisowing saves time and space during propagation, and three or four plants in a clump results in plentiful medium-sized leeks rather than a few large ones. Multisown leeks don't have perfectly straight stems, because they curve away from each other slightly when growing up towards the light. Leeks sown into 3cm (1¼in) modules will need to be potted on into 7cm (2¾in) pots after about eight weeks. They may not need potting on before transplanting if sown into 5cm (2in) modules, but if they are outgrowing the module before the ground is ready, potting on is always worthwhile. You can also sow directly outside in mid-April, for eventual transplanting as single plants or clumps.

Transplant from early June if space is available, but leeks are a great second crop for planting out in July to follow on from crops harvested in summer. Allow 22–30cm (8¾–12in) between multisown clumps,

using the wider spacing if you want larger leeks, or plant individual leeks 10cm (4in) apart. Traditionally, leeks are planted deeply in a trench or dibbed hole so that the portion of stem growing below the soil is white, rather than pale green, which makes it slightly sweeter. This is not essential, because pale green stems are still sweet and tender. I also find that shallower plantings, with the top of the root ball 3–5cm (1¼–2in) below soil level, grow more quickly because the roots are closer to the topsoil, where there's more microbial activity. For some white at the stem bottoms, dib holes deep enough so that the top of the

Transplanting leeks after clearing a cabbage crop.

root ball is about 7cm (2¾in) below the soil surface. Don't push soil back around the plants, instead water them in and the soil will gradually fill the hole over time, also helping to direct water to the roots while plants establish.

Care and protection

Leeks thrive on moisture, so keep them watered in dry summer weather, especially during late summer and early autumn as they grow large. They are mostly trouble-free, but a few specific pests can sometimes cause problems. Allium leaf miner causes pale lines within leaves as maggots feed inside the plant, and can lead to fungal disease. Covering crops with mesh for their entire life will prevent adult flies laying eggs, but if insects are already in the soil it is difficult to protect against them. Leek moth caterpillars feed inside plants, and a lack of growth in late summer is the only outward sign of a problem. If you discover that the moth is active in your area, protect plants with mesh from transplanting until early September, when adult moths are no longer laying eggs. Mesh will also protect leeks from rabbits, which love the seedlings. Rust is a common fungal disease that is more prevalent in dry conditions and causes orange spots on the lower leaves. Little can be done to prevent or treat rust, but I find it worthwhile to remove and compost any badly affected lower leaves in autumn.

Harvesting and storage

Make a note of when each variety you sowed should be harvested: summer varieties in August and September, autumn varieties from October to December, while winter varieties are best left until March or April, since they put on significant growth as soon as spring weather warms even a little. One great quality of leeks is that they can be harvested at any stage, whenever you're hungry, as long as they're

Lift leeks using a trowel to cut roots and minimize soil disturbance.

not left for too long. Summer varieties will rot or topple over by October and winter leeks form a flower stem during May, which is edible at first but becomes tough.

Harvest whole multisown clumps, using a trowel to cut through the roots so that they remain in the soil, where they are food for soil organisms. You can also use a knife or a sharp trowel to cut the largest leek from a clump and allow smaller ones to keep growing.

In winter, where temperatures don't fall below –5°C (23°F), you can harvest leeks as required. Where the soil freezes solid, another option is to lift the leeks with some soil and 5cm (2in) of roots attached. Place them in a box with extra soil around the roots and store in an outhouse or garage, with a window to allow in light for the leaves. Stored like this they can keep for a couple of months.

A multisown clump of 'Philomene' autumn leeks.

VARIETIES

SUMMER

'Bulgarian Giant', **'King Richard'**, **'Jolant'** All tall, thin, fast-growing leeks with pale green stems up to 60cm (2ft) long. Very tasty.

AUTUMN/WINTER

Autumn Mammoth group Contains many good varieties that are quite compact.

'Oarsman' F1 A reliable variety that bulks up quickly.

'Philomene' This highly productive Bulgarian variety matures from August to December.

WINTER

'Bandit' Stands well through winter with handsome blue-green leaves.

'Northern Lights' F1 Leaves develop a purple hue in winter cold.

'Musselburgh' Hardy, but this widely available open-pollinated variety (see p.37) often grows shorter stems than it used to.

KEY INFORMATION

Seed to first harvest: Summer – 4½–5 months, Autumn – 5–6 months, Winter – 10–13 months **Sowing to transplanting:** 2–3 months **Position:** Moist, tolerate some shade **Spacing:** Clumps at 20–25cm (8–10in) equidistant, singles at 10cm (4in) **Hardiness:** Hardy, but mature summer and autumn varieties can be damaged below -5°C (23°F) **Suitable for multisowing and as a second follow-on crop**

	JAN	FEB	MAR	APR	MAY	JUN	JUL	AUG	SEP	OCT	NOV	DEC
Sowing				▬								
Transplanting						▬▬▬▬▬						
Harvesting (summer)								▬▬▬▬				
Harvesting (autumn)	▬▬								▬▬▬▬▬▬▬			
Harvesting (winter)		▬▬▬▬▬										

ONIONS

Onions can be harvested young for their leaves and stem, as "salad" or "spring" onions, or after two or three months as bulb onions, when grown at a wider spacing. Shallots have a milder, sweeter flavour and are smaller than onions because they subdivide into clusters. Bulb onions and shallots can be grown from sets, which are immature onions that give earlier harvests, or grown from seed, which is cheaper and allows you to increase your crop by multisowing to grow onions in clumps. Red onions are slower to mature, slightly lower yielding, and are more inclined than yellow varieties to bolt from planting as sets.

Sowing and transplanting

If you grow from sets, wait to plant them at or after the spring equinox (21st March) in order to reduce the risk of bolting. Sow seeds for salad onions, bulb onions, and shallots from mid-February to mid-March under cover, or in a drill outdoors in the second half of March. Sow overwintering onions in late summer – not before the last week of August – to reduce the bolting risk. Continue to sow salad onions until early July; I make three sowings, in March, mid-May, and mid-June to early July. Later sowings are more prone to downy mildew in damp August weather. In late August, I also sow a variety of salad onion that's suitable to overwinter, such as 'White Lisbon', for welcome harvests in spring.

Onions and shallots swell nicely in multisown clumps to produce a heavy total yield of mid-sized bulbs or salad onions. I sow six bulb onion or shallot seeds, and ten salad onion seeds per 3cm (1¼in) cell, to transplant as clumps. Transplant spring sowings in late March or April, just a little deeper than they were growing in their module. Space all multisown clumps of salad onions 25cm (10in) apart, and shallots and multisown bulb onions 30cm (12in) apart. Transplant your late August sowings of overwintering salad and bulb onions from mid-September to mid-October.

You can also sow seed direct outside in drills about 2.5cm (1in) deep and 20cm (8in) apart, with three seeds per 1cm (½in) for salad onions and six seeds per 1cm (½in) for bulb onions to transplant. Gently lift bulb onion seedlings with a trowel five weeks after sowing, to transplant in small clumps at the same final spacing as multisown modules.

To plant sets, dib holes 10–15cm (4–6in) apart for onions or 25cm (10in) apart for shallots. Put them in with their tapered tip pointing upwards and resting about 3cm (1¼in) below soil level, before covering over.

Multisown onion seedlings in spring.

Care and protection

Although they're hardy, I cover spring plantings with fleece to speed up growth, increase yields, and protect them from rabbits. You can cover later transplants with mesh to keep rabbits off, because fleece would overheat summer crops and it holds too much moisture over winter. Watering is rarely necessary for bulb onions, unless it is dry when they start to form bulbs in June. Salad onions are tolerant of dry conditions, but will produce more good quality green growth if watered.

Keep ahead of weeds in spring by hoeing regularly while onion growth is upright, because once leaves start to fold over in early summer it becomes more difficult. If you're expecting weed growth, then space plants 15cm (6in) apart, with 35cm (14in) between rows, for easier hoeing or removal of perennial weed shoots.

Continually wet conditions in late spring and early summer can cause downy mildew to turn leaves brown, which halts growth. After that happens, bulbs do not store for long. A white dusting of powdery mildew can affect onions in late summer and autumn, but is less of a problem. Onion white rot is also a fungal disease, which becomes evident by early summer when leaves yellow and plants fall over as the roots rot away. Onion sets can carry the disease, so always check they are firm and show no sign of white mould at the base before planting. Where allium leaf miner is a pest, its maggots eat into onion bulbs and roots, badly damaging the harvest. Avoid this by transplanting in May after the first generation of egg-laying adult flies, and harvesting by August to miss the second generation in autumn.

Harvesting and storage

Salad onions will be ready to harvest within ten weeks of sowing in spring. Twist out larger plants from multisown clumps, or use a trowel to cut their roots, leaving the rest to grow on. This can give a harvest period of two months

Lay out onions to cure in the sun after harvest.

from one sowing. If left to grow beyond the salad onion stage, varieties of *Allium cepa* will make white bulbs, which taste good but don't store beyond October. For salad onions with long stems that don't form a bulb, grow varieties of *A. fistulosum*.

The harvest date of bulb onions and shallots depends on the variety and when it was sown or planted. Bulb onions can be harvested for immediate use as soon as they reach a desirable size, but they need to be reasonably mature to store. An indication of maturity is when at least a quarter of their green stems have folded downwards at the neck. You can then bend all the remaining necks to fold the stems down, and leave the plants for another week to encourage bulbs to mature and prevent onions with fat necks, which will not store so well. Harvest by cutting under a clump of onions with a trowel, to minimize soil disturbance and ensure that bulbs are intact with short roots attached.

If you have follow-on crops to plant immediately, remove all the onions and spread them out somewhere dry, like

Make several sowings of salad onions to pick for longer. These are 'Lilia' and 'White Lisbon'.

Saving seed

It is feasible to save seed from onions if you have space to allow six to ten of your best bulbs to flower, to ensure cross-pollination. Each bulb will produce up to five tall stems bearing globe-shaped flowerheads, which need support: push in corner stakes and run a string around them. Seedheads form in late summer and need to be cut to hang upside down in a dry place, then rub out the black seeds in autumn.

VARIETIES

SALAD ONIONS

'White Lisbon' Classic old *Allium cepa* variety with long white stems and the ability to bulb up, giving a wide range of harvest dates.

'Lilia' A red *A. cepa* variety that also grows into a decent bulb. Prone to mildew and bolting in early summer.

'Ishikura', 'Ramrod' Varieties of *A. fistulosum*, sometimes called "bunching onions", with longer, straight stems that don't make bulbs.

BULB ONIONS

'Red Baron' The red onion variety I recommend from seed or sets. Stores well.

'Sturon' A top variety of yellow onion. Gives good yields of round bulbs and stores well.

'Stuttgart Giant' Produces flatter-shaped bulbs of fine flavour. Stores well.

'Rose de Roscoff' The classic rose-tinted French onion from Brittany. Matures in early July.

'Senshyu Yellow' A useful overwintering onion for early summer harvest.

SHALLOT

'Matador' F1 A vigorous hybrid variety that produces large yields of pink-skinned shallots.

'Zebrune' Attractive long, brown bulbs with a hint of pink.

greenhouse staging or slatted shelves in a garage, where the leaves can turn from yellow to brown; a process called "curing". Alternatively, leave the harvested onions on the bed for a week or two so the leaves yellow and lose their bulk, before bringing them under cover to finish the drying process. Changeable weather is not a problem, because breezes help the late summer sun to dry onion plants between rain showers. But shade onions drying outdoors in very hot sun during July.

Trim the yellowed leaves off, leaving 3–5cm (1¼–2in) of neck on the onion to shrivel as it dries. This makes it easier to spread the onions out to finish drying. Once their skins are papery, store onions in a box in dry, warm conditions inside the house. Attractive plaits or bunches of onions can be created while the stems are yellow, which store well hung up in the house. Well-cured bulbs from spring plantings can keep until late spring, while overwintering onions start to sprout and soften by late December.

Cured bulbs of onion 'Rose de Roscoff' ready for storing.

SALAD ONIONS

Seed to first harvest: 2½ months **Sowing to transplanting:** 6 weeks **Position:** Full sun or some shade
Spacing: Multisown 25cm (10in) equidistant **Hardiness:** Hardy, to at least -8°C (18°F)
Suitable for multisowing

	JAN	FEB	MAR	APR	MAY	JUN	JUL	AUG	SEP	OCT	NOV	DEC
Sowing		▓	▓	▓	▓	▓	▓					
Sowing (overwintering)								▓				
Transplanting			▓	▓	▓	▓	▓	▓				
Transplanting (overwintering)									▓	▓		
Harvesting						▓	▓	▓	▓	▓		
Harvesting (overwintering)				▓	▓							

BULB ONIONS & SHALLOTS

Seed to first harvest: 4½ months from seed, 3½ months from sets **Sowing to transplanting:** 6 weeks
Position: Full sun **Spacing:** Bulb onions – multisown 30cm (12in) equidistant, sets 15cm (6in). Shallots – 30cm (12in) equidistant from seed or sets **Hardiness:** Hardy, to at least -8°C (18°F) **Suitable for multisowing**

	JAN	FEB	MAR	APR	MAY	JUN	JUL	AUG	SEP	OCT	NOV	DEC
Sowing (from sets)			▓									
Sowing (from seed)		▓	▓									
Transplanting			▓	▓								
Harvesting								▓	▓			

OVERWINTERING ONIONS

Seed to first harvest: 7 months **Sowing to transplanting:** 6 weeks **Position:** Full sun
Spacing: Multisown 30cm (12in) equidistant, sets 15cm (6in) **Hardiness:** Hardy, to at least -8°C (18°F)
Suitable for multisowing and as a second follow-on crop

	JAN	FEB	MAR	APR	MAY	JUN	JUL	AUG	SEP	OCT	NOV	DEC
Sowing (from sets)										▓		
Sowing (from seed)								▓				
Transplanting									▓	▓		
Harvesting						▓						

CUCURBITS - CUCUMBER FAMILY

Courgette and summer squash

Cucumber

Melon

Winter squash

*A harvest of fragrant, ripe melon 'Emir' F1 is
a highlight of the summer garden.*

The members of the cucumber family are tender, warmth loving summer vegetables that are killed by just a little frost. Plants grow rapidly and produce generous harvests during the summer months, except for winter squash, whose fruits ripen with hard skins at the end of summer and store through winter, even into spring. Cucurbits' soft, fibrous roots flourish in the humus rich, moisture retentive surface of no dig beds, where growth is likely to be faster than in dug soil, and managing weeds is easy.

Choosing what to grow

Vigorous cucurbits produce heavy yields, which means that one or two of each plant may suffice, unless you have a big family. Plants do grow large however, and each will need at least 1m² (11ft²) of space to reach its full potential. Courgette, summer and winter squash, and ridge cucumbers will all grow well outdoors. Melons and cordon cucumbers need extra warmth and should be grown under cover, where you can use the height of a greenhouse or polytunnel to erect supports for plants, which will increase their growth and the harvests they produce. Training cordon plants up these supports requires a regular, small input of time in summer.

Homegrown courgettes and cucumbers are slightly sweeter than shop bought vegetables, while melons are so tasty and aromatic that you will be amazed by the harvest that you achieve. A high water content means that most cucurbits do not store well, with the exception of ripe winter squash, which can be stored until May, making them hugely valuable during winter and early spring.

CROP		JAN	FEB	MAR	APR	MAY	JUN	JUL	AUG	SEP	OCT	NOV	DEC
Courgette and summer squash	Sow				▭▭▭								
	Harvest						▬▬▬▬▬▬▬▬▬▬						
Cucumber (Ridge)	Sow					▭▭▬▬▬							
	Harvest							▬▬▬▬▬▬					
Cucumber (Cordon)	Sow				▭▭▭								
	Harvest							▭▭▭▭▭▭▭▭▭▭					
Melon	Sow			▭▭									
	Harvest									▭▭▭			
Winter squash	Sow				▭▭								
	Harvest									▬▬▬			

▬▬ Outdoors   ▭▭ Under cover

VEGETABLE AND HERB DIRECTORY

Sowing, growing, and harvesting

All cucurbit seeds need warmth to germinate, and should always be sown under cover for best results. I recommend sowing seeds on their sides because it's easy and produces good germination. Don't sow too early, because young plants grow fast when conditions are warm and will need to be potted on to keep them in growth before transplanting, when they can easily run out of space if the weather remains too cold to plant them out. Wait until after your last frost date to transplant these tender plants, which thrive in full sun and sufficient space. They all need watering in dry conditions to sustain their growth, and this is especially true for cucumbers.

Pick courgettes, summer squash, and cucumbers regularly to prevent the fruit becoming seedy and hard-skinned, and to keep more harvests coming. Melons and winter squashes need to be left on plants to ripen, when they can be harvested over a shorter period of two to four weeks.

Winter squash store well as long as they are left to "cure" in the sun at about 25°C (77°F) for a week after harvest, and are then stored in dry conditions.

Common problems

Much as these plants love a plentiful supply of water when in full growth, they can easily be overwatered when small and in plastic pots, and if this happens they die almost overnight. Be careful to keep the compost in pots no more than 75 per cent moist.

Their large leaves quickly smother the ground, but as they fade towards the end of summer, weeds can grow rapidly. No dig helps at this point because there are few weeds and they are easy to remove. From midsummer, older leaves often turn white with powdery

A white dusting of powdery mildew is nothing to worry about on older courgette leaves.

mildew. This looks dramatic, but is actually not severe because the fading leaves do not contribute much to growth, so can be removed to compost if you prefer. Downy mildew is a less common fungal disease, but will kill plants within three weeks if conditions are humid in late summer. Watch for dark mould on the underside of leaves and also blotchy yellow patterns which can be mistaken for virus. Cutting off infected leaves to compost won't significantly delay the progress of this disease. Red spider mite is pink, almost invisible, and one of the worst pests on plants under cover. The first symptom is leaves turning pale, then tiny cobwebs develop, especially where stalks join onto leaves. Watering leaves can help and there are predators you can buy as biological controls, called *Encarsia formosa*.

Cordon cucumber 'Carmen' F1 fruits prolifically throughout summer.

COURGETTE AND SUMMER SQUASH

Courgettes belong to the large family of summer squash, which produce fruits of bright colours and shapes, including 'Patty Pan' and 'Yellow Crookneck'. Given warmth and plenty of space, these vigorous plants are easy to grow and prolific, producing heavy yields throughout summer and into autumn. The fruit have soft skins, pale flesh, few seeds, and are best used soon after picking, unlike thick-skinned winter squash that will store for long periods.

Sowing and transplanting

Squash plants are very frost tender so avoid sowing too early. I recommend sowing under cover, but never more than two or three weeks before the last frost date in your area, because seeds will germinate quickly and soon grow into a plant that is ready to transplant outside.

Sow singly, into either 5cm (2in) modules or small pots, by placing the seed flat on the compost, pushing down gently, and covering lightly with a little more compost. Avoid sowing into larger pots as the compost can easily become waterlogged before seedlings develop a strong root system. Keep your new sowing warm for at least five days to trigger germination. Unless you have a heated greenhouse, germinate seeds in a warm place in the house (above 16°C/61°F at night). They could even be wrapped in polythene and put in a warm cupboard, as long as you move them into the light as soon as a leaf is visible. After 15–20 days, it is best to pot on young plants into a 10cm (4in) pot, so that they can grow into sturdy plants, ready to transplant after the last frost.

Most gardeners need to wait until late May or early June before transplanting, to ensure the weather is warm enough. Make a deep, rectangular hole to accommodate the root ball so that 5cm (2in) of its stem is below surface level. Allow 90cm (3ft) between plants to give them ample room to spread. Water plants in thoroughly and, if it's not raining, water every two days for the first week or two. These squash plants also grow well in large containers, especially bush varieties and the climbing courgette 'Black Forest' F1. You can also plant them through black polythene laid to cover weeds, to produce a harvest while the weeds beneath are dying.

Young courgette plants need space to grow.

Cut courgette stalks to avoid damaging the fruit.

Care and protection

Young plants can be damaged by slugs, but when planted in warm weather they grow away quickly and are unlikely to be seriously set back. If the weather is cool and windy after transplanting, place a fleece cover directly on top of plants to help them get going and remove it as soon as days are sunny. Once established, courgettes are strong and fast growing. They need frequent watering to crop well in hot, dry weather, otherwise they tend to go dormant and produce few fruits. Plants in containers could need watering twice a day during summer, together with weekly feeding once fruits start to develop. By contrast, plenty of food is available to plants in no dig soil thanks to its healthy microbiome, so you don't need to feed.

A pretty silvering on leaves is quite normal, but after midsummer the lower leaves often start to develop a white dusting of powdery mildew. Although this can look dramatic and worrying, it's part of the natural cycle of growth, where plants allow the mildew to affect older leaves that are no longer contributing to growth. A healthy courgette plant won't have mildew on its younger leaves and will continue to produce courgettes; my advice is not to worry about it and to remove and compost mildewed leaves if you don't like their appearance. All diseased leaves can be composted, because the pathogens that cause such diseases do not affect plants at random and can only establish when conditions suit them, which often forms part of plants' natural cycles of growth and decay.

Harvesting and storage

Consider wearing gloves and long sleeves when picking and handling courgettes and squash, to avoid contact with secretions from the prickly hairs on the leaves and stems, which can cause an itchy rash on the skin for several weeks afterwards.

To harvest, either snap the fruits off the main stem or cut through their stalks; the latter results in better storage. Young plants are too small to grow fruit to full size, so pick these first fruits very small, to avoid delaying the formation of further courgettes. For tender fruits containing little seed, pick courgettes before the striking yellow flower at their tip has fully died. Both the female flowers with fruit behind them and the male flowers on thin stems, can be picked while open to eat fried in batter. Given plenty of space and a mild autumn, plants can remain productive until early October. Young squash fruits will keep well for about a week in the fridge or in a cool larder.

Harvested courgettes 'Cocozelle' and 'Defender' F1.

VARIETIES

COURGETTES

'**Early Gem**' **F1** Prolific production of long, thin, pale green courgettes. I've grown this variety over four decades and it has stood the test of time.

'**Defender**' **F1** A shiny, dark green courgette. Both fruits and the plant can grow long.

'**Cocozelle**' An Italian heirloom variety producing slightly bulbous, pale green, ribbed courgettes.

'**Parador**' **F1** Pretty fruits and, like other yellow varieties, yields are about one-third lower than green courgettes.

'**Black Forest**' **F1** This climbing variety can be grown up string, which is useful where space is tight. Remove lower leaves regularly, to reduce plant weight and help the string to hold it up.

SUMMER SQUASH

'**Yellow Crookneck**' A pretty variety, with elongated and knobbly fruit on a trailing plant.

'**Patty Pan**' Grows flattened, scallop-edged squash in a range of colours.

KEY INFORMATION

Seed to harvest: 2 months **Sowing to transplanting:** 3–4 weeks **Position:** Need warmth and full sun; won't thrive in a cold, shady spot **Spacing:** 60cm (2ft) minimum, but 90cm (3ft) gives a whole season of fruiting **Hardiness:** Not hardy; will be killed by frost **Suitable for interplanting in late summer**

	JAN	FEB	MAR	APR	MAY	JUN	JUL	AUG	SEP	OCT	NOV	DEC
Sowing					▬▬▬							
Transplanting						▬▬▬						
Harvesting							▬▬▬▬▬▬▬					

CUCUMBERS

Grown in healthy soil and eaten freshly picked, homegrown cucumbers have a flavour far superior to any you can buy. Tasting is believing! Two types are available to gardeners: outdoor ridge cucumbers trail on the ground and produce knobbly, medium-length fruit; cordon varieties need to be grown under cover for warmth and trained up supports. They repay this investment with prolific and tasty crops of smooth-skinned fruit.

Sowing and transplanting

Cucumbers are heat-loving plants, best sown under cover no earlier than mid- to late spring. Don't sow more than four weeks before your last frost date, because they will be killed by a hint of ice and need warm conditions to thrive. I sow both cordon varieties and outdoor cucumbers under cover, though you could sow ridge cucumbers directly into the soil in warm June weather.

Sow single seeds into 5cm (2in) modules by laying them flat on the compost, pushing down gently, and covering lightly with compost. Steady warmth is crucial for germination and keeping module trays in warm nighttime temperatures inside the house often produces the best results. Seedlings grow rapidly and, two weeks after sowing, need potting on into 7cm (2¾in) pots to keep them growing strongly. I lavish a lot of care on these plants because each one gives such generous harvests, often potting them on again to 10cm (4in) pots to produce large, strong plants. Avoid overwatering young plants, as their soft stems damp off easily in waterlogged compost and they will die. Lift pots and only water any that feel light.

Always transplant both indoor and outdoor cucumbers after your last frost date – even plantings under cover need warm weather before they go in the ground. Transplant ridge cucumbers into the soil at least 60cm (2ft)

Plant cordon cucumbers with a supporting string.

apart, and cordon varieties 90cm (3ft) apart. If growing in a container, choose a large 45cm (18in) one, which makes feeding and watering manageable. To provide support for tall cordon plants, place a knotted polypropylene string in the base of the hole and transplant the root ball on top of it so that the roots hold the string in place. Tie the top of the string to whatever support is available in your greenhouse or polytunnel. Plant slightly deep to support the stem, with the top of the root ball 5cm (2in) below soil level.

Care and protection

Ridge varieties sprawl across the ground with no need for support, which makes it easy to protect plants with fleece if the weather is cold or windy after transplanting. Train cordon

Remove the lower leaves of cordon cucumbers to improve ventilation.

Ridge cucumbers are rarely troubled by pests and diseases, except slugs, which can damage young plants in cool, wet conditions. Under cover, cordon plants may suffer red spider mite and whitefly, but I find that plants grown in healthy soil are less susceptible. If you're worried about red spider mite, you can release the predatory mite *Phytoseiulus* into your structure when you transplant cucumbers in May. The dusty white of powdery mildew often covers older leaves after midsummer. Affected plants still have healthy young leaves and continue to be productive, so just cut off mildewed lower leaves to improve ventilation around the base of plants. Downy mildew in late summer is more damaging and can quickly cause plants to rot and die. The first sign is yellow blotches on leaves, with a stronger discolouration and some fungal growth underneath. Little can be done for outdoor plants, but it can be prevented under cover by not wetting plants when watering on cloudy days. In sunny weather, it's fine and even beneficial to wet the leaves.

Harvesting and storage

My best advice is to keep picking! In warm weather, ridge varieties produce a cucumber every day, and cordon plants a large fruit every other day. Reduce the glut by picking smaller cucumbers, when they have softer skins and are less likely to be seedy. Ridge cucumbers have thick and knobbly skins and I peel off at least half, then slice thinly and sprinkle with salt an hour before eating, to enhance flavour and digestibility. Cucumbers are super-delicious when freshly picked, but will keep for up to a week in the fridge or for a few days at room temperature.

plants upwards by twisting their main stem around the supporting string regularly, and removing all of the sideshoots that start to grow at the axils where each leaf joins the stem. I also remove all tiny cucumbers until plants are at least 60cm (2ft) tall, to channel energy into plant growth and roots, for crops throughout summer and into autumn. I also remove every second baby cucumber from cropping plants, to produce a steady supply and avoid gluts. Once the main stem reaches the top of its string, loop it over to allow the plant to continue growing towards the ground.

These large, fast-growing plants need water. Even ridge cucumbers outside will need a good soak twice a week in dry weather, while cordon plants under cover benefit from a generous watering every two to three days. Water container plants every day, and give liquid feeds once a fortnight, or even every week in hot weather.

Cut the tough stalks of ridge cucumbers.

VARIETIES

CORDON

Some old varieties are harder to grow as they produce male flowers, which need to be removed to avoid pollinated fruits with a bitter taste. I recommend growing "all-female" F1 hybrids without male flowers to prevent this problem.

'Carmen' and **'Femspot'** Both produce abundant full-sized cucumbers 30–40cm (12–16in) in length.

'Passandra' Forms plentiful half-size cucumbers about 15cm (6in) long.

'Iznik' Mini "lunchbox" cucumbers that I've grown successfully in my conservatory.

RIDGE

'La Diva' Easy to grow outdoors for prolific crops of 15–20cm (6–8in) long fruit.

'Tanya' Another reliable variety with similar fruits to 'La Diva' that are slightly spiky.

KEY INFORMATION   ▬ Outdoors   ▬ Under cover

RIDGE

Seed to first harvest: 80 days   **Sowing to transplanting:** 4–6 weeks   **Position:** Full sun
Spacing: 60–90cm (2–3ft)   **Hardiness:** Tender; needs warmth and is killed by frost

	JAN	FEB	MAR	APR	MAY	JUN	JUL	AUG	SEP	OCT	NOV	DEC
Sowing					▬	▬						
Transplanting						▬						
Harvesting							▬	▬	▬			

CORDON

Seed to first harvest: 70 days   **Sowing to transplanting:** 4–6 weeks   **Position:** Under cover
Spacing: 90cm (3ft)   **Hardiness:** Tender; needs warmth and is killed by frost

	JAN	FEB	MAR	APR	MAY	JUN	JUL	AUG	SEP	OCT	NOV	DEC
Sowing				▬								
Transplanting					▬							
Harvesting						▬	▬	▬	▬	▬		

MELON

Melons need warmth and in areas where a warm summer is not guaranteed, grow them in a greenhouse or polytunnel. To harvest and eat your own ripe melon is a precious moment. The handful of ripe fruits per plant may not compare well to highly productive crops like cherry tomatoes, but they are worth growing if you have space. This profile concentrates on growing cantaloupe melons in temperate climates; honeydew and watermelons need extra warmth.

Sowing and transplanting

From mid-March to early April, sow single seeds into 3cm (1¼in) modules and keep them warm under cover to encourage germination. I start newly sown trays in the house, where nighttime temperatures are higher. Transfer them to the greenhouse before seedlings become too tall and leggy, but keep nighttime temperatures above 10°C (50°F) using a hotbed or electric propagating mat to keep plants growing and protect them from frost. Pot on seedlings into 7cm (2¾in) pots after three to four weeks so their growth isn't checked, and maybe again into 10cm (4in) pots in late April when growth speeds up. Be careful not to overwater young plants in pots, because roots will damp off in wet compost and plants will die. Don't water if pots feel heavy.

Transplant under cover in mid-May or soon after. Set plants deep enough to bury 5cm (2in) of stem and space 50–60cm (20–24in) apart, or into containers at least 45cm (18in) in diameter, filled with multipurpose compost. Allow plants to trail over the ground, or grow them as cordons up a string secured in the soil under the root ball when you transplant them (see pp.173–174). Plants may grow outdoors, but they will run out of warmth to ripen the fruits unless afternoon temperatures exceed 24°C (75°F) in the shade during summer.

Care and protection

Once cordon plants are growing rapidly, twist the main stem quite tightly around the supporting string every two or three days, to ensure enough support to carry the weight of heavy fruit. Unlike cucumbers, melons develop from the first node of every sideshoot. I pinch out all of the early sideshoots until plants are 1–1.2m (3–4ft) high and then allow sideshoots to develop, so that they can hang downwards without touching the ground. Once a little melon has formed, pinch out the growing tip of its sideshoot.

If your summer is not hot (below 24°C/75°F most of the time) allow just three or four melons to develop by removing all new sideshoots once those fruits are formed. This increases your chances of ripe fruit. Plants are capable of ripening many more fruit – I have picked 12 'Minnesota Midget' from a single

Removing sideshoots from flowering plants.

plant in a warmer-than-usual summer – but the downside is that they ripen later. Plants growing on the ground and in containers can be allowed to sprawl without pruning, until you see melons developing. They self-prune fruit numbers, but once you see a few melons, help ripen them by repeatedly pinching out new stems.

The fast-growing plants need consistent but moderate watering. Increase the amount in hot weather, then reduce watering to maintenance levels in late summer when the swollen fruits are ripening.

Plants are not usually troubled by pests. Knock aphids off leaves with a water spray in late spring and early summer – the period before their predators arrive. Plants tend to grow away from minor damage caused by slugs and woodlice nibbling a serrated pattern around leaf edges. Red spider mite is serious if it occurs, but will hopefully be late enough in summer that fruits are already well developed.

Harvesting and storage

Melons that look mature may remain unripe on the plant for a week or more, then suddenly yellow and fill the greenhouse or polytunnel with their amazing sweet aroma. Another clue to ripeness is a slight cracking around the stalk, sometimes with dark sap oozing out. Pick fruit as soon as you notice any of these signs, by cutting the stalk while holding the melon. They store better with a short piece of stalk attached and will keep for two weeks if cool,

Ripening 'Minnesota Midget' fruits.

but gradually lose flavour and become soft in texture.

Saving seed from open-pollinated varieties (see p.37) is easy, but grow a single variety to avoid cross pollination. Scoop out the seeds when you eat the fruit, then wash and dry them to store and sow the following spring.

VARIETIES

'Minnesota Midget' and **'Petit Gris de Rennes'** Both form delicious, small, orange-fleshed fruits and are well suited to cool climates.

'Alvaro' F1 Grows and ripens quickly, with on average four medium-sized melons per plant.

'Emir' F1 This vigorous hybrid variety produces slightly larger and longer fruit with orange flesh.

'Early Moonbeam' A tasty, green-fleshed watermelon for cooler climates, but which still needs more heat than other types of melon. Don't try watermelon until you've succeeded with other melons.

KEY INFORMATION　　　▬▬ Under cover

Seed to first harvest: 5 months　**Sowing to transplanting:** 6–8 weeks　**Position:** Full sun and sheltered, ideally under cover　**Spacing:** 50–60cm (20–24in) apart　**Hardiness:** Not hardy; needs warmth and will be killed by frost　**Suitable for saving seed**

	JAN	FEB	MAR	APR	MAY	JUN	JUL	AUG	SEP	OCT	NOV	DEC
Sowing			▬▬									
Transplanting					▬							
Harvesting								▬▬▬▬				

WINTER SQUASH

Winter squash, with their varied shapes and vivid colours, are a highlight of the summer and early autumn garden. Give each plant plenty of space and they will need little intervention, growing rapidly to cover the ground. Their skins toughen as they ripen, creating a seal that allows fruit to stand on the soil and to store easily from late autumn until early the following summer. The dense orange flesh has high nutritional value by weight and its sweetness increases after harvest. Squash are distinct from pumpkins, which are larger, thinner-skinned, and have more watery flesh, meaning they rarely keep beyond December.

Sowing and transplanting

These plants benefit from a long growing season and need warmth to grow well. If your summers are cool, it may be worth growing them under cover, or choosing Kuri varieties rather than butternuts. Lengthen the growing season in temperate climates by sowing under cover a month before your last frost date. This results in decent-sized plants, ready to transplant outside when the weather warms in late spring or early summer.

Sow the large seeds singly into 5cm (2in) modules or 5–7cm (2–2¾in) pots. Place seeds flat on the compost surface, push down gently, and cover lightly with compost. There is debate about whether seeds grow better when inserted vertically downwards, but I find it quicker to sow them flat and they germinate well. Seeds need 20–25°C (68–77°F) to germinate evenly and new sowings are best kept in the house for the first week, to benefit from the warmer nights, which encourage germination. Seedlings can then be moved into an unheated greenhouse and covered with fleece at night if the weather is cold. If this is not possible then delay sowing until late April or early May. After about two weeks you should have a strong seedling, with two large seed leaves (cotyledons). After another week or so, when the first true leaves are growing rapidly, pot them on into 9cm (3½in) pots so they grow to a good size for transplanting. Be careful not to overwater newly repotted plants to avoid flooding the roots.

Only transplant once you are certain there will be no more frosts, which could be from mid-May to early June, depending on your location. Make a straight-sided hole with a trowel and slide in the long-stemmed plants about 5cm (2in) deeper than they were growing in their pot, to help keep them stable and create a little hollow to make watering easier. Allow 1m (3ft) between plants, which means there

Winter squash are a good growing option if clearing weedy ground with a black plastic covering.

A varied harvest of 'Uchiki Kuri', 'Crown Prince' F1, and butternut 'Butterscotch' F1.

If the stalk is too hard, cut through the plant's stem instead.

will not be space for many in a small garden. It's a mistake to cram them in too close together, because this reduces the yield of each plant. The wide spacing provides an opportunity to interplant with sweetcorn, one or two between each squash, and this combination works in open ground or when planting through a black plastic mulch laid over new ground to clear weeds.

Care and protection

Water new transplants in and continue to water every two days in dry weather for about a week, to help them establish. Protecting plants from any cold or windy weather with fleece during late May can help them to get settled and start growing, but remove it as soon as conditions improve to avoid cooking leaves in bright sunshine. Once you see new growth, that usually means you need do nothing more until harvest, just enjoy watching the plants romp away to take over the garden! The speed of growth helps young plants shrug off any slug damage, but if your garden is full of slugs then go out with a torch for a few nights after they're transplanted and dispose of any you find nearby.

There is no need to prune the long stems, but if they grow over other plants or paths, then move them aside or cut them back. It's not necessary to thin the developing fruit, because squash manage this themselves. Don't worry if you see some small fruits rotting: plants set more fruit than they can sustain and then allow the surplus to decay in midsummer. The number of fruits that mature on a plant will vary depending on the variety, the weather conditions, and the space it has in which to grow.

Where summers are dry you will need to water plants as fruits develop, perhaps twice in all, but I find that is not necessary here. Powdery mildew symptoms on the older leaves during late summer are nothing to worry about because this doesn't kill the plants and is part of their cycle of growth. As the mass of leaves gradually die off the fruits are exposed to more sunlight, which helps with the ripening process.

Harvesting and storage

If you are new to growing winter squash, it can be difficult to judge when to harvest, but they must be picked before the first frost of autumn, to prevent them being damaged. Before that you are looking for most of the leaves to have died back and the stalk of each fruit to change from green, through yellow, to brown and dry. Check that the skin is hard by tapping all over the squash with your knuckle and if you hear a hollow sound it's ready to pick. If this hasn't happened by October, when fruits have run out of light and warmth to ripen, you need to pick and eat them immature, with a less dense texture and reduced sweetness.

It's easiest to harvest the whole crop of each variety at once, by carefully cutting through the

Winter squash brought indoors for curing and storage.

stalks with a sharp knife; if the stalks are fully dry and hard, cut the softer trailing stem on either side of each stalk instead. You can harvest when the stalks are yellow and still a bit juicy, but they will need to be thoroughly cured (see below) before storing. Avoid damaging skins or breaking off the stalk as this makes an entry point for mould during storage. After harvest, remove and compost all remaining growth.

Finish ripening squash to sweeten the flesh and harden the skin fully by "curing" them in a warm, sunny place, such as a windowsill in the house, for around two weeks. Properly ripened and cured squash will keep for months, anywhere indoors where it's warm and dry – even in sunshine. The tough skin seals the fruit so that it doesn't dry out and shrivel.

Seed from non-F1 varieties is simple to save from the fruit: just wash and dry it before storing. However, if you grow two or more varieties in the same season, the flowers will cross pollinate, resulting in varied fruit size, shape, and colour in the next year's crop.

VARIETIES

'Crown Prince' F1 Widely esteemed for its sweet flavour, dense texture, and excellent keeping qualities until May or longer. An average of four large (3–4kg/6½–9lb) fruit per plant with silver-grey skin and dark orange flesh. Productive in cooler climates, but less than Kuri.

'Uchiki Kuri' An orange-skinned, onion-shaped squash with a delicious chestnut flavour that is well suited to a temperate/cooler climate and usually the first variety to mature. Stores until early spring with an average of six 1–2kg (2–4½lb) fruit per plant.

BUTTERNUT SQUASH

These have a great flavour, but need a hotter summer than other winter squash to ripen the fruit.

'Waltham Butternut' Produces large, tasty fruits when summer is sufficiently warm.

'Hunter' F1, **'Harrier' F1**, and **'Butterscotch' F1** Hybrids bred to produce smaller, faster-maturing squash of 1–2.5kg (2–5½lb). Can produce a large number of fruit per plant, which store well once fully ripe and cured.

KEY INFORMATION

Seed to first harvest: 4½–5½ months   **Sowing to transplanting:** 4 weeks   **Position:** Full sun and warmth
Spacing: 1m (3ft) apart   **Hardiness:** Tender; will be killed by frost and needs summer warmth to thrive
Suitable for interplanting with sweetcorn

	JAN	FEB	MAR	APR	MAY	JUN	JUL	AUG	SEP	OCT	NOV	DEC
Sowing				▬								
Transplanting					▬							
Harvesting									▬▬▬			

UMBELLIFERS - CARROT FAMILY

Carrot

Celeriac

Celery

Florence fennel

Parsnip

Chervil

Coriander

Dill

Parsley

This hardy family of vegetables and herbs has flavours that are wide-ranging and strong, from the aniseed of Florence fennel to the punchy citrus of coriander. Parsnips are particularly frost hardy and grow sweeter as the temperature falls, while coriander, chervil, and parsley are all hardy plants that will survive frost. Fresh umbellifers can be harvested over a long season and supplemented with stored roots and seeds.

Choosing what to grow

With the exception of parsnips, umbellifers are economical with space and excellent for interplanting among other vegetables (see pp.70–71), which makes them well suited to smaller gardens. The herbs are all compact plants that crop for several months from one sowing; chervil is a fantastic herb for winter and would grow well with coriander and parsley in a container, somewhere sheltered. Growing your own carrots is a must, because their intense flavour is at a completely different level to almost any you can buy. Root crops and Florence fennel grown in healthy no dig soil also store in considerably better condition than most purchased vegetables, plus you have the option to keep parsnips in the soil through winter. Celery and celeriac are more challenging to grow well, but the results are certainly worth the effort.

Sowing, growing, and harvesting

Carrots and parsnips are the only vegetable seeds I sow direct, so that their tap roots can grow straight downwards, rather than risk damaging them by transplanting. The low number of weeds in no dig soil makes it easy to care for direct-sown seedlings. Most other umbellifers start well sown into modules and transplant successfully, because they are not grown for their tap roots. The tiny seeds of celery and celeriac are best sown into seed trays for pricking out and have an unusual quality, in that they need light to germinate.

CROP		JAN	FEB	MAR	APR	MAY	JUN	JUL	AUG	SEP	OCT	NOV	DEC
Carrot (early)	Sow			■	■		■						
	Harvest						■	■	■	■			
Carrot (maincrop)	Sow						■						
	Harvest									■	■	■	■
Celeriac	Sow			■									
	Harvest										■	■	■
Celery	Sow			■	■	■							
	Harvest							■	■	■	■		
Florence fennel	Sow		■					■					
	Harvest						■	■		■	■		
Parsnip	Sow		■	■	■	■	■						
	Harvest	■	■	■	■					■	■	■	■
Chervil	Sow							■	■				
	Harvest	■	■	■	■	■	■	■	■	■	■	■	■
Coriander	Sow		■	■	■	■	■	■	■	■			
	Harvest	░	░	░	░	░	░	░	░	░	░	░	░
Dill	Sow		■	■	■	■	■	■	■	■			
	Harvest				■	■	■	■	■	■	■	■	
Parsley	Sow		■	■	■	■	■						
	Harvest	■	■	■	■	■	■	■	■	■	■	■	■

■ Outdoors   ░ Under cover

A cover of mesh supported on hoops prevents carrot fly larvae burrowing into roots.

Florence fennel and the herbs flower in early summer during their first year, so to achieve a harvest before they bolt it's good to sow very early, in late winter under cover, and sow again in midsummer. Carrots and parsnips flower in their second spring, so can be sown any time from early spring until midsummer. Celery and celeriac are best sown in spring, but while celery is ready to cut within four months, celeriac needs the whole season to grow large.

Pull carrots as required through summer and autumn, and lift any remaining roots of maincrop varieties in December to store in a sack through winter. Parsnips can be left in the soil for winter and lifted as required, while celeriac are best cut as needed through autumn and then harvested for storage in December. Florence fennel can be eaten freshly cut, but will keep for up to a month if cut in late autumn. Celery and umbellifer herbs are best enjoyed freshly picked.

Celeriac 'Prinz' with its leaves and roots trimmed, ready for cooking or storage.

Common problems

Carrot fly is a major pest of the umbellifer family and its maggots may eat the roots of any of these plants, but affect carrots in particular. Prevent adult flies laying their eggs around plants with a carefully secured mesh cover. Where the slug population is high, they will eat tiny new leaves of seedlings even before you see them. Control slug numbers (see p.95) and sow carrots as far as possible from areas of slug habitat. Rabbits adore carrot leaves and the young foliage of other umbellifers, except parsnips, so you may need to protect plants with crop covers.

Canker damages parsnips when moisture levels are high in wet weather and heavy soil. Choose parsnip varieties bred with resistance if canker is a problem, and sow in June. Late blight (*Septoria apiicola*) can cause the leaves and stalks of celery and celeriac to turn brown, mainly in late summer and autumn. Removing and composting affected leaves improves the appearance of plants but does little to slow the spread of this disease.

Bolting (rapidly running to seed) can be a problem if the herbs or Florence fennel are sown from mid-spring to early summer, but this is easily avoided by sowing outside this window. My favourite time to sow coriander is late July, for small harvests outdoors from October to May and large winter harvests from plantings under cover.

CARROTS

Carrots are a joyful vegetable to grow. They're not easy, but there's nothing quite like the thrill of pulling your own carrots, partly because you never know what you're going to find when you grab hold of those leaves! The flavour of a fresh carrot is something money can't buy and one of the highlights of home gardening; it can be quite unexpected if you've never grown them before. Although there's a lot of fun to be had growing carrots, there are also potential problems to watch out for that can result in poor harvests.

Sowing and thinning

This is one vegetable that I always sow directly into the soil and would never raise as a transplant, because this would almost inevitably break the tap root and produce forked carrots and a smaller harvest. Carrots grow well on heavy soil in no dig beds, because seedlings get a good start in the top layer and then root down into the undisturbed soil – they do not fork, and harvests are large. It's often claimed that adding compost or manure before sowing carrot seeds results in forking. However, this happens only when the compost has been dug in.

Three sowings can provide carrots almost year-round. Start in early spring with a fast-growing early variety for a summer crop, then sow again in early summer, for autumn harvests. In the second half of June I sow a slower-growing maincrop variety, for an autumn harvest of late carrots that continues into December and stores well into spring. Initially, tiny carrot seeds grow slowly as they don't contain a lot of resources for the seedling to draw on. This makes them extremely vulnerable to pest damage, especially if they are sown too early and the seedlings struggle to establish in cold conditions. Wait until the weather warms and seedlings will establish quickly and suffer less pest damage. Avoid sowing into compost containing many weed seeds, because it is time consuming to weed around small seedlings.

The soft, friable surface of no dig beds is ideal for direct sowing and it's easy to make a drill 1–2cm (½–¾in) deep using a dibber, a metal hoe, the corner of a rake, or even your finger. Rows can be 15cm (6in) apart for early varieties or as much as 30cm (12in) apart for autumn harvests of larger roots. If it's dry, water the drill before sowing to wet the soil at the bottom. Drop approximately three seeds per centimetre along the row, being careful not to sow too thickly. If seedlings are overcrowded after about six weeks, thin out a few to leave two or three carrots per centimetre.

Thinning a row of carrot seedlings.

It can be difficult to find space for summer sowings of maincrop carrots so I often inter-sow rows between earlier plantings that are between two and six weeks away from final harvest. This works well between garlic and spring onions, or lettuce and spinach, where regularly picking the outer leaves allows space for carrot seedlings to grow.

Care and protection

Slugs can be a big problem for early sowings. Always sow carrots in a clear space where only compost has been used as a mulch and away from any overgrown area where slugs could be hiding. Weeding is especially important when early sowings are small, and the first weeding is easier if you mark carrot rows by sowing fast-growing radish seeds every 5cm (2in) along their length. This makes it easier to see tiny carrot seedlings and weed around them safely, and produces a small radish harvest.

Cover early sowings with fleece to speed up germination and early growth, and protect seedlings from rabbits. In early May, swap the fleece for cooler mesh, preferably supported on hoops, to keep away carrot root flies looking to lay their eggs in the soil around plants. Carrot fly larvae can cause serious damage and adult flies are active from mid–May through June, so it's best to have early sowings covered all the time. For summer sowings, there's a period from late June until the second week in August when flies are not laying eggs and carrots can be left uncovered, but always cover before 10th August to avoid the second generation of flies. Insect mesh will keep most root flies off, but even when the edges are secured with stones or heavy sticks, some flies will wriggle underneath. Slugs nibble roots as they mature, so if you see signs of damage it's best not to leave carrots in the ground for too long before harvesting them to eat and store.

Carrots only rarely need watering, most often during dry weather in early summer, when roots are swelling. It is important not

Pulling sweet early carrots.

to overdo it, however, because although roots grown in dry soil may be smaller, they are definitely sweeter.

Harvesting and storage

When shoulders of roots start to push above the surface, around ten weeks after sowing, you can take a first harvest by pulling those that are visible, which gives the remaining roots more space to swell. Continue to harvest by thinning like this until midsummer for sowings of early varieties, and until early autumn for maincrops, after which you can harvest large, mature roots. It's usually easy to pull carrots from no dig soil by firmly holding the leaves and easing them gently upwards. Long varieties may need the extra leverage of a trowel, inserted almost vertically close to the roots, which loosens the ground a little so carrots can be pulled out gently. Watering dry soil before harvesting makes the roots easier to pull.

Around four months after sowing, roots gradually become tougher and more fibrous as they continue to swell. This is especially the case in warmer conditions and means that the last harvest for early varieties is best made around late July. Pull harvests of maincrop carrots to store before nighttime temperatures fall below about –5°C (23°F).

For maximum flavour and sweetness, I recommend eating summer harvests freshly pulled. Early varieties have a slightly higher water content than maincrops, but they will keep for a week or two in summer if kept cool, and for two months in autumn. Maincrops will store through winter and into spring. Leave soil on the roots at harvest time to help them retain moisture, and carefully twist or snap the leaves off before storing, so that they don't pull moisture out of the harvested root. I store autumn harvests in paper sacks, which is much less effort than arranging roots in boxes of sand. Larger, undamaged roots will keep in decent, if not perfect, condition for three to five months, depending on the variety, in any shed or outbuilding where they won't freeze solid. Towards the end of winter, carrots sprout new yellow leaves and little white hairs as they start to grow again. Roots become drier, but are still good to eat at this stage and taste much better than shop-bought.

Seed saving

Producing your own carrot seed is possible but difficult. Select eight or ten of your best stored carrots at the end of winter and plant them 30cm (12in) apart, so they soon sprout new leaves and rise to flower in June. Cover plants with mesh to prevent insects causing cross pollination from any wild carrots nearby, although it's hard to secure over the tall plants. Cut off each seedhead in late August, dry fully for a week or two, and rub out the seeds.

VARIETIES

Early varieties of carrot are generally sown in spring for early summer harvests, and you can also sow them in summer for quick harvests in autumn. Maincrop varieties mature more slowly: sow them in early summer, for autumn and winter crops and storage.

EARLY VARIETIES

'Nantes Milan 2' Sweet Nantes carrots came top of a taste test by chef and restaurateur Raymond Blanc and this is the variety I recommend. It has even, cylindrical roots that are rounded at the tip.

'Nairobi' F1 A fine 'Nantes' hybrid of exceptional vigour, for earlier harvests.

'Amsterdam Forcing' This more pointed carrot is thin and tender, for smaller and exceptionally early harvests.

'Chantenay' Produces short, sweet early carrots.

'Purple Haze' Fun for its amazing purple roots with a band of orange at their centre. Their flavour is rich and less sweet than 'Nantes'.

'Flyaway' and **'Resistafly'** Bred to deter carrot fly. Some swear by them but I have suffered root fly damage when growing them.

'Sugarsnax' F1 One of many fine varieties from the 'Imperator' range. Although the extra sweetness isn't obvious, the carrot length is amazing, often reaching 22cm (8¾in).

MAINCROP VARIETIES

'Berlicum' A slower-growing variant of 'Nantes' that can grow enormous. Tastes good and stores well.

'Autumn King' A classic pointy-ended carrot, which is good to store, although sometimes a little fibrous in texture, perhaps from lack of varietal maintenance.

'Oxhella' Short, stocky roots taste good and have very high dry matter, which makes them great for storing; larger roots can keep into May. An equivalent variety is 'Oxheart'.

Twisting off leaves of maincrop carrot 'Oxhella' ready for storing.

KEY INFORMATION

EARLY VARIETIES

Seed to first harvest: 10 weeks   **Position:** Adaptable; will tolerate some shade   **Spacing:** Rows 15cm (6in) apart
Hardiness: Seedlings stand spring frosts to about -4°C (25°F)   **Suitable for intersowing as a follow-on crop**

	JAN	FEB	MAR	APR	MAY	JUN	JUL	AUG	SEP	OCT	NOV	DEC
Sowing			▬	▬		▬	▬					
Harvesting						▬	▬	▬		▬		

MAINCROP VARIETIES

Seed to first harvest: From 12 weeks for fresh carrots, 5 months for storing   **Position:** Adaptable; will tolerate
some shade   **Spacing:** Rows 30cm (12in) apart   **Hardiness:** Mature plants stand frost to about -5°C (23°F),
depending how much leaf cover is above them   **Suitable for intersowing as a follow-on crop**

	JAN	FEB	MAR	APR	MAY	JUN	JUL	AUG	SEP	OCT	NOV	DEC
Sowing						▬	▬					
Harvesting									▬	▬	▬	▬
Storage	▬	▬	▬	▬							▬	▬

CELERIAC

Celeriac needs fertile soil and a long growing season to crop well, and is not a vegetable that I would leap into growing if you're a beginner. When you get it right, you'll have large, tasty, celery-flavoured roots (actually a swollen stem just above the plant's root system), which easily store through winter until the following April. Plants thrive in heavy soil, which holds moisture; if your soil is light, add an extra 5cm (2in) mulch of compost before planting.

Sowing and transplanting

Tiny celeriac seeds need light to germinate and will not come up well if covered in even a thin layer of compost after sowing. Sow under cover in late March and avoid exposing seedlings to cold conditions at any stage, as this may result later in plants running to seed (or "bolting") before their stems swell to produce a crop.

I sow one half of a small seed tray with celeriac and the other half with celery, making sure they are clearly labelled because the seedlings look exactly the same. Fill the tray with seed compost and wet it thoroughly before sowing. Scatter the seeds thinly over the compost and spray with a fine mist to make sure they are fully moist. Cover the seed tray with a sheet of glass or a clear polythene bag, and place it in a warm (15–20oC/59–68oF) and light place. Take the covering off as soon as seedlings are visible, after about two weeks.

Tiny seedlings are ready to prick out after three or four weeks, either at the two-leaf stage or when they have one true leaf. Prick them out into 3cm (1¼in) modules and grow under cover until mid- to late May, when you can transplant them outdoors once the weather is warmer. Dib holes for the transplants, push in the module root balls about 1cm (½in) below surface level, and water in well.

Care and protection

If the weather is cool after transplanting, cover the bed with thermacrop or mesh to help plants establish quickly. A cover also protects from possible rabbit and aphid damage – sometimes aphids eat new leaves to the extent that plants barely grow. Remove the cover after about a month or so. Water twice more after transplanting and during any periods of hot, dry summer weather. Celeriac flourishes in moist soil and will need more watering if your underlying soil is chalk or sand, but it doesn't need the same plentiful watering as celery.

Removing yellow lower leaves from maturing plants is reputed to help celeriac swell, but I have never noticed a significant difference and do it only to improve the appearance of plants. Celery late blight (*Septoria apiicola*) is a fungal disease that causes brown patches on leaves in autumn. Affected leaves can be removed to compost, but this does little to prevent its spread. Slugs and woodlice love celeriac, so avoid growing them in beds with edges of decaying wood, which afford those pests the perfect place to hide.

Harvesting and storage

Celeriac swells noticeably above the ground from late summer and throughout autumn. Take your first harvest around mid-October and continue picking as required until late November. At this point, or earlier if leaves are mostly diseased, lift the remaining roots to store, because they keep well after harvest but suffer pest and disease damage when left in the soil over winter. Use a trowel, spade, or knife to cut under the swollen celeriac to leave most of its masses of fibrous roots in the ground to decompose. If you were to pull up the plants, these roots would lift and disturb the soil. Snap off the leaves individually or use the back of a knife to rub downwards and remove leaf stalks cleanly.

The dry texture of celeriac allows it to store amazingly well without shrivelling. Leave a few fibrous roots on with compost between them to retain moisture. Place roots in an open box or crate and store below 10°C (50°F) in a shed, where they will tolerate some exposure to frost. Mice like to feast on stored roots, so I keep a mousetrap in the shed all winter.

VARIETIES

I don't find much variation in flavour between different celeriac varieties.

'Prinz' A long period of healthy growth, producing a uniform, evenly shaped crop.

'Ibis' Fast growing and earlier maturing than 'Prinz', but the roots don't store quite so well.

'Mars' Can grow large and swells a decent amount above ground.

KEY INFORMATION

Seed to first harvest: 6–7 months **Sowing to transplanting:** 8 weeks **Position:** Full sun or shade in moisture-retentive soil **Spacing:** 35–40cm (14–16in) in an equidistant grid pattern **Hardiness:** Hardy to -10°C (14°F) and possibly colder **Suitable for interplanting**

	JAN	FEB	MAR	APR	MAY	JUN	JUL	AUG	SEP	OCT	NOV	DEC
Sowing			—									
Transplanting					—							
Harvesting										—	—	—

Trim the roots and leaves (here showing symptoms of celery late blight) after harvest.

CELERY

Unlike its shop-bought equivalent, which has been raised using a lot of fertilizer and water, celery grown in no dig soil has extra flavour, fibre, microbes, and I would say more nutrients. Plants flourish in warm, wet conditions that produce rapid growth, juicy celery, and lush foliage.

Sowing and transplanting

Celery can be difficult to raise successfully from seed and there is no shame in buying transplants, especially if you haven't grown it before. You can also raise plants by putting a celery stalk into a glass with water at the bottom. Keep it at room temperature for two weeks or so and when roots appear, plant the rooted stalk into a pot of compost. The seeds need light to germinate, such that even a thin layer of compost on top of the tiny seeds prevents them coming up well. Sow from the second half of March to late May, always under cover and not in frosty conditions, because this may cause plants to run to seed before producing a crop. March sowings can give harvests through summer and I recommend a second sowing in late May for a tender crop from September through October.

Fill a small seed tray with fine seed compost and make sure it's fully wet before sowing. Scatter seeds thinly onto the surface, as it's easy to sow too thickly and have too many plants. Spray with a fine mist to moisten the seeds, then cover the seed tray with a small sheet of glass or a clear polythene bag to retain the moisture. Keep the tray in a warm (15–20°C/59–68°F), light position for about two weeks. Remove the covering when you see the first tiny, green leaves.

Prick out seedlings into 3cm (1¼in) modules after about three weeks, although the timing is flexible because they grow slowly at this stage. Grow on for about another five weeks and transplant after the last spring frost, into dibbed holes with the top of the root balls about 1cm (½in) below the soil surface. Water in thoroughly.

Care and protection

Protect celery planted out during May with fleece if the weather is cool, or cover with mesh for the first month to reduce aphid damage at a time when these insect pests are prolific. Watering is more important for celery than for any other vegetable; if it's not raining give plants a good water twice a week, especially as they grow large. Celery can look healthy without the extra water, but rapid, lush growth is essential for a tender harvest and only regular watering will achieve this.

Traditionally celery was blanched or earthed up to reduce bitterness, but I find this unnecessary with modern varieties that are bred for less bitterness. Twist off any sideshoots from the base of maturing plants to keep them neat. Sometimes these sideshoots are like mini celeries and can be eaten.

Slugs love celery and will chomp into stalks to spoil the harvest. Control slug numbers by reducing habitat nearby, and don't grow celery near any favoured hiding places. Where rabbits are present, protect young plants with fleece or mesh.

Celery suffers fungal diseases, starting with early blight (*Cercospora apii*), which causes light brown spots or lesions on outer leaves during the first few weeks of early summer. It's not a big worry and you can keep removing damaged leaves to lessen its spread. Late blight (*Septoria apiicola*) is more serious, sometimes causing almost all leaves and stems to turn brown in damp conditions during late summer and autumn, especially when night temperatures are 13°C (55°F) or more. Remove affected leaves to keep the disease in check, and harvest promptly if it's spreading fast. For autumn celery, grow varieties with resistance.

Harvesting and storage

You can have a very early harvest by cutting single stalks about three months after sowing, and can regularly cut or twist off the outer stalks as needed so that plants continue to grow. Start harvesting whole heads when they are small and tender, to prolong the cropping season from one sowing. Mature celery has stringier stalks, but watering reduces this and they can be good to pick for weeks. The harvest season finishes with first frosts of –2°C (28°F).

To harvest a whole head, cut at the base with a knife. The root will regrow little shoots if left in the soil, or can be removed to make space for a new planting by cutting the remaining stem base below soil level with a trowel and putting it on the compost heap.

Harvested celery can be stored in the fridge in a polythene bag for several days (see p.102), or by placing the whole stem in shallow water in a cup or bowl. Celery leaves are packed with flavour and make a valuable ingredient for stock or used like a herb.

Cut away roots and sideshoots from harvested celery.

VARIETIES

'**Victoria' F1** An easy, vigorous, and widely grown commercial variety. Its green stalks have a good flavour and are tender.

'**Loretta' F1** Fast-growing with pale yellow stalks.

'**Granada' F1** Reliable performance from later sowings thanks to its resistance to celery late blight in autumn.

KEY INFORMATION

Seed to first harvest: 3½ months   **Sowing to transplanting:** 8 weeks   **Position:** Full sun or shade in moisture-retentive soil   **Spacing:** 25–30cm (10–12in) apart in an equidistant grid pattern   **Hardiness:** Hardy, but stalks are damaged by moderate frost   **Suitable for follow-on planting**

	JAN	FEB	MAR	APR	MAY	JUN	JUL	AUG	SEP	OCT	NOV	DEC
Sowing			▬▬▬▬▬▬									
Transplanting					▬▬▬▬▬▬							
Harvesting						▬▬▬▬▬▬▬▬▬▬						

FLORENCE OR BULB FENNEL

The tender bulbs of Florence fennel are quite a delicacy, with a pronounced taste of aniseed that is softened and sweetened by roasting. Fennel has a reputation for bolting before it forms a bulb, but sowing at the two best times prevents this and means that a successful crop is not difficult to grow. Perennial herb fennel is an entirely different plant, grown for harvests of leaves and seeds.

Sowing and transplanting

April sowings usually rush to flower before the bulb has had much chance to swell, as fennel's flowering period is in early to midsummer. With this in mind I make two sowings; one in late winter or very early spring, for harvests in early summer, and a second in midsummer, to crop through autumn, until the first moderate frost of about -3°C (27°F).

Either sow in a seed tray to prick out into modules, or sow two seeds into each cell of a 3cm (1¼in) module tray and thin to the strongest seedling once they have germinated. Although fennel is related to carrots and parsnips, it pricks out and transplants well because the tap root is not harvested. Keep early sowings in the warmth of your house for about a week to aid germination. Seedlings then need to be under cover but free of frost, coming ready to plant out in four or five weeks. To transplant, make small holes with a dibber, 20cm (8in) apart and deep enough so that the top of the module will rest at least 2cm (¾in) below ground level. This shelters and supports the long-stemmed seedlings while they establish.

There's a myth that fennel is a bad companion to other plants: I've seen no evidence of this and find that it works perfectly even as an interplant between other vegetables. I've popped fennel plants between ridge cucumbers, lettuce, and spinach during their last few weeks of picking. Then after about four weeks, when the finished crop is removed, the fennel plants are already established and quick to swell their bulbs.

Care and protection

Water transplanted seedlings, and if it's dry keep them watered until you see strong leaf growth. It's also worth watering fennel that's maturing from late May into early summer to help the bulbs swell, but it's rare that you need to do that in autumn when the weather is usually wetter.

Transplant fennel in spring or late summer.

Cover early spring transplants with fleece placed right on top of plants, to protect from frost and blustery winds. Smaller fennel seedlings tend to survive spring frost better than bigger bulbs exposed to frost in autumn. Fleece can often be left over plants until early May, by which time they're nearly half-grown. Fennel is not prone to pests, but fleece in spring will prevent rabbits eating the feathery leaves. If your garden is prone to slug damage, direct-sown fennel risks disappearing at the two-leaf stage.

Harvesting and storage

There is not a massive difference between the flavour of immature and mature bulbs, but there is an optimum moment to harvest, especially from first sowings, while the bulb is plump and in good condition. Left longer, little sideshoots appear from the base of bulbs, and bulbs also elongate in early summer as the precursor to making a flower stem. To harvest, pull the whole plant up if the soil is soft, but be gentle in case the bulb snaps. A safer alternative is to slice under the bulb and through the top of the roots, using a trowel or knife. The leaves are also edible with a subtle dill flavour.

Fennel bulbs store well in cool conditions. I harvest to store the last of my autumn crop as late as possible, just before the first frost, leaving the roots attached with a little soil, to aid storage. Bulbs can stay in good condition for up to a month in the shed at that time of year.

Florence fennel 'Perfektion', maturing.

VARIETIES

'Perfektion' The main variety I grow for all sowings, with excellent results.

'Zefa Fino' This strong, fast-growing variety swells up nicely, whether sown early or late.

'Solaris' F1 A hybrid variety that produces nicely swollen bulbs.

KEY INFORMATION

Seed to first harvest: 13 weeks early sowings, 8 weeks summer sowings **Sowing to transplanting:** 4–5 weeks
Position: Can tolerate shade, but early plantings benefit from warmth and sunshine **Spacing:** 20cm (8in)
Hardiness: Slightly hardy to about -3°C (27°F) **Suitable for interplanting and as a follow-on crop**

	JAN	FEB	MAR	APR	MAY	JUN	JUL	AUG	SEP	OCT	NOV	DEC
Sowing		▬	▬				▬					
Transplanting			▬	▬				▬				
Harvesting						▬	▬			▬	▬	

PARSNIPS

Parsnips are a winter staple, and with no dig they're easy to grow. The open soil structure created by no dig methods allows their roots to travel deeply down, such that you may need a spade to lever them out. They become sweeter when exposed to frost and keep well in the ground, on all but the heaviest soil where canker may develop.

Sowing

Sow parsnips directly into the soil, because transplanting module-raised seedlings breaks the long tap root. They have a reputation for being difficult to germinate, but in my experience they come up reliably when sown into the compost layer. I have never found that compost on the surface causes roots to fork, unlike when it's dug in. Parsnip seeds take a long time to germinate, needing moist soil around them for about two weeks. In cooler climates the ideal time to sow is mid-February to the end of March, although you can also sow later, even until mid-June, providing you keep the seedbed moist. Later sowings are less affected by parsnip canker (see opposite).

Lightly rake the compost surface to break up lumps; this is easiest when compost was spread a few weeks earlier. In weedy soil, best sow after the first flush of weed germination in spring, which you can hoe a day or two before sowing. Choose a still day for sowing, because the flaky seeds may otherwise blow away. Draw out 3cm (1¼in)-deep drills 30cm (12in) apart and drop in seeds roughly 1cm (½in) apart, then cover with the surface compost. If it's dry, water drills before sowing and tamp down the surface afterwards, to keep the moisture in. You can sow fast-germinating radish seeds every 5–10cm (2–4in) in the same row, for safer weeding once the radishes emerge to mark the row. Radishes sown along the row can be harvested after six to eight weeks.

Care and protection

Lay fleece over the seedbed after early sowings to speed up germination, keep moisture in, and protect seedlings from rabbits. Once you see the first or second true leaves, thin seedlings to 2.5cm (1in) apart for small parsnips, 5cm (2in) apart for medium-sized roots, or 10cm (4in) apart for big ones. Remove fleece before it gets too hot, which is often in late April. Weed regularly and remove any weeds before the canopy of parsnip leaves closes over. Keep your skin covered when weeding as parsnip sap can cause serious skin irritation. Parsnips thrive in moist conditions, but rarely need watering because they can root deeply for moisture, and swell nicely in the rains of autumn. After that, it's normal for the leaves to rot during winter.

A bed filled with healthy parsnips.

A long 'Gladiator' F1 parsnip grown in no dig soil.

In wet conditions and heavy soils, a fungal disease called canker causes orange-brown rotting around the shoulders of roots. This damage can be cut off after harvest and the remaining root will be edible, but if your soil is usually sodden during winter, rotting may be extensive and it's worth harvesting all parsnips in early December, to store in a shed or outbuilding (see right). Carrot root fly larvae tunnel into roots, but damage is usually superficial and can be trimmed off. Rodents may chew the crowns of overwintering roots; lift and store roots if this is a problem.

Harvesting and storage

Roots may be pulled out of soft soil by hand, but for long roots in heavy soil use a spade or fork. I prefer the precision of a spade and pull the handle towards me to lever the root from the soil, while gently pulling the shoulder of the parsnip upwards. Harvest roots as required from mid-September to March. Finish harvesting before many new leaves sprout from parsnips at the end of winter, which reduces sweetness and makes them fibrous.

To store lifted roots, remove any leaves before laying them, unwashed, in a box or two-ply paper bag kept in a shed or outbuilding. The high dry matter of parsnips means that they store into early spring, in reasonable condition.

VARIETIES

'White Gem' A good standard variety that's widely available with white, broad-shouldered roots.

'Gladiator' F1 My favourite long parsnip, which grows big to give a good yield, with some canker resistance.

'Javelin' F1 Another good hybrid that is slightly longer and thinner than 'Gladiator'.

'Tender and True' This popular old variety is reckoned to have a better flavour than others, although I don't notice a difference.

KEY INFORMATION

Seed to first harvest: 6 months   **Duration of harvest:** 6 months   **Position:** Grows in all soils, and tolerates some shade   **Spacing:** 5–10cm (2–4in) apart with 30cm (12in) between rows   **Hardiness:** Very hardy, down to at least -15°C (5°F)   **Suitable for interplanting with a quick spring crop**

	JAN	FEB	MAR	APR	MAY	JUN	JUL	AUG	SEP	OCT	NOV	DEC
Sowing			▬	▬	▬	▬						
Harvesting	▬	▬	▬						▬	▬	▬	▬
Storage	▬	▬	▬									▬

CHERVIL

Chervil thrives in cool conditions and is best sown annually in late summer for picking during autumn and winter. Although related to parsley, its leaves are more delicate, with a lovely bright green colour and a mild but pronounced taste of aniseed.

Sowing and transplanting

Sow chervil under cover from mid-July until 10th September. Germination can be erratic, so I sow into a small tray, then prick the seedlings out into module cells at the two-leaf stage. You could also sow two or three seeds per cell, then thin to one seedling for easier picking. Plants can go in the ground when they are still quite small, about a month after sowing, spaced 20cm (8in) apart each way.

Care and protection

Chervil is hardy, but will only grow new leaves during mild winter weather. For larger winter harvests grow it under cover. It's a moisture-loving plant, so watering during a dry autumn or early spring will promote growth. Few pests trouble this herb, but protect plants with bird netting, mesh, or fleece over winter where rabbits are present. Fleece laid on top of plants also insulates them from cold weather, for more rapid growth.

Harvesting and storage

Pick frequently in autumn, when growth is prolific, by gently twisting or pinching off outer leaves at the base of their stalks, which branch quite close to the main stem. Remove the whole stalk to keep the plant tidy. I prefer not to cut across the top of plants and instead leave the smaller central leaves to develop, to increase the rate of growth. Harvest until late April or early May, when plants produce edible white flowers.

Saving seed

If you have at least six plants to create a broad gene pool, allow seedheads to form after flowering and twist whole plants out of the ground in July. Hang plants to dry under cover, and then rub out the seeds, which you can sow straight away.

VARIETIES

I do not know any named varieties, but there is a distinction between plain and curled chervil. Their growth and flavour are similar.

KEY INFORMATION   ▬ Outdoors   ▬ Under cover   ▥ If mild

Seed to first harvest: 8 weeks   **Sowing to transplanting:** 4 weeks   **Position:** Adaptable, tolerates shade
Spacing: 20cm (8in) equidistant   **Hardiness:** Hardy to approx. -10°C (14°F)   **Suitable for interplanting**

	JAN	FEB	MAR	APR	MAY	JUN	JUL	AUG	SEP	OCT	NOV	DEC
Sowing							▬	▬				
Transplanting								▬	▬			
Harvesting	▥	▥	▬	▬	▬				▬	▬	▥	▥

CORIANDER

Coriander is an annual herb, which produces both strongly flavoured leaves and aromatic seeds. Plants rush to flower from late spring and throughout summer, so the best way to enjoy a long leaf harvest is to sow in late summer, as it is hardy enough to survive moderate frost.

Sowing and transplanting

My favourite sowing date here is 26th July, but sowing anytime from mid-July until mid-September will supply leaves through autumn, winter, and into early spring. If you want coriander leaves during summer, make new sowings every four to six weeks from mid-February until early July. Sow either in rows outside at 20cm (8in) apart or two seeds per 3cm (1¼in) module cell, to transplant after about four weeks at a 15–20cm (6–8in) equidistant spacing. Early autumn sowings planted under cover, either in soil or a container, will be much more productive during winter than plants grown outdoors.

Care and protection

During summer, water coriander generously to promote leafy growth and reduce flowering. Slugs can damage new plantings in particular, so remove any nearby hiding places and mount patrols to remove them after dark. I rarely experience problems with slugs through winter.

Harvesting

Start twisting or cutting off the lower stalks as soon as their leaves touch those of neighbouring plants. Good crops can be picked from outdoor plants in autumn, and from plants grown under cover in late winter and early spring. Leaves grow thinner and smaller as plants start to flower, and the first tender flower stems are edible. It's worth keeping plants growing to enjoy the flowers and a harvest of delicious seeds.

Saving seed

Saving seed is easy, as plants readily produce seed by late summer, but for re-sowing you need at least six to ten plants to provide a varied gene pool. Harvest seeds when still a little green, because they start to fall once fully dry and brown.

VARIETIES

'Cruiser' A favourite new variety with leaves that are especially broad, dark green, and tender.

'Confetti' A lovely contrast to 'Cruiser', producing feathery, light green foliage.

KEY INFORMATION ▬ Outdoors ▬ Under cover

Seed to first harvest: 8 weeks **Sowing to transplanting:** 4 weeks **Position:** Tolerates shade **Spacing:** 15–20cm (6–8in) equidistant or rows 20cm (8in) apart **Hardiness:** To -5°C (23°F) or colder

	JAN	FEB	MAR	APR	MAY	JUN	JUL	AUG	SEP	OCT	NOV	DEC
Sowing												
Transplanting												
Harvesting												

DILL

I love the sweet, zesty, anise aroma of dill, though not everyone shares my enthusiasm! If you do, it's an easy annual herb to grow but rises to flower even more quickly than coriander, and is less hardy. The flowers, feathery leaves, and strongly flavoured seeds are all edible.

Sowing and transplanting

There are two decent seasons of harvest: the first from sowing under cover in late winter or early spring, to transplant outside for picking through spring and summer, and the second from mid- to late summer, for autumn harvests. Sow two or three seeds per 3cm (1¼in) module cell, or sow into a seed tray to prick out one seedling per cell. From April, you can also sow directly outside, by dropping a seed roughly every 2.5cm (1in) into 1cm (½in)-deep drills, spaced 20cm (8in) apart.

Transplant three or four weeks after sowing, by dibbing deep holes so that plants sit 3cm (1¼in) below soil level to support their long stems. Where space is scarce in late summer, pop dill transplants between ridge cucumbers or salad plants that are four to six weeks away from being removed.

Care and protection

Even though plants are hardy enough to resist light frosts, early spring sowings and transplants are best covered with fleece for the first month, to keep them warm and protected from rabbits. For summer plantings bird netting on hoops is the best option.

Harvesting

Pick larger leaves by snapping off their stalks at the base. Harvest every few days to increase pickings before plants flower. Kept in water, long-stemmed leaves will stay fresh for a week.

Saving seed

You can save seed for culinary uses from just one plant, but save seed for sowing when you have at least five plants nearby, to ensure a wide gene pool. Cut seedheads when the seeds are brown and hard, then rub them off the stalks onto a sheet of paper. Remove any unwanted seedheads to prevent self-seeding.

VARIETIES

There has not been a huge amount of breeding in the world of dill and I haven't noticed significant variation between named varieties.

KEY INFORMATION   ▬ Outdoors   ▬ Under cover

Seed to first harvest: 6 weeks **Sowing to transplanting:** 3–4 weeks **Position:** Can grow in shade
Spacing: 15–23cm (6–9in) **Hardiness:** Some frost resistance to about -2°C (28°F) **Suitable for interplanting**

	JAN	FEB	MAR	APR	MAY	JUN	JUL	AUG	SEP	OCT	NOV	DEC
Sowing			▬	▬	▬	▬	▬	▬				
Transplanting				▬	▬	▬	▬	▬	▬			
Harvesting	▬	▬	▬	▬	▬	▬	▬	▬	▬	▬		

PARSLEY

Parsley is slow to germinate but is a fantastic source of vibrant, nutritious leaves for most of the year, from just two sowings. Choose between the ruffled leaves of curled parsley and the larger, more flavoursome foliage of flat-leaved varieties.

Sowing and transplanting

Parsley can take up to three weeks to germinate, and usually appears after you have given up on seeing any leaves. Sow into a seed tray under cover from mid-February until late July, pricking out seedlings into module cells, or sow directly into a drill outdoors once the weather warms in spring. Transplant up to six weeks after sowing, dibbing deep holes so that plants sit a little below soil level. Early sowings may rise to flower in summer, especially flat-leaf parsley, but summer sowings should survive winter, to crop through into spring.

Care and protection

Cover early spring plantings with fleece to keep them warm and protected from rabbits; they can be kept off later crops using bird netting. You may notice aphids, particularly in spring when I find that extra watering is the best remedy. Aphids can infect parsley with virus, which becomes obvious when the leaves of overwintered plants turn bright yellow in spring. Twist out any plants showing symptoms and compost them.

Harvesting

Twist or cut the stalks of the largest lower leaves close to the main stem. The smaller central leaves will grow for repeat harvests over many months. Remove and compost any yellowing older leaves. Growth is slow through winter, so grow a plant or two under cover to pick through cold weather.

Saving seed

Collect dry seed from overwintered plants in late summer, where at least six plants have been grown for cross pollination. Curled and flat-leaved varieties will hybridize, therefore save seed where you are growing only a single type.

VARIETIES

There are many varieties, most of which only have small differences in growth and appearance.

'Italian Giant' A flat-leaf variety that lives up to its name, although leaf size decreases as plants age.

'Lisette' An attractive curled parsley, with a bushy habit and light green leaves.

KEY INFORMATION

Seed to harvest: 10 weeks early sowings, 8 weeks summer sowings   **Sowing to transplanting:** 5–6 weeks
Position: Prefers sun but tolerates shade   **Spacing:** 15–20cm (6–8in)   **Hardiness:** Hardy to about -8°C (18°F)

	JAN	FEB	MAR	APR	MAY	JUN	JUL	AUG	SEP	OCT	NOV	DEC
Sowing			▬	▬	▬	▬	▬					
Transplanting					▬	▬	▬	▬				
Harvesting				▬	▬	▬	▬	▬	▬	▬	▬	

BEET FAMILY

Beetroot

Chard

Spinach

Pick outer spinach leaves with their stems to keep plants tidy and productive for longer.

These hardy plants are easy to grow, and can give you food over a long period from just a few sowings. Sow spinach either in very early spring, or in late summer to enjoy healthy harvests through autumn, before plants overwinter and then regrow for valuable pickings during spring's hungry gap. Beetroot is delicious fresh and stores beautifully, so that you can have it available to eat for ten months of the year. The colourful leaves and stems of beetroot and chard also add an attractive ornamental quality to your vegetable garden.

Choosing what to grow

Plants from the beet family remain medium-sized, which makes them easy to find space for in any garden. Chard and spinach are kept more compact when their outer leaves are picked regularly, and you do not need many plants to produce heavy harvests. All of these vegetables also make good follow-on second crops from summer sowings, and grow well when interplanted (see pp.66–70), which provides many opportunities to include them in your beds.

Homegrown vegetables from the beet family are packed with flavour at whatever stage they are picked. Beetroot remain tender and juicy when grown in no dig soil, even when they grow exceptionally large. These larger roots are ideal for storing over winter, because they retain moisture better than smaller beetroot. Fresh spinach leaves are always delicious, and develop an amazing sweetness when picked from overwintered plants after cold weather.

CROP		JAN	FEB	MAR	APR	MAY	JUN	JUL	AUG	SEP	OCT	NOV	DEC
Beetroot	Sow			▬	▬	▬	▬	▬	▬				
	Harvest						▬	▬	▬	▬	▬	▬	▬
Chard	Sow				▬	▬	▬	▬	░				
	Harvest			▬	▬	▬	▬		▬	▬			
	Harvest	░	░	░	░	░	░					░	░
Spinach	Sow			▬	▬				▬				
	Harvest	▬	▬	▬	▬	▬	▬			▬	▬	▬	▬

▬ Outdoors   ░ Under cover

Sowing, growing, and harvesting

The seeds of all three of these crops are large enough to handle easily and I find that multisowing them in modules works really well (see pp.78–79). They are all "multigerm" clustered seeds, which have the potential to produce more than one plant. These can be multisown, but with a seed or two less than normal. If the seed packet is labelled "monogerm", this tells you that the clusters have been separated into single seeds, of uniform size. Ideal timings for second sowings of beetroot, chard, and spinach are in June, July, and August respectively.

Leafy spinach and chard plants require regular watering during dry weather, but beetroot tolerates dry soil well and will produce sweeter roots if watered minimally. Keep plants tidy by removing any yellow or damaged leaves, to reduce pest problems and make picking easier. No dig methods make growing these vegetables straightforward because there is very little weeding to do, allowing you time to enjoy the frequent and bountiful harvests.

Careful picking using the right techniques will prolong the harvest period of all these vegetables and reduce the need for repeat sowings. Twist, rather than pull, the largest roots from multisown clumps of beetroot as you need them, and leave the rest to continue growing. This allows a single sowing to be harvested over a prolonged period of two to three months. Picking the largest outer leaves of spinach and chard repeatedly keeps plants productive for much longer than cutting across the top and waiting for plants to regrow.

Common problems

Few pest and disease problems affect the beet family, which really helps to make them easy to grow. It may be necessary to cover plants with mesh or bird netting in gardens where birds or rabbits are likely to cause damage. Slugs find spinach seedlings particularly attractive, but this is less of a problem in no dig beds,

Multisow vibrant chard into modules to raise many young plants in a small space.

provided that the growing space is kept tidy and there is no slug habitat nearby (see p.95). Leaf miner causes medium-sized yellow patches on leaves, where they have been sucked dry from the inside by feeding insect larvae. This can look dramatic, but I do not worry about it because the damage is only ever moderate. Cover plants with mesh to exclude the insects if you are concerned that leaf miner activity may affect plant growth. Bolting, where plants rush to flower before producing a crop, can affect all these crops, but is easily avoided by timing sowings carefully. Beetroot and chard will bolt if sown too early, so don't rush to start sowing in early spring and wait until mid-April for chard. Spinach naturally flowers in midsummer, so avoid trying to harvest at this time and make two sowings, one in early spring and another in summer, to provide pickings from autumn to late spring.

Large beds of spinach and beetroot feature prominently in late spring at Homecares.

BEETROOT

Beetroot growth is rapid, the flavour is sweet and earthy, plus they store easily so you can enjoy roots through winter. What's not to like? I recommend multisowing under cover to produce good germination and clusters of roots that can be harvested for two months or more from a single sowing, giving you ten months of eating (including stored roots) from just two sowings.

Sowing and transplanting

Sow under cover to aid germination and protect delicate seedlings from pests. The earliest sowings in February and March need warmth to germinate and are best kept in the house for five to seven days, in dark or light conditions, before moving the cold-tolerant seedlings into the greenhouse. 'Boltardy' and 'Pablo' F1 are good for the earliest sowings, because when exposed to low temperatures they are less inclined to bolt (run to seed). I don't sow other varieties until late March. The second period of sowing is June, for harvests through autumn and into early winter, with extra to store. Don't sow later than mid-July, because roots won't have time to swell.

Most beetroot seeds are multigerm clusters that can produce up to four seedlings, while single-seed monogerm varieties are available. Multisow three multigerm seeds, or five monogerm seeds, into each 3cm (1¼in)

module, aiming for four seedlings to transplant as a clump. Thin out the weaker seedlings in each module while they are small and add the thinnings to salads. After four to six weeks, use a dibber to make evenly spaced holes, 30–35cm (12–14in) apart, and transplant deep enough so that most of the stems are below soil level.

Care and protection

Early plantings grow faster with a covering of fleece for the first few weeks, supported on wire hoops if nights are frosty. This also prevents birds eating the young leaves, while you can cover later plantings with mesh or netting if birds, rabbits, or deer are potential pests. Leaf miner may cause translucent yellow blotches where insect larvae feed inside the leaves, but this rarely results in significant damage. Rats and mice enjoy beetroot, especially in autumn; if you see their teeth marks in the beets, they are still edible, but it's best to harvest straight away.

Water new transplants two or three times, then once plants are established there is no need to water for a month or more. Beetroot become sweeter in dry weather and only benefit from a little watering once roots have reached golf ball size.

Harvesting and storage

Harvest early sowings from June to August, and summer sowings from September to November, after which any remaining roots can be lifted to

Large roots remain tender in no dig soil.

Multisown clumps of beetroot 'Pablo' F1.

store. Pick the largest root from any multisown clump by grasping the base of the stems and twisting while easing the beet upwards. This leaves the smaller roots to develop and gives a harvest period of six weeks or more for sowings that mature in summer, and three months in autumn.

Lift the last roots in early to midwinter before night temperatures go below -4°C (25°F), to store in a box in a cool, dark shed until early spring. Twist off the leaves at harvest and leave a little soil on roots to hold moisture and reduce shrivelling; eat the small beets first as the larger ones keep for longer. In milder areas, leave beetroot in the ground during winter with a little new compost around them to protect from hard frost, but watch for rodent damage. Any roots still there in spring will sprout little leaves, which are pretty and delicious in a salad.

VARIETIES

Red unless stated.

'Boltardy' Ideal for the earliest sowings and resists bolting, but see Delve deeper, pp.50–51.

'Pablo' F1 Lovely globe-shaped beetroot, grows early.

'Jannis' Another good early variety.

'Burpees Golden' Sweet yellow flesh with a less earthy flavour than red beetroot.

'Cheltenham Green Top' Green leaves and long roots. Very hardy for winter use, when frost adds sweetness.

KEY INFORMATION

Seed to harvest: 13 weeks spring sowing, 10 weeks summer sowing **Sowing to transplanting:** 3–5 weeks
Position: Adaptable, tolerates shade **Spacing:** 30–35cm **Hardiness:** Hardy to approx. -4°C (25°F)
Suitable for multisowing, follow-on planting, interplanting

	JAN	FEB	MAR	APR	MAY	JUN	JUL	AUG	SEP	OCT	NOV	DEC
Sowing			███	███	███	███	███					
Transplanting				███	███	███	███	███				
Harvesting						███	███	███	███	███	███	███
Storage	███	███	███	███							███	███

CHARD

The contrast between chard's glossy leaves and vividly coloured stems looks amazing both in the garden and on the plate. It's easy to grow, but what sets it apart from most other plants is its sheer productivity – up to six months from a single sowing. Spinach beet is closely related to chard and grown in a similar way for a productive alternative to true spinach.

Sowing and transplanting

Don't be tempted to sow too early, to avoid the risk of plants bolting during summer. I make my first sowing under cover no earlier than mid-April. Pop single seeds into 3cm (1¼in) modules where they will produce two to three seedlings, as with beetroot. Either thin to one or two seedlings per module, for bigger leaves to cook, or multisow two seeds per module for harvests of smaller salad leaves. You can also sow directly into the ground in rows 30cm (12in) apart, spacing seeds 5cm (2in) apart. Thin direct-sown seedlings to leave 5cm (2in) between plants for salad chard and 15cm (6in) for larger leaves to cook.

Chard can be sown until July. Plants from later summer sowings stand a better chance of overwintering successfully outdoors. They won't be productive through cold winter weather and may be killed by frost, but those that survive will provide a useful spring harvest, until they flower in May. For a slow but steady under-cover crop through mild winters, sow chard from mid-August until early September, to transplant in a polytunnel or greenhouse in early autumn.

Transplant modules 22–30cm (8¾–12in) apart, using the wider spacing if you want to harvest larger leaves. Dib holes a little deeper than the root ball and pop the plants in so that their long stems are below the soil surface; this provides added shelter and stability while the plants establish.

Care and protection

Water after transplanting and, if the weather is dry, keep these leafy plants well watered. Slugs often chomp holes in the older leaves. Minimize damage by removing and composting

Pick only the outer leaves for regular harvests.

The vibrant stems of chard 'Rainbow'.

Tidy plants are healthy and quick to pick.

diseased and fading leaves from the outside of plants, so only healthy, vigorous leaves remain. Cover chard with bird netting or fine mesh if you find bird damage; at Homeacres sparrows often feast on the leaves.

Harvesting and storage

Pick multisown chard for salad when leaves and stalks reach 10cm (4in) tall. Allow single plants to reach over 30cm (12in) high before picking leaves for cooking. In summer, pick every few days for tender leaves and stalks, which can still be delicious when up to 50cm (20in) long while summer growth is fast, but stalks will gradually go stringy as they age. Winter leaves grown under cover do not grow large, but their bright colours are decorative in salads.

Pick by putting your thumb on top of the stalk and twisting it off the main stem at the base. Don't leave the stalk attached to the stem as these remnants will attract slugs. Pick the outer leaves, retaining those clustered at the centre to power new growth. Regrowth will be much slower if you cut across the top, to harvest all the leaves. Harvested chard keeps well in a cool, dark, moist environment, and will last for a week refrigerated in a polythene bag (see p.102).

VARIETIES

Swiss chard Vigorous with fat, white stems. Hardier than coloured varieties and very productive. Try 'White Silver' and 'Fordhook Giant'.

Ruby chard Striking red stalks contrast with glossy dark green leaves. Try 'Charlotte', 'Fantasy', or 'Peppermint' for pink stalks.

'Bright Yellow' Green leaves with vibrant yellow stalks and veins.

'Rainbow' and **'Bright Lights'** Attractive mixes of white, orange, yellow, and red chards. Thin out the white-stalked plants as they can be dominant.

Spinach beet (perpetual spinach) Thinner, mostly pale green stalks; a beet leaf with a flavour closer to true spinach and tender stalks. 'Lucullus' has a long harvest period and is resistant to bolting.

KEY INFORMATION　━━━ Outdoors　▬▬▬ Under cover

Seed to first harvest: 7–10 weeks　**Sowing to transplanting:** 3–4 weeks　**Position:** Any; tolerates shade
Spacing: 22–30cm (8¾–12in) equidistant or direct-sown in rows 30cm (12in) apart, with 5–15cm (2–6in) between plants　**Hardiness:** Will tolerate slight frost; plants hardy to -5°C (23°F)　**Suitable for multisowing and as a second follow-on crop**

	JAN	FEB	MAR	APR	MAY	JUN	JUL	AUG	SEP	OCT	NOV	DEC
Sowing					▬	▬	▬	▬				
Transplanting						▬	▬	▬	▬			
Harvesting			▬	▬		▬	▬	▬	▬	▬		
Harvesting	▬	▬	▬								▬	▬

SPINACH

Spinach (*Spinacia oleracea*) is an autumn, winter, and spring leaf with wonderful flavour and nutritional value, distinct from spinach beet (*Beta vulgaris* subsp. *cicla*) (see pp.208–210). One sowing can give eight months of harvest, because overwintering plants are incredibly hardy thanks to their production of sugars as antifreeze, which makes their leaves remarkably sweet. Don't try to replicate supermarket baby leaf spinach at home; instead, pick small leaves for salads, or let them grow larger for cooking, when they will still be tender and delicious. In healthy soil, spinach leaves can reach the size of a dinner plate.

Sowing and transplanting

Best avoid sowing spinach between mid-April and late July, because it flowers in early summer and will bolt rather than making leaf growth. I find that sowing in the second week of August (10th August at Homeacres) gives a large harvest from late September to November, and plants will overwinter to crop again in spring. Sowing anytime in August is suitable for plants to overwinter, but the later you leave it the smaller your autumn harvest will be. You can also sow in late winter or early spring, but do this as early as possible to maximize cropping before plants bolt. Make your last spring sowing by the end of March, or early April in cool areas.

Multisow 2–3 seeds into 3cm (1¼in) module cells under cover to produce clumps of two or three plants for salad leaves, or one plant for leaves to cook. Transplant two to three weeks after sowing in late summer, or four weeks after sowing in spring. Space 20–22cm (8–8¾in) apart each way, into holes dibbed 1cm (½in) deeper than the root ball. You can also sow directly in late March or in August, either in drills 20cm (8in) apart, or scatter seed thinly under summer crops like cordon tomatoes or cucumber. Spinach starts well as an understory plant, while the taller vegetables above finish cropping. If you sow direct, thin plants in drills to at least 10cm (4in) apart for larger leaves to pick for cooking, and half that for smaller salad leaves.

Multisown spinach seedlings.

Care and protection

Water new transplants and continue to water in dry weather until you see them grow strongly, which may be just five to seven days. Autumn spinach rarely needs further watering, but during spring it can be dry when plants are putting on growth, such that watering twice a week will pay off.

Although spinach is hardy to frost and wind, it is worth protecting new transplants with fleece or mesh in early spring, to speed growth and protect from pests. A mesh cover on overwintering plants will shield them from the worst of the weather and promote growth in late winter, as light levels increase.

Slugs are often an issue, so be sure to sow or plant into clear ground, with no slug habitats nearby. Leatherjackets can also damage early plantings, severing stems or even eating small plants entirely. Sift through the soil where the plant was and you can often find and dispose of the brown grub. Keep spare plants as replacements for up to two weeks after you transplant.

Harvesting and storage

Harvest spinach leaves small for salad or much larger for cooking. Exactly when to pick is your call, depending on the size you like. Pinch off leaves or use a knife if you prefer.

Picking spinach 'Medania' with its stalks.

I enjoy eating the stalks, but even if you don't, remove them to make the next picking easier and to prevent remaining stalks from rotting on the plant. Keeping plants tidy like this and removing any yellowing leaves helps to reduce slug problems.

Spinach's first leaves grow large, particularly in spring, then get smaller and more pointed with each passing week. Once you see a flower stalk in the centre of plants in early summer, you can keep picking for another week or so, but leaves will be small and thin. You cannot prevent flowering by pinching out the flower stalk, so twist out bolted plants and add them to your compost. Like most leaves, spinach will keep for up to five days in a polythene bag in the fridge (see p.102), but it is tastier and more nutritious when freshly picked.

VARIETIES

'Medania' My favourite for being so winter hardy and long-lived. Its large, soft leaves are also suitable for salad if picked smaller.

'Giant Winter' Makes big leaves in cool conditions, but I found it flowered early in spring, giving a shorter harvest, and a few plants bolted before winter.

'Missouri' F1 and **'Emilia' F1** Similar large, dark green leaves. Perhaps a little quicker to crop and more uniform than 'Medania', but the seeds are more expensive and you can't save your own.

SAVING SEED

Saving spinach seed is viable in a small garden, but you need at least three to six plants to provide a sufficient pool of genes. Stop picking plants in early May so that they become sizeable before flowering in early summer. Seed clusters develop on each stem and turn from green to pale brown during July, when plants should be twisted out and hung to dry under cover with good ventilation. Once the seed clusters feel dry, rub them off the stalks, clean by winnowing (see p.106), dry for a week in a sunny windowsill, and store in an envelope or jar. I've noticed that fresh spinach seeds don't germinate rapidly, and after storing for a year germination is as good or even better. My seed saved from 'Medania' has produced plants with darker green leaves that were slower to grow and bolt. This genetic variability is one facet of the fun you can have when saving seed.

KEY INFORMATION

Seed to first harvest: 6–7 weeks **Sowing to transplanting:** 2–4 weeks **Position:** Full sun or some shade, where slugs aren't too numerous **Spacing:** 20–22cm (8–8¾in) equidistant for multisown clumps, or direct-sown in rows 20cm (8in) apart, with 10cm (4in) between plants **Hardiness:** Hardy, down to -15°C (5°F) or lower **Suitable for multisowing and as a follow-on crop**

	JAN	FEB	MAR	APR	MAY	JUN	JUL	AUG	SEP	OCT	NOV	DEC
Sowing			▬	▬				▬				
Transplanting				▬					▬			
Harvesting					▬	▬	▬					
Harvesting	▬	▬	▬	▬					▬	▬	▬	▬

*An appetizing early autumn salad
mix containing lettuce, frisée and
escarole endive, sorrel, beetroot,
and two types of radicchio.*

LEAFY SALAD CROPS

LETTUCE FAMILY

Chichory / radicchio

Endive

Lettuce

BRASSICA FAMILY

Chinese cabbage

Mizuna and mustards

Pak choi

Rocket

WINTER SALADS

Corn salad

Land cress

Winter purslane

You can produce fresh leaves with an incredible range of colours and flavours at any time of year, by choosing wisely from the great diversity of vegetables that produce salad leaves. For best results, time sowings carefully to enjoy a long period of picking healthy leaves, and to avoid plants running to seed rapidly. Select vegetables that naturally grow strongly in the season when you want harvests and pick carefully to prolong the life of plants.

Choosing what to grow

I have divided leafy salad crops into three groups: the lettuce family, the brassica family, and winter salads. Understanding the common characteristics of the crops within each group, such as flowering time and susceptibility to particular pests, will help you to grow them successfully. For example, brassica salads flourish in autumn and winter, but quickly start to flower and suffer pest damage in spring and summer, when lettuce growth is lush and healthy. Be aware of this seasonal flow when planning what to grow, and ignore the long range of sowing dates on many seed packets.

It's possible to harvest crops belonging to the lettuce family almost year-round. Juicy lettuce leaves are abundant from spring to early autumn, but plants suffer more disease and become less productive through autumn, and their hearts are not frost hardy. Endive and chicory are both hardier – chicory especially so – and yield crisp, bitter leaves through autumn and into winter.

Salads from the brassica family produce the tastiest leaves throughout autumn, winter, and early spring. They include the attractive, vigorous and pungently flavoured oriental mustards, peppery rocket, and mild, crisp pak choi and Chinese cabbage.

Winter salad crops are also hardy enough to provide salad leaves through the coldest months. Mild-flavoured corn salad never grows large and survives exceptionally cold weather. Land cress grows quite quickly in milder winter

CROP		JAN	FEB	MAR	APR	MAY	JUN	JUL	AUG	SEP	OCT	NOV	DEC
LETTUCE FAMILY													
Chicory / radicchio	Sow						O	O					
	Harvest	O	O							O	O	O	O
Endive	Sow							O	O	U			
	Harvest	U	U	U	U				O	O	O	U	U
Lettuce	Sow		O	O	O	O	O	O	O	O			
	Harvest	O	O	O	O	O	O	O	O	O	O	U	U
BRASSICA FAMILY													
Chinese cabbage	Sow							O					
	Harvest										O		
Mizuna and mustards	Sow							O		U			
	Harvest	U								O	O	O	O
Pak choi	Sow							O					
	Harvest									O	O	O	
Rocket	Sow								O	O			
	Harvest (salad)			O					O	O	O	O	O
	Harvest (wild)			O	O	O	O	O					
WINTER SALADS													
Corn salad	Sow								O				
	Harvest	O	O	O							O	O	O
Land cress	Sow								O	U			
	Harvest	O	O	O	O						O	O	O
Winter purslane	Sow								O	O			
	Harvest	O	O	O	O						O	O	O

■ Outdoors   ▨ Under cover

---

weather, but has a strong flavour and is best used in small amounts. Winter purslane is less hardy, but worth growing in milder regions for its tender leaves.

Sowing, growing, and harvesting

Raise transplants under cover and have these fast-growing vegetables ready to plant as soon as other crops are finished, or even before that as interplants (see pp.70–71). Almost all salad vegetables can be picked regularly of outer

Transplant young pak choi into holes dibbed deep enough to bury the entire stem.

leaves, for a longer period of regular harvests compared to cutting. I harvest lettuce almost year-round from just four sowings, thanks to my leaf lettuce method of picking (see pp.224–226). Lettuce and other salad vegetables can also be grown for hearts, which need longer to mature and produce a single, larger harvest. Chinese cabbage, endive, and some varieties of chicory will make firm hearts in autumn, which blanches and sweetens the inner leaves and enables them to be stored in a cool place for several weeks.

All these salad plants are frost hardy and can survive winter outside, but often without putting on much new growth. Productivity and quality during winter can be increased by transplanting them under cover in early to mid-October, immediately after summer vegetables, such as tomatoes, are cleared.

Common problems

Tender salad leaves are a magnet for slugs and snails, which chew holes in leaves and destroy seedlings. Protect plants initially by raising them under cover, then reduce food sources and hiding places for molluscs by picking regularly and removing fading leaves. Rabbits can also decimate salad beds, but plantings can be protected at any stage with covers of mesh or bird netting.

Root aphids can damage lettuce badly in late summer. These small, sap-sucking insects feed unnoticed on roots; the most obvious sign of their presence is plants wilting suddenly and unexpectedly, especially in warm, dry weather. Endive and chicory are not affected, which makes them a good choice for autumn salads where root aphids occur. Lettuce can also be prone to downy mildew, especially later in the growing season and in damp conditions. This fungal disease causes patches of leaf to turn yellow, then brown, often with white, fuzzy growth underneath. To help prevent its spread, remove affected leaves and water plants less frequently, preferably early on a sunny day.

Lettuce 'Lollo Rossa', picked of its outer leaves, interplanted with spinach 'Medania'.

Brassica salad crops are prone to insect pests in late spring and summer, which is a good reason to wait until late summer to sow them. Protect plants under fine mesh where necessary. Flea beetles are little, black beetles which spring up when disturbed, and pepper young foliage with round holes. They spoil the appearance of crops, check the growth of plants, and can even kill seedlings. Cabbage root flies lay eggs at the base of plants and the resulting white maggots burrow down to feed on roots. This damage slows growth, results in sudden wilting when the weather is sunny, and may kill young transplants. Cabbage butterfly and moth caterpillars feed on the succulent leaves of pak choi and Chinese cabbage, often causing serious damage. Cover new tranplants with fine mesh immediately to prevent adult insects laying eggs.

CHICORY / RADICCHIO

Sow radicchio in summer, to transplant as a second planting after earlier crops, and harvest in autumn. Find good quality seeds and you can grow tight hearts of colourful, bittersweet leaves that are untroubled by most pests, and perfect in salads or gently cooked. Be wary of misleading seed packet descriptions. This profile covers raising Palla Rossa and Treviso radicchios in open ground during autumn, but you can also grow varieties specially bred for forcing chicons, and dig up their roots in early winter for forcing in any dark place.

Sowing and transplanting

Don't sow radicchio in spring or the plants will rush to flower. Sow from the second week of June to mid-July, opting for the earlier date in cool climates. The later in this window you sow, the greater the value of your late-autumn harvests, when there will be fewer fresh leaves around. Either sow thinly in a seed tray to prick out into 3cm (1¼in) modules, or sow two seeds per module and thin to one seedling.

Seedlings grow fast in summer and can be transplanted three weeks after sowing while still quite small. Where space isn't available, pot them on into 7cm (2¾in) pots, or interplant among a weed-free crop that's three to four weeks from harvest. Dib holes 30cm (12in) apart, and pop in plants with the module top below soil level, to help retain moisture, as it's often dry at planting time.

Care and protection

Water newly transplanted seedlings every couple of days in hot summer weather, until you see them growing strongly. Plants heart up in autumn when moisture isn't a problem, and carry on growing slowly in mild conditions until early winter.

The lovely thing about radicchio is that it has few problems with insect pests. Slugs will eat seedlings, but you can reduce potential damage by raising larger transplants in 5cm (2in) modules or 7cm (2¾in) pots. Keep rabbits off seedlings with bird netting or mesh – don't use fleece because the plants will get too hot. Plants withstand frost best when hearts are still loose. Protect firm hearts with fleece for a late harvest in winter, if you don't want to harvest and store them.

Harvesting and storage

The prime harvest time is September from early sowings to November from later sowings. Plants may stand the winter, but harvest before spring because in March they switch growth habit towards flowering, and leaves become bitter. To pick, slip a knife under the head and cut the main stem, then trim off a good number of the outer leaves. Each variety has a different habit; if it's not tight-hearting, the central leaves remain loose for a harvest containing many tough, bitter outer leaves.

A maturing Treviso radicchio.

Cutting a firm head of Palla Rossa radicchio '506TT'.

Left too long, the outer leaves of hearts can turn brown and rot – some varieties are more prone to this than others. Check plants regularly, and if you see a rotting heart, cut it immediately. A lovely heart can usually still be found inside the rotten outer leaves. After harvest, slide a trowel underneath old stems to remove them and prevent regrowth. Firm radicchio hearts can store for four to six weeks in a box kept in a shed below 10°C (50°F), where they will tolerate some frost. This is often a better option than leaving them in the ground during winter.

VARIETIES

BALL-SHAPED PALLA ROSSA TYPES

'506TT' My favourite Italian variety is less easily available in the UK post-Brexit, but it's worth seeking out for excellent red hearts.

'Marzatica' A red variety that performs well and hearts to a reasonable extent in autumn.

'Castelfranco' Pretty green leaves, speckled yellow and pink, which fold inwards rather than creating a tight heart. Some plants stand well through winter.

POINTED TREVISO TYPES

Select a variety suitable for growing outdoors as some are bred for forcing under cover.

'206TT' A reliable Italian variety, less easily available in the UK post-Brexit, that forms fat, conical hearts outdoors, with thick, juicy white stalks.

KEY INFORMATION

Seed to first harvest: 3 months **Sowing to transplanting:** 3–5 weeks **Position:** Prefers full sun, but will tolerate shade **Spacing:** 30cm (12in) equidistant for all types **Hardiness:** Hardy; young or looseleaf plants to -15°C (5°F), mature hearted plants to -5°C (23°F) **Suitable for follow-on planting and interplanting**

	JAN	FEB	MAR	APR	MAY	JUN	JUL	AUG	SEP	OCT	NOV	DEC
Sowing						▬						
Transplanting							▬▬					
Harvesting	▬▬▬								▬▬▬▬▬▬			

ENDIVE

Endive flowers in late spring, and is best sown in summer for abundant crops through autumn and into winter, when it resists mildew and root aphid. Choose from broad-leaved escarole and attractive frisée varieties with highly indented leaves. Endive is sometimes confused with closely related lettuce, and can be harvested in the same way for outer leaves or whole hearts. The difference is its bitter flavour, which is delicious countered with a slightly sweet dressing.

Sowing and transplanting

Sow from late June to early August for fast-growing seedlings to give harvests outdoors through autumn. If you have space to grow endive under cover through winter, sow in early September. Germination can be variable and I favour sowing into a small seed tray, to prick out seedlings individually into 3cm (1¼in) module cells. Other options are to sow two seeds per cell and thin to one, or make direct sowings thinly into rows 25cm (10in) apart, with seeds 5–10cm (2–4in) apart.

Summer-sown seedlings grow rapidly and are best transplanted after just three weeks. Endive is ideal to fill space after summer harvests of onions, summer cabbage, peas, and broad beans. Space planting holes 22cm (8¾in) apart each way for leaf harvests and 30cm (12in) apart to produce hearts. Drop plants in so that the top of the root ball sits below soil level, and water in.

Care and protection

Water generously during dry weather, because these leafy plants don't thrive in dry soil. Slugs cause only minor damage and rarely eat frisée varieties. Unlike lettuce, endive is not affected by root aphid in late summer. Rabbits and deer love endive, and bird netting is a better protection than mesh as it allows more of autumn's scarce light to pass through.

Blanching is a way to reduce the bitterness of leaves by depriving plants of light, but I enjoy the taste of endive when green, and

Freshly picked frisée and escarole endive.

firmly believe that bitter flavours are good for our health. It can also be difficult to blanch endive without at least some leaves rotting in darkness, or slugs going rampant, and I don't find it's worth the effort. If you want to blanch, cover each plant with a large pot for a maximum of one week, allowing reasonable space between the plant and cover, before harvesting the whole head of leaves.

Harvesting and storage

Harvest medium-sized, outer leaves individually from the base of plants. Place your thumb on top of a stalk and twist while gently pulling, to break it off near the main stem of the plant. Work your way round the outside of plants, always leaving a rosette of leaves at the centre, for rapid regrowth and a lovely succession of green leaves through autumn. Plants under cover will produce a few leaves over winter and many more as growth resumes in early spring.

Endive can also be left to heart up to give a single, large harvest of leaves anytime from late September to mid-November, depending on the sowing date. Cut the main stem just above soil level and trim off everything discoloured and rotting. Sometimes the leaves between the outermost and innermost leaves of hearting plants turn brown, but you can still harvest the finest heart leaves, with careful trimming. Hearts can stand for two weeks or more in reasonable condition, even in temperatures

Pick outer leaves regularly during autumn.

down to about -2°C (28°F), but harder frosts will damage the leaves. Endive leaves are drier than lettuce, which helps them to store well for up to a week in a polythene bag in the fridge (see p.102).

VARIETIES

FRISÉE

'**Wallone**' Strong growth and dark green, with plentiful leaves over a long period.

'**Pancalieri**' Prolific plants with deeply indented leaves. Seeds widely available in the UK.

ESCAROLE

'**Bubikopf**' and '**Diva**' Both have large, slightly ruffled, pale green leaves, softer in texture than frisée.

KEY INFORMATION　▬ Outdoors　▬ Under cover

Seed to harvest: 7–8 weeks for outer leaves, 11 weeks for hearts　**Sowing to transplanting:** 3 weeks
Position: Full sun is best, and they like moisture　**Spacing:** 22cm (8¾in) equidistant for outer leaves, 30cm (12in) for hearts, rows 25cm (10in) apart sown direct　**Hardiness:** Hardy to -10°C (14°F), although hearts damaged by lighter frosts　**Suitable as a follow-on crop**

	JAN	FEB	MAR	APR	MAY	JUN	JUL	AUG	SEP	OCT	NOV	DEC
Sowing						▬	▬	▬				
Transplanting							▬	▬	▬			
Harvesting	▬	▬	▬	▬	▬			▬	▬	▬	▬	▬

Use netting to protect a colourful lettuce crop from pests.

VEGETABLE AND HERB DIRECTORY

LETTUCE

I'm a lettuce fanatic and enjoy regular harvests from very few sowings. In temperate climates, its natural season of growth is spring to midsummer, but it will grow in low temperatures to crop year-round. My method of picking medium-sized leaves rather than whole heads extends the harvest period from each sowing, reduces pest and disease problems, and makes lettuce the most productive vegetable I grow. A huge range of varieties is available; harvesting Batavian and cos types (see below) as leaf lettuce makes for a salad with an enticing mix of colour and texture.

Sowing and transplanting

Sow from mid-February to mid-September in modules under cover. Within that period I recommend just four sowing times for year-round harvests of leaf lettuce: late February to early March, for harvests mid-spring through to midsummer; late-May to early June, to pick from midsummer into early autumn; mid-July for leaves from September until the first notable frosts; and early September to transplant under cover to pick from November to April. Sow more frequently for a steady supply of heading lettuce.

Either sow in a seed tray and prick seedlings into 3cm (1¼in) modules, or sow two seeds into each module and thin to one seedling. Picking is easier from single plants than from a clump. Sow a mixture of varieties for different colours and textures. Lettuce seeds need some light to germinate, so rather than covering them with compost, scatter lightly with perlite or vermiculite, or cover the seed tray with glass, to keep seeds moist while they germinate. Keep the February sowing in the house because nights are cold. Although lettuce has a reputation for failing to germinate at high temperatures, summer sowings grow well in the greenhouse when kept out of direct sunlight for the first week.

Seedlings grow fast and can be transplanted just four weeks after early sowings and three weeks after summer sowings. Dib holes 22cm (8¾in) apart for leaf lettuce or 30cm (12in) apart for hearting lettuce, and set the top of the root ball 1cm (½in) below soil level to retain moisture and ensure sturdy stems. Lettuce also thrives in wide, shallow boxes. For winter harvests, transplant a September sowing into boxes on staging under cover, rather than a windowsill with low light levels.

Lettuce can also be grown from direct sowings. Sow thinly into moist soil or containers, from mid-March to early August, for quick cut-and-come-again crops of small leaves. Or thin plants to 22cm (8¾in) for leaf picking, and 30cm (12in) for hearts.

Cover sowings with glass to aid germination.

Picking outer leaves gives harvests over a long period.

Care and protection

Water straight after transplanting and again a couple of days later, then water only in hot weather, when a good soak every two or three days is beneficial and plants in pots should be checked daily. Water in the morning to avoid wet leaves overnight, as this reduces damage from slugs and downy mildew. In winter, I hardly water lettuce in my polytunnels to keep the soil surface and leaves dry, which reduces slug numbers and fungal disease.

Cover early spring plantings with fleece for warmth and protection from pests like rabbits and birds. From May onwards, exclude these pests using cooler netting, thermacrop, or mesh. Reduce slug habitat by keeping nearby beds tidy and removing rotting wooden sides of beds. Other soil pests, like leatherjackets or wireworms, can cut young plants at the base, especially in spring. Find and remove them by rummaging in soil under the affected plant. Keep a few transplants in reserve, especially in spring, to replace any losses.

Lettuce root aphids feed mostly in late summer, sometimes causing plants to wilt quickly and dramatically. Remove affected plants to compost. To help combat root aphids, keep soil moist and add an annual compost mulch to retain soil moisture in summer.

Picking leaf lettuce regularly prevents downy mildew, which affects mainly older leaves. When daylight levels decrease rapidly in October and growth slows, leaves become more prone to downy mildew, especially in damp weather. Escarole endives are a more reliable autumn harvest (see pp.220–221).

Harvesting and storage

Harvests in spring and summer are larger and healthier than those in autumn. Pick larger outer leaves at least weekly, leaving the baby central leaves to grow on. This enables plants to "stay young" and produce new leaves for ten weeks, or even for six months from an autumn sowing, until eventually a flower head forms and leaves become smaller and bitter.

It is possible to save lettuce seed from a single plant, and you could save seed from two neighbouring plants of different varieties, because they don't cross pollinate. It can be difficult to gather dry seed from a spring sowing in the UK, because seeds ripen as late as September. An alternative is to sow in early September and overwinter seedlings under cover to plant out in spring, for plants that flower and set seed in late summer. Select your strongest plant and stake the 75cm- (30in-) tall flowering stem. About two weeks after you see the head of yellow, tufted flowers, twist out the plant and hang it up to dry. A month later, rub out the seeds from the many dry tufts.

Lettuce 'Winter Density' (top) and 'Lollo Rossa', interplanted with spinach (above).

Begin to harvest when the outer leaves of plants spaced 22cm (8¾in) apart start touching their neighbours. To pick, place your thumb over a leaf stalk close to the main stem and push down with a slight rotation to detach the leaf cleanly with its stalk attached. Do this carefully on a first pick when plants and roots are especially delicate. Remove any damaged or discoloured lower leaves and keep the stem tidy, so that it starts to resemble a little tree trunk as the plant grows upwards. Pick leaves every few days and at least once a week, whether or not you need the leaves, because unpicked plants will go to flower more quickly.

From May to September, lettuce plants easily grow one new leaf a day, and they all need picking before they start to decay and attract slugs. Establishing how often and how hard to pick takes practice. If too many small leaves are removed from the centre, plants take longer to regrow; but take advantage of this if you're going away for a week or two in summer and pick plants heavily before you go so that they are just ready to pick on your return. Wash harvested leaves, shake out excess moisture, and they will keep in a polythene bag in the fridge for a few days (see p.102). Lettuce stalks brown at the tip after a day or two, but they are still good to eat.

Cut heads of lettuce when the central leaves fold in and turn paler. Start to harvest heads before they're too tight, because they lose quality after about two weeks and begin to turn bitter as they rise towards flowering. Harvested heads can also be kept in the fridge so that leaves can be removed as required. Always harvest cut-and-come-again lettuce above the smallest leaf, otherwise the plant won't regrow. It's usually possible to make two or three cuts per sowing.

VARIETIES

COS TYPES

Easy to pick as leaf lettuce with an upright growth habit. They also make fine, sweet hearts.

'Valmaine', **'Parris Island Cos'** Both are quite large and give plentiful dark green leaves over a long period.

'Little Gem', **'Maureen'** Smaller cos varieties normally grown for heads, that also give many harvests when picked of outer leaves.

'Winter Density' Reliably forms a nice green heart or very productive picked for leaves.

'Bijou' Slower growing with attractive dark red leaves and a slightly bitter flavour. More prone to mildew.

'Rosedale' Crunchy leaves with a blush of pink colour.

BATAVIAN TYPES

Long-lived plants whose leaves are slightly firmer and crunchier than cos types.

'Grenoble Red' ('Rouge Grenobloise') Originates from the Alps and is hardy, especially over winter in a polytunnel where it can crop from November to late May.

'Maravilla de Verano' At its best in summer, when it crops for a very long period before flowering. Leaves are sweet and a good size.

BUTTERHEAD TYPES

Usually grown for their heads of soft, buttery, rounded leaves.

'Marvel of Four Seasons' This excellent hardy variety has bronzed, light green leaves and can be picked for leaf lettuce and sown for overwintering.

'Humil' Pale green and has super-soft leaves.

ICEBERG OR CRISPHEAD TYPES

Form tight heads of crisp, pale green leaves and cannot be grown as leaf lettuce. They need a warm summer.

'Webbs Wonderful' and **'Lakeland'** Both have softer, thicker leaves than supermarket iceberg heads.

LOOSE-LEAF TYPES

Never form a heart and can be picked as leaf lettuce or a cut-and-come-again crop.

'Lollo Rossa' and **'Lollo Bionda'** Frilled, deep red and light green leaves respectively add colour and texture to salads.

'Navara' Rich red, glossy leaves with some resistance to root aphid.

'Red Salad Bowl' and **'Green Salad Bowl'** Widely available oak leaf varieties that often run to seed quickly and are best avoided.

KEY INFORMATION　▬ Outdoors　▬ Under cover

EARLY VARIETIES

Seed to first harvest: 6 weeks for leaf lettuce, 10–12 weeks for hearts, 4–5 weeks for cut-and-come-again
Sowing to transplanting 3–4 weeks　**Position:** Full sun or light shade; full sun in winter　**Spacing:** Leaf lettuce, 22cm (8¾in) equidistant. Hearting lettuce, 30cm (12in). Cut-and-come-again, rows 15–22cm (6–8¾in) apart
Hardiness: Hardy, but don't thrive in regular frost. To -7°C (19°F) in a polytunnel　**Suitable for interplanting and saving seed**

	JAN	FEB	MAR	APR	MAY	JUN	JUL	AUG	SEP	OCT	NOV	DEC
Sowing (modules)		▬	▬	▬	▬	▬	▬	▬				
Sowing (direct)			▬	▬	▬	▬	▬	▬				
Transplanting			▬	▬	▬	▬	▬	▬	▬	▬		
Harvesting	▬	▬	▬	▬	▬	▬	▬	▬	▬	▬	▬	▬

Mix lettuce varieties with endive and radicchio for diverse colours and textures.

CHINESE CABBAGE

Chinese cabbage has a mild flavour and tender texture, perfect for stir-fries, salads, or roasting. It is also fast-growing, capable of withstanding some frost, and will store for up to a month. Unfortunately, caterpillars and other insects also have a taste for the puckered, pale green leaves, and the difficultly of growing plants to maturity with tight hearts free of caterpillar holes should not be underestimated.

Sowing and transplanting

Like other salads from the brassica family, Chinese cabbage is a crop for the second half of the year, best-suited to sowing in late July. They naturally rise to flower in late spring or early summer, which leaves spring sowings little opportunity to develop hearts before they start to bolt.

For insect protection, raise plants under cover by either sowing into a seed tray to prick out into modules, or sow two seeds in each 3cm (1¼in) module and thin to the strongest seedling. Growth is so fast that seedlings can be transplanted from 15 to 21 days old; don't leave plants in modules for any longer. Space plants 30cm (12in) apart each way, and up to 35cm (14in) apart to produce larger hearts. Dib holes and transplant so that the top of the module is 5cm (2in) below the soil, to support the tall stems. Protect plants with a fine mesh cover as soon as they are in the ground, to exclude as many insect pests as possible.

Care and protection

Continue to cover plants with fine mesh until harvest to provide as much protection as possible from pests, but even then, check plants and remove any caterpillars you see. Where slugs are numerous, remove and compost the older, outer leaves as they start to yellow, since this is where most slugs will hide. Twist each leaf off gently while holding the centre of the plant where the heart leaves are forming, so as not to disturb the shallow roots. This creates space for dry air to circulate around each plant, where otherwise there can be a mass of rotting leaves by October.

In late summer, new transplants need watering every two or three days in dry weather. Even once established, fast-growing Chinese cabbage plants are thirsty and benefit from a good soak twice a week, unless rainfall is plentiful. Water less as autumn advances.

Harvesting and storage

The size and tightness of the heart at the centre of each plant will vary according to the variety. Plants usually mature in October when there is a short window of about two weeks to harvest hearts in good condition, before the outer

A 24-day-old Chinese cabbage ready to transplant.

Cutting a head of Chinese cabbage 'Michihili'.

leaves start to discolour and decay. Plants are hardy, but frost can spoil mature heads by blowing them open, so harvest before the weather turns too cold. Cut through the main stem, just below the lowest leaves that you want to keep. Twist the remaining stem and roots from the soil to compost. I have tried growing Chinese cabbage to harvest by picking off the outer leaves individually, but it didn't work well and is best grown as a hearting plant.

Tight hearts, harvested in their prime, hold moisture well and can be stored in a cool shed for up to a month. Remove any loose outer leaves and check for slugs before storing.

VARIETIES

'Blues' F1 A standard short, fat, barrel-shaped variety that stands reasonably well.

'Michihili' This taller variety produces pointed hearts, 45cm (18in) high, which risk both flowering and blowing over.

'Sat 36' Compact, cylindrical heads that can reach 1.3kg (3lb) in weight.

'Granat' Sow July to early August for long, slender heads. Not suitable for storage.

KEY INFORMATION

Seed to first harvest: 10 weeks   **Sowing to transplanting:** 2–3 weeks   **Position:** Full sun for fewer slugs
Spacing: 30–35cm (12–14in)   **Hardiness:** Hardy; non-headed plants -10°C (14°F), headed plants -4°C (25°F)
Suitable as a second follow-on crop

	JAN	FEB	MAR	APR	MAY	JUN	JUL	AUG	SEP	OCT	NOV	DEC
Sowing							▬					
Transplanting								▬▬				
Harvesting										▬▬▬▬▬		

Picking individual leaves from mustards 'Green Frills' and 'Red Frills' in early autumn.

MIZUNA AND MUSTARDS

These attractive, cold tolerant crops from the brassica family put on tender new growth in cool conditions, for fantastic autumn and winter harvests. Best sown in late summer, they can also be sown very early in spring, for a short cropping period before they flower in late spring and early summer. Mizuna has mild flavour while mustard leaves are pungent, especially from older plants. Pick or cut them small for salad leaves, or let mustards grow larger for cooking in stir-fries.

Sowing and transplanting

Sow in early August, or late July in cooler climates, for leaves to harvest through autumn, winter, and into early spring. Winter harvests are small from plants outside, and if possible I recommend making another sowing in mid-September to grow under cover. Plus you can sow under cover in mid-February to mid-March, to plant outdoors for a few spring harvests.

Either sow directly into the soil, in drills 20cm (8in) apart, or multisow three seeds in 3cm (1¼in) modules to raise plants under cover. Direct sowing works well if you want to grow a thick sward of leaves to cut small for salad; mizuna is more suitable for cutting than mustards, because each plant grows many smaller leaves rather than few large ones. Multisowing to give two plants per module results in larger leaves to pick individually. This uses less seed and plants live for longer.

In late summer, water the bed before transplanting if it is dry after harvesting the previous vegetable crop. Transplant when young, from two to three weeks after sowing, dibbing holes deep enough to bury the seedlings' long stems. Space modules 20–22cm (8–8¾in) apart, whether they contain one or three plants in the module – clusters of plants just produce smaller leaves. Thin seedlings in direct-sown rows to 2.5cm (1in) apart for salad leaves or 10cm (4in) apart for large leaves.

Transplant mustard seedlings small.

Care and protection

Growing mizuna and mustards in the latter part of the year avoids problems with many of the insect pests that affect brassicas, but a mesh cover is worthwhile for about three weeks after transplanting and five weeks after sowing, to protect the tender young plants. Cover spring transplants with fleece to give warmth and protection from the weather, as well as to keep off rabbits and pigeons. Slug damage is a common problem, particularly on juicy mizuna leaves, so it may be worth growing more mustards in slug-prone spots. Water transplants in and continue to water if the weather is dry. Although moisture-loving, plants are unlikely to need further watering

Mustard 'Red Frills' has richly coloured leaves.

during cool autumn weather. The flavour of mustards becomes hotter in dry conditions and watering dilutes this if you prefer a milder taste. Plants under cover need regular watering, but I find that once weekly, and less in midwinter, is enough through winter for plants in my polytunnel.

Harvesting and storage

Leaves can either be picked individually from plants or harvested as a cut-and-come-again crop. If you choose to cut, do it above the smallest leaf at the centre of each plant so they can regrow. It's a quick and easy harvest, but the total yield will be smaller and over a shorter period, because plants will regrow only two or three times. I prefer to spend a bit more time picking leaf-by-leaf, little and often, as this extends the life of the plants. Pick when leaves

reach your preferred size, at the base of the stalk, either between thumb and forefinger, with scissors, or a knife, while taking care not rock the plants and damage their fragile roots. Mustard leaves are agreeable to eat raw when small, but grow more pungent as their size increases and plants age. The stalks are best picked even if you want to eat leaves only, to prevent them rotting on the plant.

Leaves will keep for five days in the fridge, kept moist in a polythene bag (see p.102).

VARIETIES

MIZUNA

Seed is usually sold under its generic name and this is what I recommend you grow.

MIBUNA

Similar to mizuna, but with slender, smooth-edged leaves and less green on each stalk.

MUSTARDS

'Red Frills' and **'Green Frills'** Ideal for salads. Elegant, finely divided leaves in rich burgundy or vibrant green (sometimes called 'Red Lace' and 'Green Streaks').

'Red Giant' Puckered, rounded, red leaves have a strong flavour and suit stir-fries.

'Pizzo' Broad, green, frilly leaves, lovely for cooking.

'Red Dragon' Pretty and can be picked small for salad or large for cooking.

KEY INFORMATION ▬ Outdoors ▬ Under cover ▭ If mild

Seed to first harvest: 5–6 weeks **Sowing to transplanting:** 2–3 weeks **Position:** Cool, moist conditions. Grow well in some shade **Spacing:** 20–22cm (8–8¾in) equidistant or in rows 20cm (8in) apart
Hardiness: Fairly hardy; mizuna to -3°C (27°F) and mustard to -5°C (23°F) **Suitable for multisowing and as a second follow-on crop**

	JAN	FEB	MAR	APR	MAY	JUN	JUL	AUG	SEP	OCT	NOV	DEC
Sowing			▬	▬			▬	▬	▭			
Transplanting			▬	▬				▬	▬	▭		
Harvesting	▭	▭	▭	▬	▬				▬	▬	▬	▭
Harvesting	▭	▭	▭	▭	▭					▭	▭	▭

PAK CHOI

Fast-growing and highly productive, pak choi is an attractive proposition, but pest problems can make it one of the most difficult vegetables to grow well. The best harvests are in autumn, when plants thrive in lower temperatures and benefit from the presence of fewer insects. Nonetheless your plants will have more holes than pak choi on supermarket shelves, but will certainly boast more flavour and crunch.

Sowing and transplanting

By far the best option is to sow in early August, when there will be fewer caterpillars and flea beetles, which plague pak choi during summer. Sowing in mid-February can also give a brief harvest in early spring, until plants rise to flower. Always sow under cover, either three seeds in a 3cm (1¼in) module, or a few seeds in a little seed tray, to prick out into modules within five days of sowing, at the two-leaf stage (see p.83).

Transplant pak choi at just two, or a maximum of three, weeks old, because they grow so fast. Dib holes 20–25cm (8–10in) apart, deep enough to bury the long, spindly stems. You can grow multisown plants at a 25cm (10in) spacing, with two or three in a clump for smaller heads.

Care and protection

Watering is particularly important in dry weather, because pak choi is so fast-growing and full of water. The beauty of growing them in autumn is that it rains more, and usually less watering is required than in spring. To reduce slug damage, water in the morning so that most leaves are dry before nightfall.

Protect spring crops from cold weather and pests with a covering of fleece. In late summer, cover pak choi with fine mesh supported on hoops immediately after transplanting to keep out flea beetles, thrips, pigeons, and egg-laying butterflies. The first month is critical and after

Mature pak choi in early autumn with winter radish.

that plants toughen up and suffer less pest damage: it may then be possible to take the mesh cover off, but you have to judge for your own garden. Remove any yellow or rotting lower leaves as plants mature, to keep the bed tidy and reduce habitat for slugs.

Harvesting and storage

There are two ways to harvest pak choi, which will be ready once the leaves of neighbouring plants are close to touching each other. The first is to cut the outer leaves from plants regularly and allow younger leaves to continue growing. This needs care and works best if you hold the centre of the plant while cutting the outer leaves, because the roots are fragile and easily disturbed. Alternatively, harvest a whole plant by cutting through the base of its main stem. This works nicely for multisown clumps,

Harvesting a whole pak choi 'Karaoke' F1.

because the biggest one can be cut first, leaving the others to grow on. In autumn, a few plants from August sowings may flower, but most will carry on growing into November, until frost damages plants. Plants don't stand for as long in spring, and all need to be harvested before flower stems develop.

The watery leaves of pak choi don't store well, but you can keep them in a polythene bag in the fridge for a few days (see p.102).

VARIETIES

'Joi Choi' F1 The main variety for me, which forms large, handsome plants with thick white stems and dark green leaves.

'Karaoke' F1 Another good variety with white stems and dark green leaves.

'Canton White' Has a squat habit and nicely curled, fat stalks with pale green leaves.

KEY INFORMATION

Seed to first harvest: 6 weeks   **Sowing to transplanting:** 2–3 weeks   **Position:** Full sun or shade, but beware of slugs   **Spacing:** 20–25cm (8–10in) equidistant   **Hardiness:** Hardy down to about -3°C (27°F), but mature plants go soft if they freeze   **Suitable for multisowing and as a second follow-on crop**

	JAN	FEB	MAR	APR	MAY	JUN	JUL	AUG	SEP	OCT	NOV	DEC
Sowing		▬					▬▬	▬				
Transplanting			▬					▬▬				
Harvesting				▬▬	▬				▬▬	▬▬		

ROCKET

The name rocket is used for two quite different plants: large-leaved salad rocket (arugula) and wild rocket, with its slimmer, serrated leaves. Both have a peppery flavour, especially wild rocket, which means you don't need many leaves to pep up a salad and a few plants go a long way. Salad rocket is productive through autumn and winter, while wild rocket grows most leaves through spring and into June. Grow both types for a long period of harvest.

Sowing and transplanting

Although rocket can be sown directly outdoors, the seedlings are so vulnerable to damage by slugs, flea beetles, and caterpillars that I recommend sowing in 3cm (1¼in) modules under cover. Multisowing three seeds of salad rocket per cell gives clumps of two or three plants that yield numerous mid-sized leaves, rather than fewer large ones from single plants. Wild rocket has tiny seeds that are difficult to multisow, so I sow into a small seed tray and prick out the seedlings singly into modules.

Sowing both types of rocket in late summer gives a much longer period of harvest, with significantly less flea beetle damage than spring sowings, which rush to flower soon after they are ready to pick. Early August is my top time to sow salad rocket, but it can be sown for growing outdoors until early September. Salad rocket can also be grown under cover in a greenhouse or polytunnel from a mid-September sowing, for a long and generous winter harvest. Transplant salad rocket two to three weeks after sowing. Dib a hole deep enough to pop plants in with their long stems below ground level.

For the best harvest of wild rocket, I keep young plants under cover in 7–9cm (2¾–3½in) pots during late autumn and winter when, unlike salad rocket, it doesn't produce many leaves. It's then transplanted outdoors very early in spring, using a trowel to make a straight-sided planting hole, when the sturdy plants with strong roots grow rapidly.

Care and protection

Both rockets are prolific in moist conditions, so water regularly in dry weather. Plants are susceptible to brassica pests, most notably flea beetles, which eat the same tender leaves that we want. Cover beds with fine mesh after transplanting, and keep wild rocket protected until it finishes cropping in summer. Mesh will also protect plants from pigeons. Both types of rocket are hardy, although even salad rocket will not grow much through winter when planted outdoors.

Salad rocket has large, lobed leaves.

Use mesh to protect wild rocket from pests.

Harvesting and storage

My favourite harvest is the first flush of tender leaves; in September from salad rocket, and in April for wild rocket. Later harvests have a more pungent flavour.

As soon as salad rocket plants are touching their neighbours, start to pick the outer leaves every few days. Remove any yellowing leaves at the same time, to keep plants tidy, reduce pests, and make subsequent picking quicker. Return to pick from the same plants every few days in early autumn when growth is rapid, then reduce the frequency of picking as the weather cools and days darken. Plants that survive winter will flower in spring.

Either pick the thin leaves of wild rocket individually, or cut the leaves from a whole plant with a knife, above the level where you see the tiniest leaves developing. This allows regrowth for another cut in two to three weeks, becoming weekly through May and June. Pick or cut off flowering stems to prolong the harvest. Leaves are best eaten freshly picked, or will keep for only a few days in a polythene bag in the fridge (see p.102).

VARIETIES

Some named varieties are available, but both generic salad rocket and wild rocket yield lovely leaves.

SALAD ROCKET

'Apollo' Larger, more rounded leaves compared to the serrated edges of normal salad rocket.

WILD ROCKET

'Athena' Strong leaf growth over a long period.

KEY INFORMATION ▬▬ Outdoors   ▬▬ Under cover   ⸱⸱⸱⸱⸱ If mild

SALAD ROCKET

Seed to first harvest: 4–5 weeks   **Sowing to transplanting:** 2–3 weeks   **Position:** Moist soil in full sun or some shade   **Spacing:** 22cm (8¾in) equidistant   **Hardiness:** Hardy to at least -6°C (21°F)   **Suitable as a second follow-on crop**

	JAN	FEB	MAR	APR	MAY	JUN	JUL	AUG	SEP	OCT	NOV	DEC
Sowing								▬▬	▬			
Transplanting								▬▬		▬		
Harvesting		⸱⸱⸱	⸱⸱⸱	⸱⸱⸱					▬	▬	▬	▬
Harvesting	▬	▬	▬	▬							▬	▬

WILD ROCKET

Seed to first harvest: 10–30 weeks   **Sowing to transplanting:** Up to 6 months   **Position:** Moist soil in full sun or some shade   **Spacing:** 22cm (8¾in) equidistant   **Hardiness:** Hardy to at least -6°C (21°F)   **Suitable as a second follow-on crop**

	JAN	FEB	MAR	APR	MAY	JUN	JUL	AUG	SEP	OCT	NOV	DEC
Sowing									▬			
Transplanting		▬	▬									
Harvesting				▬	▬	▬	▬					

CORN SALAD

Also known as lamb's lettuce or mâche, corn salad is amazingly frost hardy and easy to grow. The soft, slightly waxy leaves have a nutty flavour that is milder than other winter salads. Grow a good number of plants to see you through winter, as the harvests per plant are small.

Sowing and transplanting

I recommend sowing in early September for valuable leaves to harvest through winter. You can also sow in late August for autumn harvests. I avoid spring sowings, as they only occasionally thrive when the weather stays cool and wet.

Direct sowing is viable, because seed is fairly cheap and big enough to sow evenly. Space rows 15cm (6in) apart, sow seeds every 1–2cm ($^1/_2$–$^3/_4$in), and thin to 7–10cm ($2^3/_4$–4in) apart. You can also sow two or three seeds per 3cm ($1^1/_4$in) module under cover. Seeds need constant moisture and take at least a week to appear. Transplant after four weeks, 10cm (4in) apart, setting the root balls only a little below soil level.

Care and protection

Corn salad is mostly ignored by pests, which makes it easy to grow. It's tough enough to stand outside all winter, but can be protected with fleece during really cold spells. Powdery mildew affects August-sown plants during autumn if the soil is dry; keep plants well watered and sow in early September to avoid this problem.

Clusters of new shoots in April after cutting the main head in February.

Harvesting and storage

From mid-October, cut a whole plant at the base with a knife, for a one-off harvest. Alternatively, cut a bit higher to pick the central leaves and return about a month later for a smaller second harvest of sideshoots. There is little growth over winter, but plants produce new spring leaves, before rising to flower from mid-April.

VARIETIES

There are only small differences between varieties.

'Vit' and **'Verte de Cambrai'** Both widely available and worth trying.

KEY INFORMATION

Seed to harvest: 2–4 months **Sowing to transplanting:** 4 weeks **Position:** Adaptable; full sun or part shade
Spacing: 10cm (4in) equidistant **Hardiness:** Very hardy to approx. -10°C (14°F) **Suitable as a follow-on crop**

	JAN	FEB	MAR	APR	MAY	JUN	JUL	AUG	SEP	OCT	NOV	DEC
Sowing								▬				
Transplanting									▬			
Harvesting	▬▬▬▬	▬▬▬▬	▬▬▬▬	▬▬▬						▬▬	▬▬▬	▬▬

LAND CRESS

Also called American land cress, this incredibly hardy winter salad tastes like watercress, but is spicier and more pungent. Grow it outside in temperate climates, for small pickings from late autumn until mid-spring, or under cover for abundant larger leaves, even in cold conditions.

Land cress has a powerful peppery flavour.

Sowing and transplanting

Sow in seed trays to prick out into 3cm (1¼in) modules, or two to three seeds per module and thin to the strongest plant. Sowings made under cover in August are ideal to follow on from summer crops, or sow directly into beds during early August. Sow by mid-September for plants to grow under cover through winter.

Transplant 22cm (8¾in) apart each way, to give plants space to produce larger leaves over a longer period. Pop plants into dibbed holes slightly deeper than their modules.

Care and protection

Water new transplants until they show new growth and after that outdoor-grown land cress is unlikely to need watering again. In my polytunnel, I water every two to three weeks through winter, or weekly if it's sunny.

Cover with bird netting or mesh during winter to keep out pigeons. Flea beetle damage in early spring will not set back established plants. Small slugs often hide under leaves, but rarely cause much damage.

Harvesting and storage

Once the leaves of neighbouring plants are touching, harvest through winter and early spring until plants flower in late April. Flower stalks are also edible, but plants self-seed if left too long. Twist larger leaves from the base of each plant, or gather leaves in one hand and cut through their stems. Ensure the smallest, central leaves are left to regrow for further harvests. Leaves are best picked fresh, but keep for a few days in cool, damp conditions.

VARIETIES

No cultivated varieties are available.

KEY INFORMATION ▬ Outdoors ▬ Under cover

Seed to harvest: 10 weeks **Sowing to transplanting:** 4–5 weeks **Position:** Full sun or shade **Spacing:** 20–22cm (8–8¾in) equidistant **Hardiness:** Very hardy to -15°C (5°F) or lower **Suitable as a follow-on crop**

	JAN	FEB	MAR	APR	MAY	JUN	JUL	AUG	SEP	OCT	NOV	DEC
Sowing								▬▬				
Transplanting									▬▬			
Harvesting	▬▬	▬▬	▬▬	▬▬	▬					▬	▬▬	▬▬
Harvesting	▬▬	▬▬	▬▬	▬▬	▬					▬	▬▬	▬▬

WINTER PURSLANE (*CLAYTONIA*)

Winter purslane is a prolific winter staple, hardy enough to grow outdoors in temperate climates. Plants provide repeat harvests of soft, mild leaves from November to April. It is also known as *Claytonia* and miners' lettuce, and is entirely different to summer purslane (*Portulaca oleracea*).

Sowing and transplanting

Sow under cover from mid-August to early September for outdoor harvests and until mid-September to grow under cover. Spring sowings are not productive, because plants flower in April. Sow the tiny seeds in a seed tray to prick out into 3cm (1¼in) modules, or into module cells to thin to one – and certainly no more than three – seedlings, for easier harvest. Barely cover the seeds with compost to aid germination. Transplant about four weeks after sowing, into equidistant holes dibbed 20cm (8in) apart; I often interplant between the last lettuce of autumn (see p.70). Finding space for direct sowings can be difficult in late summer, so it's useful to have transplants ready to follow autumn harvests.

Care and protection

New transplants need little attention, apart from initial watering, and are untroubled by pests. Plants are hardy, but moderate frosts cause brown discolouration on older leaves. Remove any stalks of white male flowers that appear during winter, because their flavour is poor.

Harvesting and storage

Harvest bushy plants from late autumn, by gently cutting above small developing leaves. The leaf stalks are good to eat, so cut as much of them as you can. Cut again within four weeks, depending on the temperature. Growth stops in midwinter, but restarts in February, as light levels and warmth increase. Remove plants by late April, to prevent self-seeding.

VARIETIES

Varieties of *Claytonia perfoliata* are not available.

Winter purslane has succulent, spade-shaped leaves.

KEY INFORMATION   ▬ Outdoors   ▒ Under cover

Seed to harvest: 10 weeks **Sowing to transplanting:** 4–5 weeks **Position:** Adaptable, will grow in shade
Spacing: 22cm (8¾in) equidistant **Hardiness:** Very hardy, to -10°C (14°F) **Suitable as a follow-on crop**

	JAN	FEB	MAR	APR	MAY	JUN	JUL	AUG	SEP	OCT	NOV	DEC
Sowing								▬▒				
Transplanting									▬▒			
Harvesting	▬	▬	▬								▬	▬
Harvesting	▒	▒	▒								▒	▒

SOLANUMS, BASIL, AND SWEETCORN

Aubergine

Sweet peppers and chillies

Basil

Potatoes

Sweetcorn

Tomatoes

Aubergine 'Black Pearl' F1 from my greenhouse,
where summer heat ripens fruit by July.

Plants in this group need summer warmth and are damaged or killed by frost. Many are best grown under cover, except in climates with hot summers. Choose varieties carefully for outdoor growing and don't sow or plant them too early. They are all exciting to grow; potatoes for their rapid growth and the joy of unearthing buried tubers, and the rest for their intense flavours that are highlights of the summer and early autumn garden.

Choosing what to grow

All of these vegetables thrive in no dig soil, and potatoes in particular produce heavy yields of tubers that are easy to harvest from the soft surface of no dig beds. In this group, potatoes yield the earliest crop, store most easily, and are ideal to grow while weeds are dying under a mulch of cardboard and compost, or plastic.

The flavour of homegrown tomatoes, sweetcorn, and freshly harvested new potatoes is remarkable, so no matter how small your garden, I recommend that you find space for at least a few! All except sweetcorn, chillies, and basil make large plants however, so be careful to avoid overcrowding when growing them under cover. Potatoes also need plenty of space, but it only takes three months to grow a crop of second earlies to lift and store, which leaves ample time for a follow-on crop.

Sowing, growing, and harvesting

Sow all except potatoes under cover in warmth, but not so early that your plants grow large and leggy before it's warm enough to transplant them, after the last frost. Seed potatoes can be planted directly outdoors earlier in spring

CROP		JAN	FEB	MAR	APR	MAY	JUN	JUL	AUG	SEP	OCT	NOV	DEC
Aubergine	Sow		▓▓▓	▓▓									
	Harvest								▓▓▓▓▓▓▓				
Sweet peppers and chillies	Sow		▓▓▓										
	Harvest							▓▓▓▓▓▓▓					
Basil	Sow				▓▓▓▓▓▓								
	Harvest						▓▓▓▓▓▓▓▓						
Potatoes (first earlies)	Sow			▓									
	Harvest						▓						
Potatoes (second earlies)	Sow				▓								
	Harvest							▓					
Potatoes (maincrop)	Sow				▓								
	Harvest								▓				
Sweetcorn	Sow				▓▓								
	Harvest									▓▓▓▓			
Tomatoes	Sow			▓									
	Harvest						▓▓▓▓▓▓▓						
	Harvest								▓▓▓				

▬▬ Outdoors   ▬▬ Under cover

because their first growth is underground, but their new shoots need to be protected from spring frosts with fleece.

It's easiest to grow aubergines, sweet peppers, and tomatoes in open soil where possible, but they also thrive in pots, given regular feeding and daily watering in summer.

Chillies and basil make more compact plants that are excellent for containers and will flourish in a sunny, sheltered position. Cordon tomatoes and aubergines need to be trained up tall supports, but this effort is worthwhile to make efficient use of space and produce healthy, high-yielding plants. It is important to water plants consistently once fruits and tubers are swelling.

Pick fruit and cobs when ripe, or before that to increase the productivity of capsicums. Know the signs of ripeness to look for, as these vary according to each crop and individual varieties, which can be different sizes, shapes, and colours when mature. Harvest no dig potatoes once you see the leafy tops begin to yellow, by pulling the stems rather than digging the tubers out. Pinch off the shoot tips of basil to use as required.

Second early potato 'Lily Rose' has unusual pink-fleshed tubers.

Common problems

Late blight is a disease that affects tomatoes and potatoes and can be a major issue during wet and dull summers. Periods of consistently high humidity with temperatures above 10ºC (50ºF) allow spores to infect plants with wet leaves and stems, and reproduce within just a few days. In most of the UK, these conditions are only likely to occur after the third week in June. Symptoms develop very quickly and affected plants turn brown, limp, and soft within just three days.

Aubergine plants grown under cover are prone to damage by red spider mites, which feed on their sap and cause pale mottling of foliage that can be difficult to notice at first. Significant damage may kill plants. Aphids suck sap from the leaves and stems of all these vegetables, but are a short-term problem in spring, which is brought under control when their natural predators, including ladybirds, arrive in early summer. Water directly onto leaves to knock aphids off plants and reduce damage. Slugs are mainly a concern where potatoes are left in the ground for too long before lifting, because they eat holes in tubers, which allow easy access for other pests and diseases, and mean that the crop can't be stored. Eelworms and other soil grubs may also damage tomato roots and potatoes, but rarely to a worrying extent. Ripe sweetcorn is a favourite food for badgers, rodents, and birds, which will sometimes eat cobs just before you plan to harvest. It's worthwhile picking cobs slightly underripe anywhere that there is a possibility of this happening.

Picking tomato 'Sungold' F1 from cordon plants trained up string supports in the polytunnel.

AUBERGINE

Aubergine plants demand warmth to grow well. In temperate climates where summer temperatures average around 21°C (70°F) in the afternoon, grow them under cover, or perhaps in a sunny and sheltered position outdoors. I don't notice a marked difference in flavour between homegrown and purchased aubergines, but the fruits look beautiful at all stages of development and the fancy varieties are fun to grow.

Sowing and transplanting

Sow aubergines under cover by the end of March, to give them the warmth and long growing season they need. Sow seed thinly in a small seed tray to prick out into 3cm (1¼in) module cells. Pot plants on into 7cm (2¾in) pots when about six weeks old or 5cm (2in) high, for good-sized plants to transplant in mid-May, or after the last frost date if planting outdoors.

Transplant in open ground 40–50cm (16–20in) apart, where more space gives a longer cropping season, or in large pots 30cm (12in) in diameter. Bury the stem by 5cm (2in), because plants are often drawn up when raised

together in small pots. Plants under cover can be grown as bushes or trained as cordons with two stems. To support cordon aubergines, place two knotted polythene strings in the bottom of the planting hole, slide the rootball in on top of them, and water each plant in. Tie the tops of the string to the greenhouse or polytunnel frame or wire, in a narrow v-shape.

Care and protection

Be careful not to overwater seedlings and young plants. Water more when fruits start swelling, but each plant's requirements will vary according to the weather and its size. Remove older, lower leaves as they naturally brown and die off.

To train a cordon plant with two stems, remove all sideshoots between the main stem and leaves until the plant reaches 30–35cm (12–14in) tall. Then leave a strong sideshoot near the top to become the second stem. Gently twist each stem around its supporting string as it grows, removing any sideshoots. Pinch off the first flower bud to channel the plant's energy into growth rather than fruiting. Grow outdoor plants without removing their sideshoots, to form a bush. Provide support by looping string around the outside of the plant, about halfway up, and tying it to a central cane, pushed into soil close to the main stem.

Remove the first flower to promote growth.

Using a knife to cut aubergine 'Black Pearl' F1.

Aubergines are prone to aphids and whitefly, mostly in late spring, but vigorous plants grown in healthy soil are less vulnerable to damage. Spray aphids off plants with a hose and natural aphid predators should soon arrive to restore balance. Tiny red spider mites are barely visible, so a problem is often serious by the time it's noticed. Watch for the undersides of young leaves turning pale and matt. Wetting the leaves of plants under cover can help, but biological controls are probably too expensive for anyone just growing one or two plants.

Harvesting and storage

It is not always obvious when aubergines are fully grown and ripe. Check the size and colour of your variety so you know what to expect. The flesh of over-mature aubergines becomes fibrous, seedy, and loses flavour, while their glossy skin turns more matt. Pick by pulling the chosen aubergine upwards to snap its stalk from the main stem, or cut the stalk with a knife or secateurs. Keep picking to encourage the production of new fruits. Aubergines keep well for about a week at ambient kitchen temperature, rather than in the fridge.

VARIETIES

'Black Pearl' F1 A reliable variety producing large, deep purple fruit.

'Slim Jim' Long, slender, purple fruits.

'Pot Black' F1 Small plants that grow well in containers and produce round fruits.

'Rosa Bianca' Egg-shaped fruits with skin streaked purple and white.

'Thai Long Green' Long, thin fruits ripen to pale green.

KEY INFORMATION ▬ Under cover

Seed to harvest: 4 months **Sowing to transplanting:** 2–3 months **Position:** Under cover or outdoors in a sheltered, sunny position with as much warmth as possible **Spacing:** 40–50cm (16–20in) apart
Hardiness: Will not tolerate frost; need nighttime temperatures above 10°C (50°F) for strong growth

	JAN	FEB	MAR	APR	MAY	JUN	JUL	AUG	SEP	OCT	NOV	DEC
Sowing		▬	▬									
Transplanting					▬							
Harvesting							▬	▬	▬			

SWEET PEPPERS AND CHILLIES (CAPSICUMS)

These tender crops are killed by frosts and need a long, warm growing season, so they need special care in cooler climates. Waiting for sweet peppers to ripen from green to the vibrant reds and yellows familiar from the supermarket results in low yields: pick fruit green for a bigger harvest. Chillies are prolific plants that are easier to grow, and ripen fruit in slightly cooler conditions. They grow well in 25cm (10in) pots, which means there is always space for them on a sheltered patio, greenhouse staging, or even a windowsill.

Sowing and transplanting

Sow early, from mid-February to mid-March, to allow capsicums the long growing season they need to grow, flower, and develop fruits. Where summers are really hot, you can sow in late March or April. Germinate seeds under cover, with added warmth, which is easiest to provide in the house. You could also buy plug plants in early April, to reduce the work involved.

Sow seeds singly into 3cm (1¼in) modules or scatter a few over the compost in a small seed tray, cover with a little compost, and water well. Prick out seedlings from a seed tray into 3cm (1¼in) modules when they develop their first true leaf, and continue to pot young plants on about every three weeks – first into a 7cm (2¾in) pot, then into a 9cm (3½in) pot. This keeps plants growing, without overwhelming them with too much compost and moisture at any stage, and will produce sturdy plants by mid-May that have been raised entirely under cover.

Always wait until after your last frost date and for the weather to warm up before planting capsicums, especially if growing them outdoors. Grow sweet peppers in 30cm (12in) containers, or space them 45cm (18in) apart in open soil. Plant deeply so that 5cm (2in) of the stem is below the surface.

Care and protection

Capsicums need less water than aubergine and tomato plants. Lift plants in pots and only water when they feel light. Chilli plants in particular are slow growing, and plentiful moisture encourages lush grow at the expense

Transplant sweet peppers after the last frost.

Ripe sweet pepper 'Gogorez' F1.

of flowering and fruiting. Water sweet pepper plants more when fruits start to swell, but reduce watering for both sweet peppers and chillies in late summer, to slow new growth and help intensify the flavour. Feeding is not necessary for plants in open ground, but feed sweet peppers in containers regularly with an organic liquid fertilizer. I tend not to feed container-grown chillies.

Chillies usually make compact plants that grow without support or with just their central stem tied to a cane. Sweet pepper plants need support, however, because stems can snap under the weight of large fruits. The bushy plants are difficult to train, so I wait until they are well established before looping string around the outside of the plant and tying it to a cane close to the main stem, to prevent branches dropping outwards. From mid-August until the end of the growing season, pinch out all new stems and small flowers, so that plants concentrate resources on developing and ripening the last fruits.

These plants are fairly trouble free and healthy soil, good husbandry, and careful watering all keep problems to a minimum. If aphids appear on new growth in spring, wash them off plants with water, to keep them in check until predators arrive.

Harvesting and storage

It's your choice whether to harvest fruit green or delay picking by up to a month waiting for them to colour as they ripen. In cool climates it might be better to enjoy the green fruit, because ripening diverts energy away from forming new fruits, resulting in a small crop.

All capsicums are ready to pick when the matt, pale green fruit become darker green and glossy. After that they slowly ripen and colour, developing sweeter, more tender flesh. Pick chillies by gently snapping the stalk off with an upward rotation, being careful not to break the fragile stems. Use secateurs to cut the thick stalks of sweet peppers to avoid damaging the plant. Keep picking through autumn, but get your harvest in before it is spoiled by the first frost, or move plants in pots under cover to continue cropping. Try pruning chilli plants down by two-thirds to overwinter in their pot. Watered very sparingly and kept frost-free during winter, they may grow away again when spring arrives.

Fruit that has started to colour will continue to ripen if it is kept at room temperature after picking. Eat sweet peppers within two weeks of harvest. Chillies are easy to store either by drying them on a sunny windowsill, or packing them in jars under oil.

VARIETIES

SWEET PEPPERS

'California Wonder' Large, red, square-shaped fruit.

'Sweet Banana' Long, pointed, yellow fruit.

'Bell Boy' F1 Heavy, block-shaped fruit with thick flesh. Slower to ripen but prolific picked green.

'Gogorez' F1 Slightly flat, ribbed, thick-walled fruit that ripen to deep red.

'Cayenne' Long, slender fruit with a slight chilli heat. Ripens to red and grows well in cooler conditions.

CHILLIES

'Fire flame' F1 Long, thin fruit ripen to red and are hot. Can be grown outdoors.

'Little Bomb' Small, rounded fruits ripen to dark red and have plenty of heat.

'Jalapeño Early' Extra-hot, red, semi-long fruits with rounded tips.

'Purple Gusto' F1 Mild, purple fruits ripen to red.

'Poblano' The mildest of these chillies. Long fruits ripen from purple to red.

'Hungarian Hot Wax' Pointed fruits ripen through yellow to orange, with variable heat.

Chilli 'Purple Gusto' F1 (top) and 'Little Bomb' (above).

KEY INFORMATION

Seed to first harvest: 4 months for green fruits under cover   **Sowing to transplanting:** 3 months   **Position:** Grow under cover or outdoors, in a warm (over 21°C/70°F), sunny, sheltered position   **Spacing: Sweet peppers** 45cm (18in) apart in open ground. **Chillies** 30cm (12in) apart in open ground   **Hardiness:** Not hardy; some of the most warmth-demanding plants

	JAN	FEB	MAR	APR	MAY	JUN	JUL	AUG	SEP	OCT	NOV	DEC
Sowing		▬	▬									
Transplanting					▬	▬						
Harvesting							▬	▬	▬	▬		

BASIL

Basil thrives in warmth and bright sunlight, making it an easy summer annual. It is less abundant and more prone to disease in cool, damp weather, and is killed by frost. Grow basil under cover in cool climates. Different varieties have distinctive spicy or fruity flavours.

Sowing and transplanting

Make your first sowing in April, under cover with a propagation mat, or on a windowsill indoors. This could provide basil all summer, but you can continue to sow under cover until June. The roots decay in soggy compost, so add up to 60 per cent sand, vermiculite, or perlite to the sowing compost, and water as little as you dare. Multisow three seeds per module and, after ten days, thin to one or two plants for easy picking. Alternatively, buy pots of supermarket seedlings and divide them up to pot on into 9cm (3½in) pots. Transplant once your last frost date has passed and the weather is warm. Basil grows well in containers.

Care and protection

Water plants growing in open soil twice a week, while those in containers may require daily watering in summer. Seedlings are vulnerable to slug damage, especially if planted when temperatures are low. Green caterpillars sometimes cause slight damage in high summer.

Harvesting and storage

Pick 5cm (2in) from the top of each plant before it flowers, then pinch out the tops of all new stems every few days. This promotes tender new sideshoots throughout summer. Remove flower stems. Keep picked stems in water for a few days and take leaves as needed. You can also make new plants like this because stems in water are quick to make roots. You can then move them to small pots of compost.

VARIETIES

'Sweet Genovese' A popular, high-yielding variety, with large, dark green leaves and classic basil flavour.

Sweet Thai basil Strong aniseed flavour, which is great for Asian dishes.

Many other varieties are named according to their flavour, such as Lemon, Cinnamon, and Lime basil, which are all remarkably intense.

KEY INFORMATION

Seed to harvest: 7 weeks **Sowing to transplanting:** 4–6 weeks **Position:** Full sun **Spacing:** 22–30cm (8¾–12in) apart **Hardiness:** Killed by frost; grows best when nighttime temperatures are above 12°C (54°F)

	JAN	FEB	MAR	APR	MAY	JUN	JUL	AUG	SEP	OCT	NOV	DEC
Sowing				▬	▬	▬						
Transplanting					▬	▬						
Harvesting						▬	▬	▬	▬			

POTATOES

Potatoes grow quickly and easily for a plentiful crop that will store well and taste better than anything you can buy. No dig potato plants root deep into the ground while, compared to dug soil, the potatoes themselves develop close to the surface and can be harvested with minimal soil disturbance. The huge range of varieties is divided into three types according to the speed at which they mature: first early, second early, and maincrop. First and second earlies crop in half a growing season, freeing up bed space in late summer. Maincrops take longer, making them susceptible to late blight.

Sowing and transplanting

Potatoes are grown from "seed potatoes", saved from the previous year's harvest. Put seed potatoes in a box on a light windowsill in late winter and they will form sturdy green shoots that remain compact until it's time to plant – a process known as "chitting". Avoid keeping seed potatoes in darkness, where new shoots will grow long, pale, and unmanageable for planting.

Non-organic potatoes sold in supermarkets may have been treated to prevent them sprouting, which means they probably won't grow if used as seed potatoes. You can save your own seed potatoes (see p.254), buy seed potatoes from seed merchants, or try planting organically grown eating potatoes – just check the variety and its pattern of growth.

It's risky to plant seed potatoes more than three weeks before the last frost date, because damage to leaves and stems may set back their growth. But in much of the UK, first earlies can be planted in late March, provided their leaves are protected from late frost with fleece, then second earlies from mid- to late April and maincrops from mid-April to mid-May.

Rather than dig a trench, use a trowel to plant potatoes individually in the soft top layer of no dig beds. Look closely and you will see that new shoots are concentrated at one end of the tuber, called the "rose end"; plant with these shoots at the top. Push the trowel straight down, pull it towards you to make a slit, and drop in the potato with its top at least 5cm (2in) below the soil surface. If you plant deeper you're more likely to need to dig them out. Potatoes can also be planted through a mulch of black plastic sheeting over a new patch of weedy ground (see pp.40–41). Push the trowel through a slit in the plastic and plant in the same way. Shoots will grow up through the slit towards the light, although you may occasionally need to ease them out.

Planting seed potatoes is easy in no dig soil.

Spring frost damage on potato foliage.

Late blight is a disease of wet, dull summers, which can cause the leaves and stems of previously healthy plants to turn grey-brown, limp, and soft within three days (see p.243). Watch out for it in warm, wet weather and at the first sign of infection, cut plants at ground level to prevent blight reaching the tubers. You can compost the tops, because blight spores survive only in living plant tissue and die in a compost heap, even if it's not hot. After removing diseased foliage, leave potatoes in the soil for a few days, to allow blight spores on the surface to die before harvesting. It's said that blight persists in soil, but it does not. I have trialled growing potatoes in the same bed for the last seven years, and in year seven the harvest was superb with no disease problems.

Care and protection

Once the leaves of early plantings are above ground they risk being singed by frost. When a night of 3°C (37°F) or lower is forecast you can protect the leaves by "earthing-up" and pulling compost over them, or covering plants with a double layer of fleece. These spring frosts do not kill the roots because there's insufficient time for ice to penetrate into the soil, and by late May growth will be rapid.

If exposed to light, tubers produce solanine which turns them green and is mildly poisonous with an unpleasant taste. To prevent this, watch for new potatoes breaking the surface, and drop more compost on top to cover them. For second earlies, I use a shovelful of compost per plant, which is also a long-term investment to improve the soil, and benefits subsequent plantings. Watering is unlikely to be necessary in moist spring soil. As harvest approaches in early summer, growth is phenomenally rapid and you'll get a bigger crop by watering generously twice a week for the last two weeks, should the weather be dry.

Earthing up plants with extra compost.

Harvesting baby new potatoes in early June.

VEGETABLE AND HERB DIRECTORY

Common scab is a disease that causes surface disfigurement, and having to peel away discoloured tissue reduces the edible portion of each potato. Scab usually occurs on disturbed soil with a high pH, and potatoes developing close to the surface in no dig beds are rarely affected. Potato blackleg comes from infected seed potatoes and usually occurs on those isolated plants. Diseased stems turn black at ground level, rot, and fall over, halting development, but any potatoes are still edible. You can compost the tops in a hot heap. In my experience it doesn't persist in the soil, just don't save tubers from infected plants for seed.

Soil-dwelling slugs chew into potatoes, allowing entry to other pests and diseases, which is good reason to lift tubers promptly. Eat slug-damaged tubers first because they won't store well.

Wireworms can be a pest in ground that was grassland or weed-covered before planting. These yellow-brown beetle larvae burrow thin tunnels deep into tubers, making it hard work to cut away damage and allowing rot to set in. Check for wireworms and reduce the population by baiting them in spring with half an old potato left on the soil surface overnight; wireworms will have begun to feed on it by the following morning. Pop them in your compost heap and continue to lay bait until no more wireworms are found.

Harvesting and storage

The first harvests of fresh potatoes have a high sugar content and that prized "new potato" flavour, both of which diminish after harvest and as tubers grow to maturity. Flowering is a first sign that harvest is imminent, although flowers can be inconspicuous or non-existent, especially on first early varieties. A more reliable signal that potatoes are ready is the dark green leaves losing their lustre and turning pale or yellow. Don't wait for the tops to die off completely, because this increases the likelihood of slug damage and reduces

Plentiful 'Lily Rose' tubers under black plastic.

the window of time for a second planting after the potato harvest.

Pull rather than dig your potatoes from no dig soil. Grasp a plant's stems, give a gentle upward pull, and three-quarters of the tubers will lift with the top, leaving some nestling in the ground. Rummage with your fingers to unearth the remaining tubers, which come out with very little soil sticking to them. Potatoes may develop more deeply in sandy soils, where a trowel or fork helps to remove them. Harvest even the tiniest potatoes because any left behind will grow like weeds.

Tubers store well in 2- or 3-ply paper sacks, which exclude light and prevent them turning green. Remove any damaged tubers and check that the skins are dry before putting them in the sack. Leave lifted potatoes on the soil in the sun for a few hours, or lay them in crates or boxes in the shed for two or three days. Keep the sacks somewhere dry and dark. Warmth

Dry potatoes keep well in a thick paper sack.

VARIETIES

FIRST EARLIES

'Swift' Extra-fast with cream, oval-shaped tubers, but an unremarkable flavour.

'Sharpe's Express' Slower to mature, almost a second early, with tasty yellow tubers.

'Red Duke of York' Red-skinned tubers have pale flesh of fine flavour.

'Casablanca' Matures a week later than true first earlies for a good yield of large, slightly watery tubers.

SECOND EARLIES

'Estima' and **'Charlotte'** Both give high yields of large potatoes, with a waxy consistency and lovely flavour.

'Apache' Unusual pink skin mottled with yellow patches and delicious yellow flesh.

'Linzer Delikatess' A yellow salad potato, with a good yield of small, waxy tubers.

'Lily Rose' The striking dark pink-red colour of the skin also extends into the flesh.

'Mayan Gold' Long, yellow tubers with a buttery texture and amazing flavour. Cook in just five minutes.

MAINCROPS

'Desiree' A delicious, dense potato with purple skin and yellow flesh. Less prone to scab in no dig beds.

'King Edward' Deservedly popular for its fine flavour and good yields.

'Sarpo Mira' and **'Sarpo Axona'** From the 'Sarpo' range of reliably blight resistant varieties which are tall and can grow into autumn. Cut their tops back at the end of August to prevent tubers becoming starchy and dry.

during late summer is no problem for storage, but don't allow them to freeze in winter. Empty sacks every few weeks and remove any rotten potatoes to prevent infection spreading. Remove sprouts from tubers in late winter. First earlies sprout sooner, so are not usually stored, but second earlies like 'Charlotte' keep until April. By mid-spring stored potatoes look slightly shrivelled, but remain tasty.

Saving seed potatoes

I recently began using my own potatoes as seed and the results have been brilliant. To save your own seed, put some egg-sized tubers from healthy plants to one side at harvest time – this is an ideal use for any potatoes that are slightly green. Keep them in a paper bag, labelled with the variety, away from rodents. In mid-winter, when they start to sprout, place them in light to chit as normal.

Second earlies 'Lily Rose' and 'Linzer Delikatess'.

FIRST EARLIES

Seed to first harvest: 2 months **Position:** Full sun is best, to keep leaves dry **Spacing:** 35–40cm (14–16in) or 30cm (12in) for a small, very early harvest **Hardiness:** Not frost hardy

	JAN	FEB	MAR	APR	MAY	JUN	JUL	AUG	SEP	OCT	NOV	DEC
Planting			▬									
Harvesting						▬						

SECOND EARLIES

Seed to first harvest: 3 months **Position:** Full sun is best, to keep leaves dry **Spacing:** 45–50cm (18–20in) **Hardiness:** Not frost hardy

	JAN	FEB	MAR	APR	MAY	JUN	JUL	AUG	SEP	OCT	NOV	DEC
Planting				▬								
Harvesting							▬					

MAINCROPS

Seed to first harvest: 4 months **Position:** Full sun is best, to keep leaves dry **Spacing:** up to 60cm (2ft) **Hardiness:** Not frost hardy

	JAN	FEB	MAR	APR	MAY	JUN	JUL	AUG	SEP	OCT	NOV	DEC
Planting				▬▬								
Harvesting								▬				

SWEETCORN

Freshly picked sweetcorn has a special flavour and sweetness that you cannot buy. The sugars in cobs are only temporary and soon turn to starch, before the kernels eventually become dry corn or maize. Sweetcorn is easy to grow when summers are warm, but it can be difficult to protect ripening cobs from the many animals and birds who also have a taste for them. When I lived in France I noticed that farmers grew maize, but never ate it at the sweet stage. I tried to sell sweetcorn at the market only to receive comments like "duck food"!

Sowing and transplanting

Sow a combination of early and later varieties at the same time, for a succession of cobs to harvest in late summer and early autumn. Where summers are cool, choose an early variety that needs less time to mature.

Sweetcorn needs warmth to thrive, so there is no point sowing it too early in spring. Wait until about a month before your last frost date to sow under cover, and only sow outdoors once the risk of frost has passed. Sowing under cover is more reliable because warmth gets

germination underway quickly, and the fat seeds are protected from rodents and birds, although it may still be worth setting a mousetrap near the trays.

Sow seeds singly about 1cm (½in) deep, into 3cm (1¼in) or 5cm (2in) modules under cover, or sow directly by dibbing holes 1–2cm (½–¾in) deep, every 25cm (10in) across a bed. Transplant seedlings after about four weeks, always after the last frost. Sweetcorn is often grown in a block, with plants 25–30cm (10–12in) apart, to aid pollination. This makes sense as pollen drifts down from male flowers at the top, onto the hairs of cobs growing on surrounding plants, enabling sweet kernels to swell. However, I also harvest fat, well-pollinated cobs from plants growing in rows. Transplanting tall sweetcorn between sprawling winter squash plants makes efficient use of space, but the UK climate is not hot enough to grow climbing beans up the corn, for harvesting both at a dry stage, which is known as "the three sisters" method.

Care and protection

If it is cold after you transplant, lay fleece over plants for the first two or three weeks to help them establish. In cool conditions plants will just sit there and turn yellow but grow away rapidly once the soil warms up. Water after

Male flowers drop pollen onto the cobs below.

Peeling a cob to reveal ripe yellow kernels.

transplanting. Soak twice a week if the weather is dry when the cobs are swelling.

Maturing cobs are vulnerable to rodents, badgers, and birds. My only advice is to beat them to it: harvest mature cobs immediately, or even slightly under-ripe, when they are extra tender. Sideshoots from the base of stems can be removed or left to bear smaller, often poorly pollinated cobs.

Harvesting and storage

Watch for the hairy tassels at the tops of cobs turning brown as they ripen. You can also pull the outer green sheath apart enough to check the kernels' size and colour; look for pale yellow-cream, which will darken to golden-yellow when cooked. Push down to snap a cob off the stem and eat it as fresh as possible, either raw or lightly boiled. The harvest period is short, and is one to relish.

VARIETIES

'Tramunt' A fantastic open-pollinated (see p.37), late, extra-sweet variety, which retains sweetness well after picking.

'Mezdi' A medium-early, open-pollinated (see p.37), extra-sweet variety that produces smaller cobs than 'Tramunt'.

'Northern Extra Sweet' F1 and **'Earlibird' F1** Both good early varieties, well suited to growing in cooler summers.

'Sweet Nugget' F1 A reliable, mid-season variety for good-sized cobs.

Babycorn 'Minipop' F1 Produces a succession of small baby cobs, for fun rather than to fill your plate.

KEY INFORMATION   ▬ Outdoors   ▬ Under cover

Seed to first harvest: 3 months for early varieties **Sowing to transplanting:** 4–5 weeks **Position:** Full sun and warmth **Spacing:** 25–30cm (10–12in) equidistant **Hardiness:** Tender, will be killed by frost **Suitable for interplanting**

	JAN	FEB	MAR	APR	MAY	JUN	JUL	AUG	SEP	OCT	NOV	DEC
Sowing					▬	▬						
Transplanting						▬						
Harvesting								▬	▬			

TOMATOES

Raised under cover and transplanted outdoors after the last frost, tomato plants grow fast in full sun where summers are warm. I recommend growing at least half of your crop under cover in damp climates, to protect plants from the summer rain, which brings late blight and ruins potential harvests. Long-stemmed, upright varieties are called "cordon" or "indeterminate", while compact types are known as "bush" or "determinate". Cordon tomatoes take time to train up supports, but their varied colours, shapes, amazing flavours, and high yields are your reward. Tomatoes also grow well in containers, given regular feeding and daily watering during summer.

Sowing and transplanting

When to sow depends on your last frost date. I sow six to eight weeks before that date, which is the second half of March, in warmth under cover. This allows time to grow good-sized transplants and maximize the chance of fruit ripening during our temperate summers. Resist the temptation to sow in February, because seedlings will quickly become overcrowded and spindly under cover, while waiting to be planted out.

Sow seeds thinly into a small seed tray or sow one seed into each cell of a 3cm (1¼in) module tray. Avoid sowing into bigger pots, to save space and prevent seeds rotting in excessively moist compost – the trick is to pot plants on regularly into slightly larger containers as they grow. Prick out from a tray into 3cm (1¼in) modules when seedlings have their first two seed leaves (cotyledons). After about three weeks, once plants have two true leaves, pot them on into 7cm (2¾in) pots, then after roughly 10–12 days pot them on again into 9cm (3½in) pots. Ten days later, you should have a sturdy young plant, perhaps with a truss of flower buds visible, ready to transplant.

When the last frost date has passed, transplant into open soil, large containers,

or grow-bags in a greenhouse or polytunnel, or outdoors where summers are reliably warm. Tomato plants have long stems, which grow additional roots when buried, so always transplant deeper than they were growing in their previous pot. Allow at least 45cm (18in) between plants, and up to 55cm (22in) for cordon plants under cover, and grow two plants per grow-bag rather than the three sometimes suggested.

Bush tomato varieties grow well in pots where they can be left to do their own thing and drape over the sides. When grown in open ground their stems trail over the soil and fruit may be eaten by slugs. Cordon tomatoes need

Under cover, bury a supporting string under the roots.

Gently twist the main stems of young plants around their string as they grow.

support, either with a sturdy stake driven into the soil close to the root ball after planting or with robust polypropylene strings, secured under the root ball and tied to supporting bars in the roof of the greenhouse or polytunnel. When transplanting, tie a knot in one end of the string and place it in the hole under the root ball, so that it will be held in place by the plant's roots, then secure the top using a simple loop knot.

Care and protection

Support cordon plants either by loosely tying in the main stem to the stake every 15–20cm (6–8in), or gently twisting it around the string as it grows. Snap off sideshoots that appear where leaves join the main stem, so the plant retains a single stem and is easy to maintain. I cut off the lower leaves of cordon plants from about a month after transplanting, before they are too yellow. This makes access easier for watering and picking, and improves ventilation around plants so that leaves dry quickly, reducing the risk of disease. Pinch out the tops of plants in early August, to limit development

of new flower trusses and reduce the quantity of unripe fruit at the end of the growing season.

Pruning flower trusses helps improve the quality of fruit. Cut off about half of the first truss, to prevent the bottom tomatoes lying on the ground and being damaged by slugs or woodlice. Removing the last few flowers from the ends of trusses prevents them growing so long that their last tomatoes take ages to develop. Later trusses generally need less pruning, but this depends on variety; to produce large beefsteak tomatoes leave only three or four fruits on each truss.

More problems come from overwatering than under-watering tomatoes, so go steady with the can or hose. The reservoir of moisture in no dig soil makes water management easier for plants in the ground than those in pots. In summer, I water plants growing in soil in my polytunnel twice a week, or every two days if it's really hot. From July, apply water directly onto the soil or compost around the plant, without wetting the leaves, to reduce the

Symptoms of late blight on leaves (top) and blossom end rot on fruit (bottom).

calcium deficiency caused by a lack of water, so the remedy is to water more.

Aphids may cluster on leaves and stems in spring but can be sprayed off with water to help reduce damage until predators arrive in late May and aphid numbers therefore diminish. Leaves rolling upwards occurs in some varieties when there is a big difference between day- and nighttime temperatures but is not a major problem.

Late blight can cause major damage, particularly on outdoor tomatoes, but understanding how infection occurs will reduce the risk (see p.243). Fortunately those sheltered from rain under cover will have dry leaves and are much less likely to be affected. At the first sign of rapidly spreading grey-brown rotting of foliage, remove and compost the affected leaves to help slow the spread. Blight spores do not survive in soil or compost, so it's fine to compost diseased material. Once you see blackened stems or stalks the plant is lost and should be removed, including any fruit, which, although it tastes unpleasant, is not poisonous.

Harvesting and storage

Tomatoes left on the plant until fully coloured have the sweetest flavour, but you can encourage higher yields by picking half-coloured fruit and allowing them to finish ripening at room temperature. Pick single fruits when they are mostly coloured and before they over-ripen, when tomatoes go soft and lose the acidic edge to their flavour. They keep best if picked by lifting upwards to snap the stalk, leaving the green calyx attached. This is often difficult with beefsteak varieties, which are best harvested with a sharp knife to cut the stalk of each tomato. Handle them carefully to avoid bruising or damaging their thin skin.

chance of late blight. Irregular watering can cause fruit skins to split, especially for varieties such as 'Sungold' and 'Rosella'. Reduce watering to just once a week in September, to concentrate plant energy on ripening fruits rather than growing more leaves, and intensify the sweetness of the fruit.

There is no need to feed tomatoes growing in no dig soil, where soil organisms provide a healthy balance of nutrients under the compost mulch. In contrast, tomatoes in containers or grow-bags need regular feeding with an organic liquid feed according to the manufacturer's instructions, as well as watering daily or even twice daily during summer. Avoid saturating the compost in pots, but if you see the leaves wilting on a sunny afternoon, it's a signal to water a little more. Striking black patches on the bottom of fruits, known as blossom end rot, result from

Keep harvested fruit at room temperature, out of sunlight, where they will continue to ripen gradually. Avoid placing them near bananas, which increase the chance of rotting, and never put them in the fridge, as this reduces flavour. Once light levels drop in early October, no further ripening will occur on the plant, so pick all remaining fruit to ripen indoors. Pull plants out to make space for winter crops.

SAVING SEED

Save seeds from any open-pollinated variety (see p.37). Scoop the seeds from a ripe tomato into a cup, add some water, label, and leave at room temperature for about a week. Soft tissues surrounding the seeds ferment, forming a mouldy, grey layer on top of the water, while clean seeds drop to the bottom. This process removes a germination inhibitor present around the tomato seeds. Remove the mouldy crust before draining and rinsing the seeds. Leave them to dry in the sun on a piece of card, before scraping them into a labelled envelope.

A colourful crop of cherry tomatoes 'Sakura' F1, 'Sungold' F1, and 'Rosella'.

Clockwise from top right: 'Red Brandywine';
'Black Russian'; 'Red Alert'; 'Berner Rose';
'Sungold' F1.

VARIETIES

These perform well in my garden and appeal to my taste, but I'd encourage you to try many more and find your own favourites.

CORDON VARIETIES

CHERRY Small, sweet, bite-sized tomatoes that ripen earliest and suit cooler climates with short growing seasons.

'Sungold' F1 My number one for its extraordinary fruity, sweet flavour and ability to ripen orange fruit under cover a week before other varieties. Tall plants with a long stem between each truss.

'Sakura' F1 Good yields of larger, dark red cherry tomatoes, with a full and sweet flavour.

'Rosella' Small fruit of a dusky purplish colour, with a pleasant and not over-sweet flavour.

MEDIUM-SIZED Standard salad tomatoes.

'Matina' Open-pollinated (see p.37) with round, red, mid-sized fruit and a decent flavour.

'Orkado' F1 Grown commercially for a high yield of uniform red fruit; tasty but not remarkable.

BEEFSTEAK Large, dense fruit, with much more flesh and few seed cavities. Slow to ripen and need hot summers.

'Black Russian' Yields large, dark red fruit with a fantastic flavour, but plants often look unhealthy!

'Brandywine' One of the loveliest open-pollinated (see p.37) beefsteak tomatoes, with excellent flavour and large ribbed fruit. Comes in pink, red, and yellow.

'Gigantomo' F1 and **'Big Boy' F1** Hybrids bred for exceptionally large, red tomatoes, and good flavour.

'Berner Rose' Medium-large, pink-red fruit. Not the biggest but they taste wonderful.

'Sonnenherz' Fleshy, heart-shaped, orange striped fruits.

Tomato 'Crimson Crush' F1 grown outdoors.

BUSH VARIETIES

'Red Alert' Amazing earliness and tasty small to medium-sized red fruit, with quite a thick skin.

'Maskotka' My favourite bush variety. Easy to grow, and trusses of good-sized, tasty red fruit drape over the edge of the container.

'Tumbling Tom Red' Widely available and pretty bog standard, producing small, red fruit with an average flavour.

BLIGHT-RESISTANT VARIETIES

Much less prone to blight than standard varieties, but not immune to infection.

'Crimson Crush' F1 A cordon variety with large fruit, going towards beefsteak, and crimson coloured. Delivers decent flavour and quite a high yield when grown outdoors.

'Mountain Magic' F1 Also a cordon for round, red, medium-sized tomatoes, with an average flavour.

KEY INFORMATION ▬ Outdoors ▬ Under cover

Seed to first harvest: 3 months for cherry varieties, 4 months for medium to large fruit under cover, 4½ months outdoors **Sowing to transplanting:** 6 weeks **Position:** Full sun, and shelter for cordon varieties
Spacing: 40–55cm (16–22in) apart **Hardiness:** Not hardy, killed by frost, but more cold tolerant than aubergines and peppers

	JAN	FEB	MAR	APR	MAY	JUN	JUL	AUG	SEP	OCT	NOV	DEC
Sowing			▬									
Transplanting					▬▬							
Transplanting					▬							
Harvesting							▬▬▬▬▬▬▬					
Harvesting							▬▬▬▬					

The tall stems and ferny foliage of asparagus make an attractive feature in the late summer garden.

PERENNIALS

Asparagus

Perennial kale

Rhubarb

Sorrel

Chives

Mint

Rosemary

Thyme

Perennial vegetables and herbs regrow year after year, following a lull through winter, although perennial kale, rosemary, and thyme can still be picked through the coldest months. In good soil they can be very productive and one plant may be enough to give you all you need. All of these plants are hardy and straightforward to grow, but require a reasonable amount of maintenance to keep them healthy and cropping well.

Choosing what to grow

Apart from sorrel, perennial vegetables grow large, so think carefully about how many you might need, and where to situate them so they don't shade or cover other crops. Asparagus and rhubarb are seasonal delicacies in spring and early summer, and are both expensive to buy, yet easy to grow. The same is true of these perennial herbs and planting just one of each can give you richly flavoured harvests close to hand, whenever they are needed in the kitchen. It's a myth that herbs need to be grown on poor soil. In fact, feeding the soil organisms with an annual mulch of compost will increase the growth and productivity of your herbs, with no loss of flavour. Herbs also grow well in containers – indeed mint must be planted in a pot to prevent it spreading rapidly through the soil.

Sowing, growing, and harvesting

Except for the kale, all these perennials can be raised from seed. It's also easy and economical to buy young plants, especially when you need only one or two of each. The best results come from planting in early spring or mid- to late autumn, when the weather is relatively cool and the soil is moist. Once plants are growing strongly you can raise more by taking cuttings or dividing roots.

CROP	Activity	JAN	FEB	MAR	APR	MAY	JUN	JUL	AUG	SEP	OCT	NOV	DEC
Asparagus	Sow			▇									
	Plant			▇							▇	▇	
	Harvest				▇	▇	▇						
Perennial kale	Plant			▇	▇	▇	▇	▇	▇				
	Harvest	▇	▇	▇	▇	▇	▇	▇	▇	▇	▇	▇	▇
Rhubarb	Sow			▇									
	Plant			▇	▇	▇	▇	▇	▇	▇	▇	▇	
	Harvest			▇	▇	▇	▇	▇					
Sorrel	Sow		▇	▇	▇	▇	▇						
	Plant				▇	▇	▇	▇	▇				
	Harvest			▇	▇	▇	▇	▇	▇	▇	▇	▇	
Chives	Sow			▇	▇								
	Plant				▇	▇	▇	▇					
	Harvest			▇	▇	▇	▇	▇	▇	▇	▇	▇	
Mint	Plant			▇	▇	▇	▇						
	Harvest				▇	▇	▇	▇	▇	▇	▇	▇	
Rosemary	Sow			▇	▇								
	Plant			▇	▇	▇	▇	▇	▇	▇	▇		
	Harvest	▇	▇	▇	▇	▇	▇	▇	▇	▇	▇	▇	▇
Thyme	Sow			▇	▇	▇	▇	▇	▇				
	Plant			▇	▇	▇	▇	▇	▇	▇	▇		
	Harvest	▇	▇	▇	▇	▇	▇	▇	▇	▇	▇	▇	▇

Allow plants time to establish before taking a first harvest: this might be just two months after planting sorrel and mint, a year for rhubarb, and as much as three years after planting for asparagus. It is also important to stop picking, even from productive older plants of asparagus and rhubarb, by the summer solstice and late July respectively, to allow the growth of sufficient foliage to feed the roots before winter and ensure a good crop the following year. To maximize productivity, remove flowering stalks from rhubarb and sorrel as soon as they appear, cut back herbs after flowering, and cut chives to ground level before their flowers set seed in summer. You should also cut tall asparagus stems close to ground level at the end of autumn.

Raise young mint plants by taking cuttings from an established plant.

Regular weeding is necessary but not onerous, once you are free of perennial weeds thanks to thorough mulching in the first year. Annual mulches in subsequent years, with enough compost to cover soil to a depth of about 2cm (³⁄₄ in), will maintain healthy growth and make weeding easier.

Common problems

The two main pests that trouble perennials only affect specific crops and may not be found in your area, but it pays to be alert for their presence. Asparagus beetles are black with prominent pale yellow and red markings, and both the adult beetles and grubs feed on the foliage and stems of asparagus plants. This pest is hard to eradicate, but the damage it causes is less significant where plants are regularly watered and mulched. Green dock beetle is an attractive iridescent green and makes holes in sorrel leaves as it feeds. Little can be done to protect plants, but picking and composting affected leaves helps to reduce the damage.

Weeds are potentially a time-wasting chore if they become established among perennial plants, but they are easy to manage in no dig beds as long as they are removed before they seed. Older rosemary and thyme plants have a tendency to become sparse at the centre, which can be prevented by cutting them back hard each year after they finish flowering.

Mulch rhubarb with compost every year, in late autumn, to promote strong growth.

ASPARAGUS

Despite the long wait of up to four years for a significant harvest, asparagus is an excellent investment anywhere you plan to put down roots yourself. Delicious, freshly cut spears come at a time in spring and early summer when not many other vegetables are ready to harvest. Stop picking after the longest day to allow new spears to grow into a forest of ferny leaves. These feed energy back to the roots, promoting strong new growth every spring, for up to 25 years.

Sowing and transplanting

One often sees advice to plant asparagus on ridges of soil with trenches between, but this is beneficial only to keep roots proud of sodden soil that floods in winter. I've successfully grown asparagus without ridges on soggy, but not waterlogged, clay soil in a normal no dig bed. Another reason to grow on ridges would be to produce white, blanched spears beneath the mounded soil, but here, I describe how to grow green asparagus, where shoots are cut above soil level.

The easiest way to start an asparagus bed is to buy crowns – the spidery white roots of one-year-old plants. This is more expensive than growing from seed, but brings harvests forward by one year. To grow from seed, sow singly into modules in early spring and keep in the warmth of the house for a week to germinate, before moving seedlings into the greenhouse. After five or six weeks, pot young plants on into 7cm (2¾in) pots, and into a larger pot again after a couple of months, to keep them growing strongly.

Crowns and seed-raised plants can be transplanted in late autumn or early spring: I find early spring gives best results. Think long term and find them a suitable position in full sun. Established plants grow tall and thick in summer, and will cast shade like a hedge. Run the line of plants north–south if practical, to provide both sides of the row with sunlight in summer. One line can fill a 1.2m (4ft)-wide bed. Allow a generous 60cm (2ft) between plants and 1–1.5m (3–5ft) between lines.

Make a shallow, dish-like hole, about 10cm (4in) deep and slightly domed in the centre. Place a crown at the centre and spread the roots out, so that they reach slightly deeper into the soil at the periphery. Cover over with compost. This is easy in the soft surface of a no dig bed, where growth is better too – I spoke with a gardener whose asparagus planting failed for

Harvest by snapping spears at the base.

Weeding the asparagus bed in summer.

five years running in thoroughly dug soil, but had excellent results after planting crowns in surface compost without digging.

Care and protection

Watering may be necessary during the first spring, especially for seed-raised plants, but will not be needed after that. Weeding is a priority and is easy in the soft surface of no dig soil, but check the bed regularly to prevent any weeds going to seed. Laying cardboard between rows for the first year or two helps to reduce weed growth.

Long-stemmed asparagus ferns are liable to blow over, so put a permanent post and wire system in place to support them. Run parallel wires between sturdy fence posts at each end of the bed, with one wire on each side of the posts. Guide new stems between the wires as they grow upwards in summer.

If you grow an open-pollinated variety (see overleaf), go through the row in early autumn and remove any female stems with red berries, to prevent them dropping seeds; any seedlings that germinate need to be weeded out. In late autumn when leaves turn yellow, cut the stems down close to soil level. Chop up the debris before composting, or pile stems between two rows of asparagus and walk on them, so they decompose into a straw-like mulch. I add compost on top of the plants in November in the same way as I mulch other beds (see p.47). As a seaside plant, asparagus will thrive given a mulch of seaweed, or a sprinkling of salt at about 100g (3½oz) per 10m (33ft).

Treading down asparagus stems in late autumn to mulch the path between rows.

Harvesting and storage

Watch for the first spears emerging from bare soil as weather warms in spring. Pick a few spears as a taster three years after sowing seed, or two years after planting crowns, but wait another year for your first significant harvest. Spears are usually at their best at 15–20cm (6–8in) long, whatever their thickness, when you can cut or snap them close to soil level. I prefer snapping, because spears snap cleanly just above where they are fibrous, giving you only the tender part. Stop harvesting in midsummer, to allow new stems to grow up and make leaves. Spears are best enjoyed freshly picked, and can be eaten raw, but will store for a few days in cool conditions.

VARIETIES

'Connovers Colossal' This old open-pollinated (see p.37) variety produces tasty spears, but female plants yield a bit less and form berries.

'Gijnlim' and **'Backlim'** Highly recommended, productive "all-male" hybrids with great flavour. The difference between the cropping season of "early" and "late" varieties is not obvious.

'Ariane' A prolific hybrid with fat, tasty spears.

'Stewarts Purple' Open-pollinated (see p.37) with amazing, sweet, purple spears that are excellent raw. Less prolific than green varieties.

Sometimes rabbits or slugs will graze on the earliest spears in spring, but damage is usually insignificant for healthy plants. Asparagus beetle feeds on leaves and stems and can be a problem in drier areas. I find here, though, that plants grow strongly enough that asparagus beetles, which we see in spring, barely affect the harvest.

KEY INFORMATION

Seed to harvest: First small harvest 3 years from seed or 2 years from crowns **Sowing to transplanting:** 7–12 months **Position:** Full sun **Spacing:** 60cm (2ft) apart, 1–1.5m (3–5ft) between lines **Hardiness:** Roots hardy to at least -10°C (14°F), but spears damaged by frost

	JAN	FEB	MAR	APR	MAY	JUN	JUL	AUG	SEP	OCT	NOV	DEC
Sowing			▬									
Transplanting			▬									
Harvesting					▬							

PERENNIAL KALE

Perennial kale can be harvested throughout the year, including spring, when seed-grown kale is beginning to flower. These undemanding, long-lived plants don't produce seed, so you need to buy them as young plants, or propagate them from cuttings.

Planting and propagation

Plant at any time of year, but spring or summer is best for stronger and quicker establishment. Mature plants are large and grow multiple heads of leaves, so you are unlikely to need more than one. Plant tall varieties in a sheltered corner, where they may need to be tied in to a strong 1.5m (5ft) stake.

Propagate from an existing plant by snapping off 15cm (6in)-long sideshoots. Placed in a part-filled glass of water or a 7cm (2¾in) pot of moist compost, they should root within three weeks. As soon as stems in water develop roots, pop them into a pot.

Care and protection

Water new plants until they show strong growth. Although established plants tolerate dry conditions, watering promotes more leaves for picking. Limit the number of stems on older plants by twisting off unwanted new stems or cutting near the base with secateurs.

To protect from pigeons, make a wooden frame over plants and cover just the top with bird netting, to allow easy access for harvesting. In spring, spray grey aphids off new leaves with water. I leave caterpillars to feed, as they don't kill the plant and I don't pick leaves in summer. Pick off yellow or damaged leaves regularly.

Harvesting and storage

It's possible to pick leaves year-round, but growth is minimal in winter. Pick weekly, taking the older leaves from each stem by pushing down at the base of stalks.

VARIETIES

'Daubenton kale' Less than 1m (3ft) tall and easy to manage, with tender leaves.

'Taunton Deane' Can reach 2.5m (8ft) tall and prone to snapping; cut back by half to keep it under control.

'Taunton Deane', in its tenth year, is reclining!

KEY INFORMATION

Planting to harvest: Minimum 2 months   **Position:** Any; tolerates shade   **Spacing:** 75–90cm (30–35in) apart
Hardiness: Very hardy to approx. -15°C (5°F)

	JAN	FEB	MAR	APR	MAY	JUN	JUL	AUG	SEP	OCT	NOV	DEC
Planting												
Harvesting												

RHUBARB

Pink-tinged rhubarb stalks are a valuable harvest in early spring. With careful preparation and a little sweetening, the unique acidic taste of rhubarb makes it quite the delicacy, especially when stalks are forced in darkness for an earlier and sweeter crop. On all but dry, sandy soils, these large, hardy plants will flourish in a corner of the garden with very little attention, to regrow reliably every spring.

Planting and propagation

One plant is enough for most households, so it's easiest to buy a pot-grown plant or bare-root crown. Plant pot-grown rhubarb any time from spring to autumn, while crowns are sold while dormant for immediate planting between November and March. Alternatively, cut a piece of root from the edge of an existing clump in mid- to late autumn, once leaves have died down, to replant in your chosen spot. Remove a section about 10cm (4in) in diameter with dormant buds at the top. Plant it with the buds at surface level or slightly lower and they will grow away in spring.

You can also start rhubarb from seed by sowing in 7cm (2¾in) pots in early spring, under cover to speed up early growth. Once growth is strong, pop plants into a 9cm (3½in) pot before transplanting them in summer. If no space is available, pot them on again into a slightly larger container, for transplanting in autumn.

Care and protection

Water established plants regularly during dry spring or summer weather to increase the yield of stems, because growth slows in dry conditions. Rhubarb is a greedy grower and responds well to a mulch of compost or rotted animal manure, around the crown and on surrounding soil, after leaves have died back in autumn. Some varieties send up towering stems of white fluffy flowers in spring and summer, but these divert energy away from leaf production so are best cut out at ground level promptly. Crowns are remarkably resistant to pests and diseases and remain productive for many years, continually growing until they run out of space. To keep plants manageable and maintain vigour, you can remove a section of the crown and fill the hole with compost to create more space.

Forcing is not obligatory, but for tender, sweet stalks in early spring, try covering all or

Emerging rhubarb leaves in spring.

Harvest stalks with a firm twist and snap.

part of a crown with a tall pot or bucket in late winter. Depending on the temperature, after about a month you can harvest beautiful candy-pink stalks. Depriving the plant of light will weaken it, so remove the cover after two months at most, and if you want to force every year, grow at least two plants so that you can alternate between them.

Harvesting and storage

Allow new plants to establish for a year before you begin picking stalks. March to July is the main season of harvest, after which it's best to stop picking to allow remaining and new leaves to feed the roots. The earliest stalks are short and small, but larger stalks develop later for frequent picking. Grasp each stalk near the base and give it a twist with a firm pull to snap it off where it leaves the crown. The large leaves are inedible and even slightly poisonous, but are ideal for composting once cut from the top of each stalk.

VARIETIES

'Timperley Early' My favourite variety lives up to its name, producing early growth and fat, pale red stalks from March to July.

'Champagne' A really pretty variety with tender, thin, red stalks, which turn pink when forced.

'The Sutton' An old, late-cropping variety with short, dark red stalks of good flavour.

KEY INFORMATION

Seed and plants to harvest: 1 year   **Position:** Full sun is ideal, but will grow in shade. Moist soil
Spacing: 1m (3ft) apart   **Hardiness:** Hardy to approx. -15°C (5°F)

	JAN	FEB	MAR	APR	MAY	JUN	JUL	AUG	SEP	OCT	NOV	DEC
Sowing			▬									
Planting (seed-raised)						▬▬▬▬						
Planting (division from crown)										▬▬▬		
Planting (potted plants)			▬▬▬▬▬▬▬▬▬									
Harvesting			▬▬▬▬									

SORREL

These perennial plants grow easily and abundantly in no dig soil mulched with compost. Sorrel has a citrus flavour with a keen acidic "edge", and is great eaten raw or cooked in soups, omelettes, and stews. Broad-leaved sorrel is the most common and productive type, while buckler-leaved or French sorrel is more tender and delicious. Remove the flower stalks regularly from late spring to early summer, to promote continued leafy growth.

Sowing and transplanting

Sow at any time through spring and summer: either multisow in 3–5cm (1¼–2in) modules, thinning to one or two plants per cell, or sow in a tray to prick out into modules. Seeds are tiny and early growth is slow, but within five weeks the small plants can go into the ground, spaced 30cm (12in) apart. It's also possible to make direct sowings in early spring. Plants are hardy but germinate faster in warm temperatures, so cover new sowings and plantings with fleece for about a month. You can also propagate new plants by cutting a piece of root from the outside of an established clump for transplanting.

Care and protection

Sorrel is tolerant of dry conditions, but watering is worthwhile, to increase productivity and make plants less prone to beetle damage (see opposite) and bolting. There are various ways to manage flowering and encourage leaf growth, for continual harvests. You can keep picking leaves while also allowing plants to flower until early or midsummer, then cut the plant down almost to ground level, for a flush of new leaves from late summer. I use a scythe, or even a lawnmower, to cut my large buckler-leaved sorrel down in mid-July, and cut broad-leaved sorrel to about 5cm (2in) above soil level with a knife in June, before spreading

Established buckler-leaved sorrel, recently picked.

Broad-leaved sorrel rising to flower.

conditions. During dry summers, buckler-leaved sorrel develops brown spots on leaves, which increase during autumn.

Harvesting and storage

Pick from new plantings once the leaves of neighbouring plants touch. Small leaves are softer, so pick every few days if you like to eat sorrel raw. New growth is especially strong in spring, until plants send up their flower stems. Leaves pull off easily, with a variable amount of edible stalk, and can store for a week after picking when you keep them moist. Clusters of leaves can be cut from buckler-leaved sorrel to save time, but you will need to remove discoloured ones and any flowering stems.

Saving seed

Sorrel is a long-lived perennial, but you can save seed easily by allowing flower stems to develop and dry on plants, before rubbing out the seeds. You could also leave a few stems to flower and drop seeds, then use a trowel to lift and transplant any resulting seedlings.

a 2.5cm (1in) mulch of compost. Alternatively, remove flowering stems regularly from late spring, for harvests between March and November.

From early summer, you may notice damage caused by larvae of the green dock beetle *Gastrophysa viridula*, which eat small, round holes in leaves until autumn. Regular picking and composting of affected leaves will reduce the numbers of beetles and larvae feeding. Slugs live in clumps of sorrel without causing severe damage, especially when you remove those you notice while picking. Leaf quality is highest before the summer solstice and in damp

VARIETIES

I do not know of different varieties of broad-leaved and buckler-leaved sorrel.

Red-veined sorrel has small leaves with strikingly patterned foliage and an astringent flavour. I use it for ornament rather than eating in large amounts.

KEY INFORMATION

Seed to harvest: 10 weeks **Sowing to transplanting:** 4 weeks **Position:** Adaptable; tolerates shade and prefers moisture **Spacing:** 30cm (12in) **Hardiness:** Very hardy to approx. -20°C (-4°F)

	JAN	FEB	MAR	APR	MAY	JUN	JUL	AUG	SEP	OCT	NOV	DEC
Sowing			▬	▬	▬							
Transplanting				▬	▬	▬	▬			▬	▬	
Harvesting			▬	▬	▬	▬	▬	▬	▬	▬	▬	

CHIVES

This tough herb comes into its own in spring, when greens are in short supply and the slender leaves add a mild onion flavour to dishes. Chives die back in cold winters, but will produce leaves through the other seasons if they are cut back hard in early summer.

Sowing and transplanting

Buy pot-grown chives or divide an existing clump, because in my experience, seed-raised chives run to seed quickly. Sow, divide, or plant chives in spring, when plants will put on rapid growth. To divide a clump, cut through the roots near its edge with a trowel and replant this section at the same depth in open soil or in a 9cm (3½in) pot. Sow three seeds per 7cm (2¾in) pot under cover, thin to one or two plants per pot, and transplant about six weeks later. Chives can be grown in containers, but have moisture-hungry roots and will be more prolific in open ground.

Care and protection

Plants need little care, and thrive in soil with a compost mulch. Cut them back in early summer, to prevent self-seeding and to promote a fresh flush of leaves through summer and autumn. Watering keeps plants productive in a dry summer. Chives are generally untroubled by pests and diseases, but grow them in containers if you have onion white rot or allium leaf miner on your plot.

Harvesting and storage

Cut chives close to ground-level, from early spring to late autumn, using scissors or a sharp knife. Regular harvesting stimulates healthy new growth.

VARIETIES

Common chives (*Allium schoenoprasum*) Narrow, tubular leaves 20–30cm (8–12in) tall and purple, globe-shaped flowers in late spring.

Garlic chives (*A. tuberosum*) Taller, flatter leaves with a garlic flavour and white flowers.

Siberian chives (*A. nutans*) Thicker, blue-tinged leaves, reach 40cm (16in). Similar flavour to common chives.

Common chives will regrow after cutting.

KEY INFORMATION

Seed to harvest: 3–4 months **Sowing to transplanting:** 6 weeks **Position:** Unfussy, but like moisture
Spacing: 25–30cm (10–12in) **Hardiness:** Hardy to approx. -15°C (5°F)

	JAN	FEB	MAR	APR	MAY	JUN	JUL	AUG	SEP	OCT	NOV	DEC
Sowing			▬	▬								
Transplanting				▬	▬	▬						
Harvesting			▬	▬	▬	▬	▬	▬	▬	▬	▬	

MINT

Mint is a hardy, long-lived herb with invasive roots. Limit its spread by growing in pots, which can be buried in beds with the rim just above ground level. Its resilience is proven by an apple mint that flourishes in a crack between the wall and concrete path outside my back door!

Sowing and transplanting

It's easiest to buy mint as small potted plants and propagate from them if you need more. Plant in spring, spacing 40cm (16in) apart, or in a 25–30cm (10–12in) pot. Propagate in spring by lifting and transplanting sections of root, or taking 10cm (4in)-long cuttings from healthy new stems and pushing them into 5cm (2in) modules or 7cm (2¾in) pots, filled with a free-draining mix of 70 per cent compost and 30 per cent vermiculite or perlite.

Care and protection

Mint looks after itself but thrives in moist soil. Water regularly for vigorous growth, especially when it's in a container, and to prevent powdery mildew on older leaves. Early summer flowers are popular with insects, so allow them to bloom and die, before cutting stems back hard in late summer to promote new growth. In late autumn, once plants have lost their leaves, cut all stems to about 5cm (2in) above ground level.

Harvesting and storage

Pinch out the tips of new shoots as needed from mid-spring. Chop tender new leaves into salads, and use older leaves to flavour beans, peas, and potatoes during cooking, or to make tea. Cut stems to hang indoors to dry for winter storage.

VARIETIES

Apple mint (*Mentha suaveolens*) Round, fuzzy leaves.

Peppermint (*M. piperata*) Readily available with the classic mint aroma. Swiss mint is excellent for tea.

Pennyroyal (*M. pulegium*) Good ground cover in moist soil. Small leaves have a strong flavour.

Garden mint (*M. sativa*) Hardy, with a good flavour.

Spearmint (*M. spicata*) Strong, sweet flavour. Try the tasty variety 'English Lamb'.

Swiss mint buried in a pot to limit its spread.

KEY INFORMATION

Planting to harvest: 6 weeks **Position:** Sun or shade **Spacing:** 40cm (16in) apart **Hardiness:** Very hardy, perhaps to -30°C (-22°F), but dormant even in mild winters

	JAN	FEB	MAR	APR	MAY	JUN	JUL	AUG	SEP	OCT	NOV	DEC
Planting			▬	▬	▬	▬						
Harvesting				▬	▬	▬	▬	▬	▬	▬	▬	

ROSEMARY

Rosemary is a vigorous evergreen herb, which can provide a generous harvest of aromatic leaves year-round. It thrives in any soil with good drainage. The small, late-spring flowers are an unostentatious blue and a welcome source of pollen and nectar for visiting insects.

Sowing and transplanting

One plant will usually be enough for most gardens, so it's easiest to buy a pot-grown specimen to plant in spring. You can also take cuttings from an existing plant in early spring. Push 10cm (4in) lengths of new growth into module cells, filled with multipurpose compost mixed with one-third vermiculite, and they will root readily. Either pop the rooted cuttings straight into compost-mulched ground in late spring or pot them on into 9cm (3½in) pots for transplanting in summer. Set the top of the root ball a little below the surface and water in well.

Care and protection

New growth may suffer a little frost damage in cold springs, but rosemary is hardy enough in temperate climates. In midsummer, cut back the recently flowered stems over the entire plant, using either shears or a knife, to keep the bush compact. Using shears allows you to shape the bush to fit the space available. After seven to ten years, take cuttings to replace existing plants that have become bare at the base or have outgrown their space.

Pick rosemary as needed, throughout the year.

Harvesting and storage

Cut 4–6cm (1½–2½in) from the tip of green, tender stems using a knife or scissors. The leaves remain full of flavour through winter, for harvests throughout the year.

VARIETIES

Rosemary (*Salvia rosmarinus*) The common type makes an upright bush and is hard to beat.

Pink rosemary (*S. rosmarinus* 'Rosea') Slightly smaller, with thinner leaves and pretty pink flowers.

KEY INFORMATION

Plant to harvest: 12 weeks; small pick in first summer **Position:** Full sun or part shade **Spacing:** 50cm (20in) apart **Hardiness:** Hardy to about -8°C (18°F), sometimes lower

	JAN	FEB	MAR	APR	MAY	JUN	JUL	AUG	SEP	OCT	NOV	DEC
Sowing			▬	▬								
Planting			▬	▬	▬	▬	▬	▬	▬	▬		
Harvesting	▬	▬	▬	▬	▬	▬	▬	▬	▬	▬	▬	▬

THYME

This hardy, compact, evergreen herb is available to harvest year-round and delivers a rich, savoury flavour from tiny amounts. Thyme is easy to grow in well-drained no dig soil, as long as you can buy or raise healthy plants. In fact, established thyme will self-sow in late summer.

Sowing and transplanting

Thyme sold in garden centres has often been raised in perfect conditions in a greenhouse, and in my experience these soft plants then struggle to grow outside. I recommend raising robust plants from seed, even though this means waiting longer to harvest. In March, sow two or three seeds per small pot or module, or take 4cm (1½in) cuttings from new growth and push them into modules filled with an equal mix of compost and sand or vermiculite. Keep both in warmth under cover initially and transplant in early summer. Water summer plantings every two days for a week or two; plantings at other times of the year just need watering in.

Care and protection

Thyme is frost hardy and needs little care. Cut plants back after flowering in midsummer, leaving a short amount of the new, greener wood, to keep them compact and prevent them becoming bare at the centre. Use shears on older bushes and be quite severe. Add a 2cm (¾in) mulch of compost around plants every autumn.

Harvesting and storage

Use a knife or scissors to cut new growth from the stem tips. A few of the strong-flavoured leaves go a long way, so harvests should be possible all year round, even though growth almost stops in winter.

Lemon thyme has small, citrus-scented leaves.

VARIETIES

Common thyme (*Thymus vulgaris*) Widely available, with an excellent savoury flavour.

Lemon thyme (*T. citriodorus*) Has a lovely hint of citrus.

Compact thyme (*T. vulgaris* 'Compactus') A neat, slightly smaller incarnation of common thyme.

KEY INFORMATION

Plant to harvest: 8 weeks **Sowing to transplanting:** 6–8 weeks **Position:** Full sun is best; shade is possible
Spacing: 30cm (12in) apart **Hardiness:** Hardy to about -30°C (-22°F)

	JAN	FEB	MAR	APR	MAY	JUN	JUL	AUG	SEP	OCT	NOV	DEC
Sowing			▬	▬	▬	▬	▬	▬				
Transplanting			▬	▬	▬	▬	▬	▬	▬	▬		
Harvesting	▬	▬	▬	▬	▬	▬	▬	▬	▬	▬	▬	▬

INDEX

Page numbers in **bold** indicate where the main information about a vegetable or herb will be found. Page numbers in *italic* refer to illustrations.

SUPPLIERS AND RESOURCES

SEEDS

Seed Cooperative
seedcooperative.org.uk
Supplier of organic and biodynamic seeds that are open-pollinated so you can save your own.

Real Seeds
realseeds.co.uk
For unusual vegetable varieties.

Marshalls Seeds
marshallsgarden.com
Large supplier with a comprehensive range of well-maintained varieties.

Bingenheimer Saatgut
bingenheimersaatgut.de
German supplier of good quality seed for strong and even growth.

TOOLS AND EQUIPMENT

Suppliers of Charles Dowding designed module trays:
containerwise.co.uk (UK)
thefarmdream.com (Europe)
allaboutthegarden.com (USA)

Implementations
implementations.co.uk
For copper gardening tools.

Garden Imports
gardenimports.co.uk
For Charles Dowding designed long-handled dibber.

Gardening-naturally
gardening-naturally.com
Supplier of a large range of crop covers and biological controls.

Reddifast steels
reddifast.co.uk
Stock and straighten wire supports for crop covers.

First tunnels
firsttunnels.co.uk
Suppliers of a huge range of polytunnels.

Biodynamic Association
biodynamic.org.uk
For biodynamic preparations.

CHARLES DOWDING ONLINE AND ON SOCIAL MEDIA

Website charlesdowding.co.uk
Regularly updated and packed with no dig advice and online courses.
YouTube channel Charles Dowding
Instagram charles_dowding
Twitter @charlesdowding

FURTHER READING

Organic Gardening: The Natural No-dig Way by Charles Dowding (Green Books, 2018)

Salad Leaves For All Seasons by Charles Dowding (Green Books, 2021)

How to Grow Winter Vegetables by Charles Dowding (Green Books, 2021)

Gardening Myths and Misconceptions by Charles Dowding (Green Books, 2014)

Charles Dowding's Veg Journal by Charles Dowding (Frances Lincoln, 2014)

How to Create a New Vegetable Garden by Charles Dowding (Green Books, 2015)

Charles Dowding's Vegetable Garden Diary (*3rd edition*) by Charles Dowding (No Dig Garden, 2019)

Charles Dowding's Vegetable Garden Calendar (No Dig Garden, published annually)

No Dig Organic Home & Garden by Charles Dowding and Stephanie Hafferty (Permanent, 2017)

Charles Dowding's No Dig Gardening Course 1: From weeds to vegetables easily and quickly by Charles Dowding (No Dig Garden, 2020)

Charles Dowding's Skills for Growing by Charles Dowding (No Dig Garden, 2022)

Hot Beds: How to grow early crops using age-old techniques by Jack First (Green Books, 2013)

Gardening and Planting by the Moon 2022 by Nick Kollerstrom (W Foulsham & Co Ltd, 2021)

Teaming with Microbes: The organic gardener's guide to the soil food web by Jeff Lowenfels and Wayne Lewis (Timber Press, 2010)

Entangled Life: How fungi make our worlds, change our minds and shape our futures by Merlin Sheldrake (Vintage, 2021)

Finding the Mother Tree: Uncovering the wisdom and intelligence of the forest by Suzanne Simard (Allen Lane, 2021)

Mycelium Running: How mushrooms can help save the world by Paul Stamets (Ten Speed Press, 2005)

Back Garden Seed Saving: Keeping our vegetable heritage alive by Sue Stickland (Eco-Logic Books, 2008)

Gardening Without Work by Ruth Stout (Echo Point Books & Media, 2013)

The Ruth Stout No-Work Garden Book by Ruth Stout and Richard Clemence (12 Sirens, 2021)

REFERENCES

16–17 E. R. Ingham, "The Soil Food Web", *The Soil Biology Primer*, ch.1, https://www.nrcs.usda.gov/wps/portal/nrcs/detailfull/soils/health biology/?cid=nrcs142p2_053868. **M. E. Rout**, "Genomes of Herbaceous Land Plants – 2.1 Plant uptake and release", *Advances in Botanical Research* (2014). "Mycorrhizal fungi", Royal Horticultural Society [web article], www.rhs.org.uk/biodiversity/mycorrhizal-fungi. **L. VanSomeren**, "How do mycorrhizae work?", Untamed Science [web article] untamedscience.com/biology/ecology/mycorrhizae/. **A. L. Neal et al**, "Soil as an extended composite phenotype of the microbial metagenome", *Sci Rep* 10, 10649 (2020), https://doi.org/10.1038/s41598-020-67631-0.

24–25 A. L. Neal et al, "Soil as an extended composite phenotype of the microbial metagenome", *Sci Rep* 10, 10649 (2020), https://doi.org/10.1038/s41598-020-67631-0

30–31 M. Al-Kaisi, (2008) "Impact of tillage and crop rotation systems on soil carbon sequestration", https://www.researchgate.net/publication/265354997_Impact_of_Tillage_and_Crop_Rotation_Systems_on_Soil_Carbon_Sequestration. **D. Comis**, (2002) "Glomalin: Hiding Place for a Third of the World's Stored Soil Carbon." https://agresearchmag.ars.usda.gov/2002/sep/soil. **A. T. O'Geen** (2013) "Soil Water Dynamics". *Nature Education Knowledge* 4(5):9. **L. Lombardo et al**, (2019) "Mechanical Tillage Diversely Affects Glomalin Content, Water Stable Aggregates and AM Fungal Community in the Soil Profiles of Two Differently Managed Olive Orchards." *Biomolecules*, 9, 639. https://doi.org/10.3390/biom9100639

Project Editor	Jo Whittingham
Project Art Editor	Geoff Borin
Senior Editor	Alastair Laing
Senior Designer	Barbara Zuniga
Jacket Designer	Amy Cox
Jacket Coordinator	Jasmin Lennie
DTP and Design Coordinator	Heather Blagden
Senior Production Editor	Tony Phipps
Production Controller	Stephanie McConnell
Managing Editor	Ruth O'Rourke
Design Manager	Marianne Markham
Art Director	Maxine Pedliham
Publishing Director	Katie Cowan
Consultant Gardening Publisher	Chris Young
Photographer	Jonathan Buckley
Cover artwork	Jonathan Gibbs
Illustrations	Nicola Powling

First published in Great Britain in 2022 by
Dorling Kindersley Limited
DK, One Embassy Gardens, 8 Viaduct Gardens,
London, SW11 7BW

The authorised representative in the EEA is
Dorling Kindersley Verlag GmbH.
Arnulfstr. 124, 80636 Munich, Germany

Text copyright © Charles Dowding 2022
Photography copyright © Jonathan Buckley 2022
Copyright © 2022 Dorling Kindersley Limited
A Penguin Random House Company
10 9 8 7 6 5 4 3 2 1
001–327337–Sep/2022

A CIP catalogue record for this book
is available from the British Library.
ISBN: 978-0-2415-4181-4

Printed and bound in China

For the curious
www.dk.com

This book was made with Forest Stewardship Council™
certified paper – one small step in DK's
commitment to a sustainable future.
For more information go to www.dk.com/our-green-pledge